Modal Logics and Philosophy

Modal Logics and Philosophy

2nd edition

Rod Girle

McGill-Queen's University Press
Montreal & Kingston • Ithaca

© Rod Girle, 2000, 2009
Second edition 2009

ISBN: 978-0-7735-3648-7 (bound)
ISBN: 978-0-7735-3653-1 (pbk.)

Legal deposit fourth quarter 2009
Bibliothèque nationale du Québec

Published simultaneously outside North America
by Acumen Publishing Limited

Library and Archives Canada Cataloguing in Publication

  Girle, Roderic A.
    Modal logics and philosophy

  Includes bibliographical references and index.
  ISBN 0-7735-3648-7 (bound) - ISBN 0-7735-3653-1 (pbk.)

    1. Modality (Logic) I. Title
  BC199.M6G57 2000   160   C00-900897-7

Printed and bound in the UK by Cromwell Press Group, Trowbridge, Wiltshire

Contents

Preface

The second edition was prompted by two things. First there was the feed-back from several readers asking for something about conditionals, especially since many modern conditional logics use possible worlds semantics. So there are two new chapters, one in Part 1 presenting the formalities of a range of conditional logics, and one in Part 2 with philosophical discussion of some of the issues raised by conditionals.

Secondly, the use of the volume in teaching has suggested some revisions and corrections and re-ordering of content in the first part of the text.

I wish to thank all those who have sent me comments, questions and corrections.

Preface to the first edition

This text is a second level logic text. It introduces students to modal logic as an extension of classical first-order logic. The emphasis is on introducing the object language and some of the applications of modal logic in philosophy and artificial intelligence.

This text is not intended to be a metatheory text for modal logic. There are several excellent texts in that area. (For example: Brian F. Chellas, *Modal Logic: an introduction*, Cambridge, London, 1980; and G. E. Hughes and M. J. Cresswell, *A New Introduction to Modal Logic*, Routledge, London, 1996.) Our main focus will be on presenting the logics at an object language level, with a minimum of metatheory. The emphasis will be on the possible worlds semantics. There will be only a brief mention of axiom systems.

The idea is to present the languages of modal logic in such a way that the various applications can be sensibly discussed, and arguments containing modal terms can be analysed. The aim is to present a relatively small range of logics and then introduce the discussion of alethic, temporal, dynamic, epistemic and deontic applications.

The logical "machinery" that is used is the machinery of semantic tableaux. I assume that students will be familiar with Jeffrey style truth-trees. The approach overall is semantic, with an informal presentation of Kripke style possible worlds semantics. Axiomatic proof systems and natural deduction systems appear in only one chapter.

Acknowledgements

I wish especially to acknowledge the introduction to modal logic given me by Malcolm Rennie. His brilliant teaching and wide scope of presentation has been the main impetus to my work. I have drawn on his tense logic notes for material in the chapter on temporal logic.

CHAPTER 1

Argument and modality

1.1 Introduction

One of the main tasks of logic is to give an analysis of argumentation. Traditionally this analysis is of premise–conclusion argumentation. If formal methods are used, one begins with propositional logic.

The most common form of propositional logic is truth-table logic. Truth-table logic extends very easily into truth-tree logic. We assume that the reader is familiar with propositional logic in both truth-table and truth-tree forms. From this point we shall use the term propositional logic to refer to truth-table and truth-tree propositional logic unless we make it clear otherwise. Most of this text can be read with a knowledge of propositional logic only.

Propositional logic is usually extended to predicate or first-order logic. To read the whole of this volume the reader should be familiar with predicate logic and the system of truth-trees for predicate logic. Several texts introduce the reader to propositional and predicate logic and the truth-tree system. They are listed in the further reading at the end of the chapter.

1.2 Argument analysis

There are arguments that are clearly valid, but that cannot be shown to be so by propositional logic. Arguments such as:

> "All Athenians are Greeks.
> Socrates is Athenian.
> So Socrates is Greek."

require a more detailed analysis of their logical form than can be given by propositional logic. We need a logic that can deal not only with the negation, disjunction and conjunction of propositions, but also with quantifiers (*all, some*), predicates (*is Φ*) and relations (*loves*). The result is predicate logic.

Similarly, there are yet further valid arguments that cannot be shown to be valid by propositional or predicate logic. Such an argument is:

[A]   If a new course is to be offered next year, then submissions must be made to the Faculty Board before April. If submissions are to be made to the Faculty Board before April, then a Departmental meeting must be called. A week's notice must be given if a Departmental meeting is to be called. Since it is not possible to give such notice, it follows that it is not possible to offer a new course next year.

To give a proper account of how this argument is valid we have to display what is expressed by *must* and what is expressed by *possible*. These English words express *modal* notions. Other such notions are expressed by the terms *necessarily, might* and *can*.

In the 1950s a group of logicians, chief among them Saul Kripke, developed the idea that the notions of possibility and necessity could be captured in terms of *possible worlds*. The idea is really quite simple. We live in one possible world. It is the actual world. A work of fiction can be seen as a description of a possible world other than the actual world. Some works of fiction are descriptions of possible worlds very like the actual one. Some, such as works of fantasy, describe worlds quite remote from the actual world.

The explanatory idea in the possible worlds logics is the idea that if someone says "It is possible that giant squids live in the sea", then this is true just in case there is a possible world in which giant squids live in the sea. One such possible world could be the actual world. In the possible worlds logics a statement is true-in-a-world rather than just true. Furthermore, statements are said to be necessarily true just in case they are true in all possible worlds. If we say that statements such as "If it is raining then it is raining" are true in all possible worlds, then possible worlds logic holds us to be assuming that it is necessarily true that if it is raining then it is raining.

The possible worlds approach to modal terms provides a semantics for modal notions. That is, possible worlds provide an account of modal notions in terms of truth-values. Before the Kripke semantics, the main approach was by means of axiomatic and proof systems. In the following chapters we shall deal with both semantic and proof system approaches to modal logics, but, apart from Chapter 5 and sections of Chapter 6, we shall focus on the semantic approach.

The possible worlds approach to modal terms is quite persuasive. It is, in a sense, intuitively simple. But, does possible worlds logic really match the meaning that modal terms have in ordinary English? If the answer is "no", then how great is the difference? This question is important if we are going to use modal logic to assess the validity of arguments couched in English. This question is a question about the *reliability* of modal logic for argument analysis.

It is quite difficult to answer this question about the relationship between modal logic and ordinary English when we have not yet explored modal logic. So, we shall first explore some of the standard modal logics in possible worlds terms. Then, when we have a picture of how the logics work, we shall return to the question of the relationship between modal logic and ordinary English, and the concepts embedded in English.

In the chapter devoted to reliability questions we shall look at some of the problems which have concerned logicians for centuries. They are questions to do with conditionals, with modality itself, and with identity. But first, we turn to modal logic.

1.3 Possibility and necessity

The possible worlds approach assumes that, as well as negations, conjunctions, disjunctions and conditionals, we shall be dealing with statements of the forms:

It is possible that p
It is necessary that p

These are usually translated into the symbols of modal logic by:

$\Diamond p$
$\Box p$

respectively. The $\Diamond$ symbol is a *diamond*, and the $\Box$ is a *box*. In some texts an "M" is used for diamond and an "L" for box. It is easy to remember which is which, because the "M" contains the bottom half of a diamond and the "L" contains the bottom left half of a box.

$\Diamond p$ is standardly translated as *possibly p* or *it is possible that p* or *p might be true*.
$\Box p$ is standardly translated as *necessarily p* or *it is necessary that p* or *p must be true*.

Just as there is a clear set of equivalences in predicate logic between $\forall$ and $\exists$, so is there too with box and diamond. In fact, the equivalences are analogous. There are four important logical equivalences:

1. $\sim\Diamond p \equiv \Box\Diamond\sim p$
2. $\Diamond\sim p \equiv \sim\Box p$
3. $\Box p \equiv \sim\Diamond\sim p$
4. $\Diamond p \equiv \sim\Box\sim p$

These are the four **modal negation (MN) equivalences.** We can take each of these in turn and get a fairly reasonable grip on the equivalences by virtue of an intuitive understanding of the meanings of the terms involved. Let us assume that p is translated as "It is raining".

Equivalence 1 translates to:
> *It is not possible that it is raining iff it is necessary that it is not raining.*

Another translation of equivalence 1 is:
> *It is impossible for it to be raining iff it must not be raining.*

We translate equivalence 2 as:
> *It might not be raining iff it does not have to be raining.*
> Here we use "have" to express necessity.

Equivalence 3 is translated as:
> *It must be raining iff it is impossible for it not to be raining.*

Equivalence 4 is translated as:
> *It might be raining iff it is not necessary for it not to be raining.*

A great variety of expressions of ordinary language can be translated into modal logic. Not only do *possibly* and *necessarily* fall into this group, but all the other expressions we have already encountered such as *must, might* and *have* (in some cases). There are also phrases such as "is consistent with". We turn to some of these. First we consider the monadic expressions.

When it is said that *p is contingent*, what is usually meant is that it is possible for p to be true and also possible for p to be false. This would give:

p is contingent translates to $(\Diamond p \ \& \ \Diamond\sim p)$

Similarly, despite shudders from some followers of Quine, we translate *p is analytic* to $\Box p$. Some people use *analytic* in a general way so that *p is analytically true* becomes $\Box p$, and *p is analytically false* becomes $\Box\sim p$. We would then have:

p is analytic translates to $(\Box p \lor \Box\sim p)$

Given the translations above:

p is not contingent translates to $\sim(\Diamond p\ \&\ \Diamond\sim p)$

By De Morgan's equivalences this is equivalent to:

       p is not contingent translates to $(\sim\Diamond p \vee \sim\Diamond\sim p)$

or   p is not contingent translates to $(\Box\sim p \vee \Box p)$

In other words, p is not contingent iff p is either analytically true or analytically false. We can also translate:

p is contradictory by $\Box\sim p$

On the basis of these translations of "analytic" and "contradictory", and since $(p \vee \sim p)$ is analytic, we would expect

$(p \vee \sim p)$

to be a logical truth of modal logic. Similarly, since $(p\ \&\ \sim p)$ is a contradiction, we would expect

$\sim(p\ \&\ \sim p)$

to be a logical truth of modal logic. They both are.

Sometimes we have the abbreviation of the translation of p is contingent as ∇p, where:

$\nabla p =_{df} (\Diamond p\ \&\ \Diamond\sim p)$

The ∇ is the "grad" symbol. It is easy to remember for contingency by means of the mnemonic that it is an unstable wedge that could tilt over to the true or the false.

We now turn to some dyadic operators. When it is said that the truth of p is compatible with (or consistent with) the truth of q what is usually meant is that it is possible for both p and q to be true. So we can have:

       p is consistent with q translates to $\Diamond(p\ \&\ q)$
       p is compatible with q translates to $\Diamond(p\ \&\ q)$

Sometimes we have the abbreviation of the translation of

p is compatible with q as $(p \circ q)$

where $(p \circ q) =_{df} \Diamond(p\ \&\ q)$

We also have the abbreviation of the translation of

p is incompatible with q as $(p \ominus q)$

where $(p \ominus q) =_{df} \sim(p \circ q)$

As always, care must be taken in translating ordinary language. This is especially so with conditionals. For example, the first premise of argument A (p. 2) is:

If a new course is to be offered next year, then submissions must be made to the Faculty Board before April.

If we let

N = A new course is to be offered next year.
S = Submissions will be made to the Faculty Board before April.

then the conditional should be translated to:

$\Box(N \supset S)$

The "must" qualifies or operates on the *If ... then ....* In other words, we assume that what is being said is that the truth of the antecedent *necessarily implies* the truth of the consequent, not that the truth of the antecedent implies the necessary truth of the consequent. This is so in spite of the grammatical position of the "must" in the English expression of the conditional. The grammatical position of the "must" might be taken (incorrectly) to indicate that the translation should be $(N \supset \Box S)$.

The $\Box$ operates on the whole conditional in the correct translation. The word "scope" is used to indicate what the $\Box$ operates on. So, the scope of the $\Box$ in the correct translation is the whole conditional. In the incorrect translation, the scope of the $\Box$ is just the consequent of the conditional. This scope difference has quite an effect when we set about evaluating the argument for validity.

If we let

D = A departmental meeting is to be called.
W = A week's notice is to be given.

then we correctly translate argument [A] as:

(A′)
$$\square\,(N \supset S)$$
$$\square\,(S \supset D)$$
$$\square\,(D \supset W)$$
$$\sim \lozenge\, W$$
$$\therefore \quad \sim \lozenge\, N$$

At this point I forbear from incorrectly translating A, but we shall return to this argument later. We shall consider not only the correct translation, but also the incorrect translation.

When we translate arguments we shall often find that the word "must" is linked with the conclusion in English. But what is often being said is not that the conclusion is necessarily true, rather that the premises necessarily imply the conclusion, or that the conclusion follows necessarily from the premises.

For example:

[B]   If Tiger is a cat then Tiger is a mammal. Since Tiger is a cat, it follows that he must be a mammal.

Translated with

$C = $ Tiger is a cat.
$M = $ Tiger is a mammal.

we have:

(B′)
$$(C \supset M)$$
$$C$$
$$\square \therefore \quad M$$

where the modal operator really modifies the "therefore", or in the original B, the modal operator modifies the "it follows that". The argument would have been the same had its second sentence been couched as:

Since he is a cat, it must follow that he is a mammal.

If we were (incorrectly) to translate B as:

(B″)
$$(C \supset M)$$
$$C$$
$$\therefore \quad \square M$$

then, as we shall see later, the argument would turn out to be invalid in modal logic. Necessary implication is often called **strict implication**. Strict implication first appeared in its own right in the work of C. I. Lewis, where he constructed systems of logic for conditionals. Several logicians in the first part of the twentieth century were convinced that the use of the material conditional to translate *if ... then ...* conditionals was a serious mistake. Lewis used $(p \prec q)$ instead of $(p \supset q)$ for *If p then q*. We now know that Lewis's $(p \prec q)$ can be defined as a strict implication:

$$(p \prec q) =_{df} \square(p \supset q)$$

We shall return to the question of conditionals in Chapters 6 and 14.

The sort of strict implication found in valid arguments, where the conjunction of the premises necessarily implies the conclusion, is often called **entailment**.

1.4 Other modalities

The use of modal logic to give some account of *possibility* and *necessity* is only one of the applications of modern modal logic. Modal logics have been used to give accounts of many other notions. Some of these are *implication, knowledge, belief, time, change* and *obligation*. When modal logic is used to give an account of implication we have a **conditional** logic. The modal logics for knowledge are called **epistemic** logics, and those for belief are **doxastic** logics. Logics for time are called **tense** logics in the early literature, but are now mostly called **temporal** logics. Logics for change are called **dynamic** logics. Logics for obligation are called **deontic** logics. The logics for necessity and possibility are **alethic** logics. We begin with the alethic logics.

1.5 Plan of the text

This text is divided into formal and application sections. In the formal section we shall set out a range of logics. In the application section we discuss the use of these logics for the modalities mentioned above.

The formal systems are all introduced as *alethic modal logics*. The first, in Chapter 2, is a simple propositional modal logic. In Chapter 3 we look at variations of this propositional modal logic. These variations give us other logics known as the **normal** modal logics.

In Chapter 4 we look at some modal logics in the group known as the **non-normal** modal logics. These logics enable us to consider what happens when possibility and necessity change from possible world to possible world.

In Chapter 5 we set out both natural deduction and axiomatic proof systems for some modal logics. This is done for the sake of giving a broad treatment, but the emphasis is semantic. This chapter is required for a large section of Chapter 6. Both could be skipped.

In Chapter 6 we discuss conditional logics. In some cases these are simply the **alethic** modal logics applied to conditionals in the spirit of Lewis. Other conditional logics use the possible world semantics in novel ways to try to solve issues to do with conditionals.

In Chapter 7 and 8 we look at modal predicate logics. The modal predicate logics are extensions of classical first-order logic. The various logics show how one might look at quantification and identity in and across possible worlds.

In these formal chapters we shall base our intuitive understandings on the alethic modalities of possibility and necessity. There will be additional discussion of the alethic modalities in Part II.

The method for establishing the validity of arguments and formulas is *the method of truth trees*. The method is easy to use, and has the advantage that if an argument or formula is not valid, then a counter-example can be retrieved from the tree.

Finally, to repeat the comments in the Preface, this text is not a metatheory text for modal logic. We shall hardly ever use the terminology of "soundness" or "completeness", and will not prove any soundness or completeness results. There are many excellent texts that deal with meta-theoretical issues in modal logic.

In Part II we discuss in turn several of the applications of modal logic. We begin in Chapter 9 with the *alethic* applications, then in the following chapters we discuss in turn, time, change, knowledge and belief, obligation, and application to conditionals. Finally, in Chapter 15, we consider syntheses of these applications and the status of possible worlds.

1.6 Summary of translations

At this stage the following summary of standard translations is intended only as a guide:

$$\Diamond p = \text{ It is possible that } p \qquad \Box p = \text{ It is necessary that } p$$
$$\qquad \text{ Possibly } p \qquad\qquad\qquad \text{ Necessarily } p$$
$$\qquad \text{ It might be } p \qquad\qquad\quad \text{ It must be } p$$

$$(\Diamond p \ \& \ \Diamond {\sim} p) \ = \ p \text{ is contingent}$$
$$\nabla p \ = \ _{df} (\Diamond p \ \& \ \Diamond {\sim} p)$$
$$(\Box p \lor \Box {\sim} p) \ = \ p \text{ is analytic}$$

$$\Delta p \;=\; {}_{df}(\Box p \vee \Box \sim p)$$
$$\Box(p \supset q) \;=\; p \; strictly \; implies \; q$$
$$(p \prec q) \;=\; {}_{df}\Box\,(p \supset q)$$
$$\Diamond(p \;\&\; q) \;=\; p \; is \; compatible \; with \; q$$
$$(p \circ q) \;=\; {}_{df}\Diamond\,(p \;\&\; q)$$
$$\sim\Diamond(p \;\&\; q) \;=\; p \; is \; incompatible \; with \; q$$
$$(p \ominus q) \;=\; {}_{df}\sim\Diamond(p \;\&\; q)$$

References and further reading

Bradley, R. & N. Swartz 1979. *Possible Worlds*. Oxford: Blackwell.

Girle, R. 2003. *Possible Worlds*. Stocksfield: Acumen.

Kripke, S. A. 1959. "A Completeness Theorem in Modal Logic". *Journal of Symbolic Logic* 24: 1–14.

Kripke, S. A. 1963. "Semantical Analysis of Modal Logic I, Normal Propositional Calculi". *Zeitschrift für Mathematische Logik und Grundlagen der Mathematik* 9: 67–96.

Lewis, C. I. & C. H. Langford 1932. *Symbolic Logic*. New York: Dover.

White, A. 1975. *Modal Thinking*. Oxford: Blackwell.

PART ONE

Formal systems

CHAPTER 2

A simple modal logic

2.1 Introduction

In this chapter we set out a propositional modal logic. The logic is known as S5. It was given its name by one of the most important modal logicians of the early twentieth century; C. I. Lewis (1883–1964). Lewis constructed five axiomatic systems of modal logic and named them S1 to S5 (System 1 to System 5). It turns out that the simplest of the logics based on possible worlds is the same as Lewis's S5.

In this chapter I set out S5 in terms of modal truth trees, or modal semantic tableaux. The trees for S5 make the simplest possible use of the idea of possible worlds. I will not set out S5 in axiomatic form in this chapter, but will look at an axiomatic formulation in a later chapter.

S5 is often seen as a system capturing the idea of logical possibility. The diamond and box symbols can be used to translate as follows:

$\Diamond p$ = *It is logically possible that p*
   Possibly p
   It might be the case that p

$\Box p$ = *It is logically necessary that p*
   Necessarily p
   It must be the case that p

This supposition, that S5 sets out the logic of the notions of logical possibility and logical necessity, while intuitively reasonable, is not without difficulties and is discussed in Chapter 9.

2.2 Propositional modal logic

I begin with propositional modal logic. I will extend this to modal predicate logic in a later chapter. The well formed formulas of modal logic (WML) are simply the formulas of standard propositional logic with two additional monadic propositional operators: *diamond* and *box*. Formally we have:

Symbols

Propositional variables: $p, q, r, s, \ldots$

Propositional translation constants: $P, Q, R, S, \ldots$

> A *propositional letter* is either a propositional variable or a propositional translation constant.

Monadic operators: $\sim$ $\Diamond$ $\Box$

Dyadic operators: $\&$ $\lor$ $\supset$ $\equiv$ $\not\equiv$

Parentheses: ( )

Formation rules

BL: Any propositional letter standing alone is a WML.

R~:   If α is a WML then so is $\sim\alpha$

R$\Diamond$:   If α is a WML then so is $\Diamond\alpha$

R$\Box$:   If α is a WML then so is $\Box\alpha$

R*:   If * is any dyadic operator and α and β are WML, then so is $(\alpha * \beta)$

T: Nothing else is a WML.

2.3 Semantics and trees for a modal logic

The idea of truth in a possible world is crucial for the semantics. In ordinary propositional logic we have the "blanket" semantic condition for negation, for example (with $\Leftrightarrow$ for "if and only if", "iff"):

$$\sim\alpha = 1 \Leftrightarrow \alpha = 0$$

In modal logic we have the more complex condition:

$$\sim\alpha = 1 \text{ } in \text{ } world \text{ } \omega \Leftrightarrow \alpha = 0 \text{ } in \text{ } world \text{ } \omega$$

where ω is any possible world.

The conditions for the other standard operators become:

$(\alpha \ \& \ \beta) = 1$ *in world* $\omega \Leftrightarrow \alpha = 1$ *in world* ω and $\beta = 1$ *in world* ω
$(\alpha \lor \beta) = 1$ *in world* $\omega \Leftrightarrow \alpha = 1$ *in world* ω or $\beta = 1$ *in world* ω
$(\alpha \supset \beta) = 1$ *in world* $\omega \Leftrightarrow \alpha = 0$ *in world* ω or $\beta = 1$ *in world* ω
$(\alpha \equiv \beta) = 1$ *in world* $\omega \Leftrightarrow \alpha = 1$ *in world* ω and $\beta = 1$ *in world* ω
　　　　or $\alpha = 0$ *in world* ω and $\beta = 0$ *in world* ω

We are assuming that there are possible worlds. They are labelled with indices *n, m, l, k, j, ...*

The condition for diamond is:

$\Diamond \alpha = 1$ *in world* $\omega \Leftrightarrow \alpha = 1$ *in some world, say* υ

The condition for box is:

$\Box \alpha = 1$ *in world* $\omega \Leftrightarrow \alpha = 1$ *in every world*

The relationship between box and diamond is defined to give the following equivalences:

[1]　　$\sim \Diamond \alpha \equiv \Box \sim \alpha$

[2]　　$\sim \Box \alpha \equiv \Diamond \sim \alpha$

In what follows we shall generally use:

$\alpha(\omega) = 1$ for α *is true in* ω
$\alpha(\omega) = 0$ for α *is false in* ω

In truth-tree rules we shall use:

$\alpha \ (\omega)$　　for　　α *is true in* ω

These conditions, together with equivalences [1] and [2] give us the tree diagrams set out below for modal operators. The first two rules are **MN** rules. The third is ($\Diamond$S5) (the possibility rule) and the fourth is ($\Box$S5) (the necessity rule):

(MN)　　　　$\sim \Diamond \alpha \ (\omega)$　　$\checkmark$　　　　　　$\sim \Box \alpha \ (\omega)$　　$\checkmark$
　　　　　　　　$\vdots$　　　　　　　　　　　　　　$\vdots$
　　　　　　　　$\Box \sim \alpha \ (\omega)$　　　　　　　　$\Diamond \sim \alpha \ (\omega)$

($\Diamond$S5)　　　　　$\Diamond\alpha$　(ω)　　✓υ　　　　($\Box$S5)　　$\Box\alpha$　(ω)　　\υ
　　　　　　　　　　⋮　　　　　　　　　　　　　　　　　⋮
　　　　　　　　　α　(υ)　　　　　　　　　　　　α　(υ)
　　　　where υ *is* NEW *to this*　　　　　*where* υ *is* ANY *index*
　　　　　　path of the tree

A formula of modal logic is a logical truth iff it is *true in every possible world.* For the purpose of trees, this is best formulated in the negative. A formula is a logical truth of modal logic iff its negation is not true in even one possible world. The negative formulation of this definition means that if a formula is false in at least one possible world then there is a *counter-example*, and the formula is not a logical truth.

The logical truths of S5 are the S5-Valid formulas. We write "α is S5-Valid" as "S5-Valid(α)". So, the notion of logical truth in S5 is set out as:

　　　S5-Valid(α) $\Leftrightarrow$ ~α is not true in any world

or　　S5-Valid(α) $\Leftrightarrow$ α is true in every world.

Suppose we wish to test an ordinary propositional logic tautology for S5-Validity with a modal truth tree.

　　　$(p \supset (q \supset p))$

A truth-tree is a mechanism that searches for a counter-example. So we assume that the formula is false and let the tree do its search. If the search leads only to contradiction, then there is no counter-example, and the formula is S5-Valid.

We begin by negating the formula *in some arbitrary world*, say *n*.

1.　　~$(p \supset (q \supset p))$　　(*n*)　　NTF (Negate the Test Formula)

If the formula is true in *n*, then the antecedent is true in *n* and the consequent is false in *n*

2.　　　　p　　　　(*n*)　　from 1

3.　　　~$(q \supset p)$　　(*n*)　　from 1

The last formula decomposes:

4.　　　　q　　　　(*n*)　　from 3

5.　　　　~p　　　(*n*)　　from 3

Since we now have p and $\sim p$ both true in the same world, the tree closes:

×

There are two things to note about modal truth trees. First, you will see from the tree above that trees for propositional logic can all be converted to trees for S5 by the simple device of indexing every formula for some arbitrary world such as n. So, all the tautologies of propositional logic are S5-Valid.

The second thing concerns the trees which we set out in this text. The tree rules show that formulas should be *ticked off* after they have been decomposed. The rule □S5 is ticked off with a backslash. The last tree, when completed with ticks and not interspersed with comments should look like:

1. $\sim(p \supset (q \supset p))$ (n) ✓   NTF

2. p (n) from 1

3. $\sim(q \supset p)$ (n) ✓   from 1

4. q (n) from 3

5. $\sim p$ (n) from 3

×

From this point on, formulas will rarely be ticked off. I shall use annotations to indicate where the lines of the tree come from, and by what rule. When the rule is a propositional logic rule, I shall simply indicate which line was decomposed to give the annotated line. This means that the trees will be less cluttered. If the text were dynamic, in the sense that we could have the trees unfold as you watched them, then ticking off would make sense, but in a static text, ticks make for clutter. Nevertheless, when you do the exercises, tick off formulas as you decompose them. This will let you know, as you go, what you have dealt with, and what remains to be considered. As you do exercises the trees are dynamic, and unfold.

Let us now consider a formula with modal operators:

Consider $(\Diamond \sim p \supset \sim \Box p)$.

1. $\sim(\Diamond \sim p \supset \sim \Box p)$ (n) NTF

2. $\Diamond \sim p$ (n) from 1

3. $\sim\sim\Box p$ (n) from 1

4. $\Box p$ (n) from 3

Thus far we have used only tree rules for propositional logic. We now have to deal with formulas at 2 and 4. We use the modal rule for possibility for

2, and then for necessity at 4. These rules are applied in a way analogous to Existential Instantiation (**EI**) and Universal Instantiation (**UI**) for predicate logic trees. Just as we generally use **EI** before **UI**, so we use the possibility rule before the necessity rule.

5.   ~*p*   (*k*)   from 2, ◊S5

6.   *p*   (*k*)   from 4, □S5

         ×

So we see that S5-Valid(($\Diamond$~*p* $\supset$ ~□*p*)).

The testing of modal formulas does not always involve a shift from one world to another. For example, consider (□*p* $\supset$ *p*).

1.   ~(□*p* $\supset$ *p*)   (*n*)   NTF

2.   □*p*   (*n*)   from 1

3.   ~*p*   (*n*)   from 1

4.   *p*   (*n*)   from 2, □S5

         ×

So S5-Valid((□ *p* $\supset$ *p*)).

The truth-tree rules for **S5**, including the modified rules for propositional logic, are as follows:

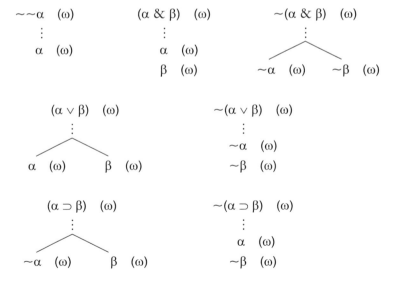

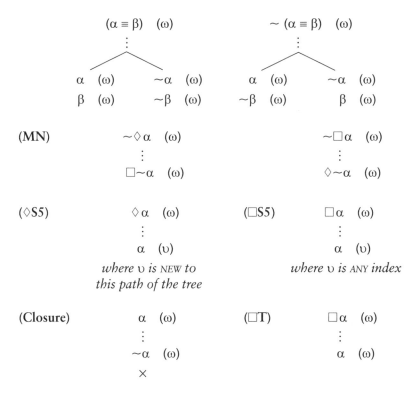

There are good reasons, which will emerge later, for adding the last rule, (□T). The rule is redundant given (□S5). When the index υ is actually the same as ω, then the rule (□S5) becomes the same as (□T). So (□T) is included in (□S5).

We now test two formulas and an argument form for S5-Validity.

Test (~□p ⊃ ◊~p).

1.	~(~□p ⊃ ◊~p)	(n)	NTF
2.	~□p	(n)	1
3.	~◊~p	(n)	1
4.	◊~p	(n)	2
5.	□~~p	(n)	3
6.	~p	(k)	4, ◊S5
7.	~~p	(k)	5, □S5
	×		

The formula is S5-Valid.

Test $(\Box(p \supset q) \supset (\Box p \supset \Box q))$.

1.	$\sim(\Box(p \supset q) \supset (\Box p \supset \Box q))$	(n)	NTF
2.	$\Box(p \supset q)$	(n)	1
3.	$\sim(\Box p \supset \Box q)$	(n)	1
4.	$\Box p$	(n)	3
5.	$\sim\Box q$	(n)	3
6.	$\Diamond\sim q$	(n)	5, **MN**
7.	$\sim q$	(k)	6, $\Diamond$S5
8.	p	(k)	4, $\Box$S5
9.	$(p \supset q)$	(k)	2, $\Box$S5

10. $\sim p$ (k) q (k) 9

          ×   ×

So, the formula is S5-Valid.

Test $\Box(p \supset q)$
              $\sim\Diamond q$
$$\therefore \quad \sim p$$

1.	$\Box(p \supset q)$	(n)	premise
2.	$\sim\Diamond q$	(n)	premise
3.	$\sim\sim p$	(n)	negated conclusion
4.	p	(n)	3
5.	$\Box\sim q$	(n)	2, **MN**
6.	$\sim q$	(n)	5, $\Box$T
7.	$(p \supset q)$	(n)	1, $\Box$T

8. $\sim p$ (n) q (n) 7

     ×   ×

So the argument form is S5-Valid.

We can look now at the argument with which we began – argument A. We test its translation [A']. The tree is:

1.	$\Box(N \supset S)$	(n)	Pr
2.	$\Box(S \supset D)$	(n)	Pr

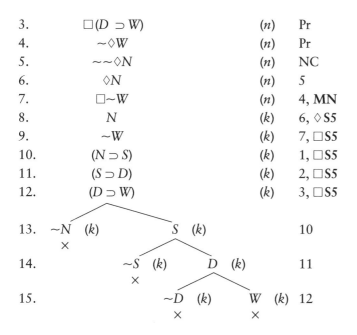

3.	$\Box(D \supset W)$		(n)	Pr
4.	$\sim\Diamond W$		(n)	Pr
5.	$\sim\sim\Diamond N$		(n)	NC
6.	$\Diamond N$		(n)	5
7.	$\Box\sim W$		(n)	4, **MN**
8.	N		(k)	6, $\Diamond$ S5
9.	$\sim W$		(k)	7, $\Box$S5
10.	$(N \supset S)$		(k)	1, $\Box$S5
11.	$(S \supset D)$		(k)	2, $\Box$S5
12.	$(D \supset W)$		(k)	3, $\Box$S5

So the argument is valid in S5.

We can cut down on the work in trees by simply omitting the indices from trees for formulas with no modal operators. By means of this work-saving convention all propositional and predicate logic trees become S5 trees.

2.3 Exercises

1. Show the following formulas to be S5-Valid:

a. $(\Box p \supset p)$
b. $(\Diamond p \supset \Box \Diamond p)$
c. $\Box\Box(p \supset p)$
d. $\Box(p \supset q) \supset \Box(\Box p \supset \Box q)$
e. $(\Diamond\Diamond p \supset \Diamond p)$

f. $\Diamond(p \vee q) \equiv (\Diamond p \vee \Diamond q)$
g. $\Box(p \& q) \equiv (\Box p \& \Box q)$
h. $(\Box(\sim p \supset p) \equiv \Box p)$
i. $(\Box(q \supset p) \& \Box(\sim q \supset p)) \equiv \Box p$
j. $\Box(p \vee \Box q) \equiv (\Box p \vee \Box q)$

2. Translate the following arguments into S5 and test for validity. Use only the dictionary provided.

a. The facts clearly established by Fanshawe's experiments are incompatible with the acceptability of the theory proposed by Brown. The facts were clearly established by Fanshawe's experiments. So, the theory proposed by Brown is not acceptable.
   [F = The facts were clearly established by Fanshawe's experiments.
   B = The theory proposed by Brown is acceptable.]

b. If it rains then moisture must be in the air. If moisture is in the air then the gauge will show a reading. Since the gauge shows no reading, it is not raining.
    [*R* = It is raining.
    M = Moisture is in the air.
    G = The gauge shows a reading.]

c. If the object has mass then it must attract all other objects. Since there is an object other than itself which it does not attract, it must have no mass.
    [*M* = The object has mass.
    A = The object attracts all other objects.]

d. We can't have two staff members away and offer all the usual courses. Therefore not having two staff members away is a necessary condition for our offering all the usual courses.
    [*A* = We have two staff members away.
    U = We offer all the usual courses.]

e. If I can see my hands then I do see my hands. Seeing my hands is incompatible with my hands' not being there. Since I can see my hands, it must follow that they are there.
    [*S* = I see my hands.
    H = My hands are there.]

2.4 Counter-examples in modal propositional logic

Modal logic counter-examples are similar to propositional logic counter-examples. The difference is that propositional letters can have different truth values across several different worlds.

Remember that formulas of modal logic are true or false *in worlds*.

So, a propositional letter can have one truth value in one world, and another in another world. Within any one world a letter can have only one truth value. For example, with the letters p and q, and the worlds n and k:

	n	k
p	1	0
q	0	1

The set of worlds, $\{n, k\}$, is a system of worlds. Systems of worlds such as the one above with two worlds and truth-values for p and q are also known as **models**. For S5, if a formula, α, is true in every world in a system then $\Box\alpha$ is true in every world in the system. But if α is false in even one of the worlds in a system then $\Box\alpha$ is false in every world in the system.

In the system above, $\Box(p \lor q)$ is true in every world because $(p \lor q)$ is true in all worlds. But $\Box(p \supset q)$ is false in every world because $(p \supset q)$ is false in n.

In the system above, $\Box p$ is false in every world because p is false in k. Also, $\Box q$ is false in every world because q is false in n.

If a formula, α, is true in at least one world of the system then $\Diamond\alpha$ is true in every world in the system. For $\Diamond\alpha$ to be false in all worlds α has to be false in all worlds.

In the system above $\Diamond(p \supset q)$ is true in every world because $(p \supset q)$ is true in one world, world k. Note also that in the system above $\Diamond(p \lor q)$ is true in every world because $(p \lor q)$ is true in at least one world.

These facts, and a couple more, can be tabulated as:

	n	k			n	k			n	k
p	1	0		$\Box p$	0	0		$\Diamond p$	1	1
q	0	1		$\Box q$	0	0		$\Diamond q$	1	1
$(p \lor q)$	1	1		$\Box(p \lor q)$	1	1		$\Diamond(p \lor q)$	1	1
$(p \supset q)$	0	1		$\Box(p \supset q)$	0	0		$\Diamond(p \supset q)$	1	1

The definition of a counter-example is:

> *A system is a counter-example to a formula's being S5-Valid iff the formula is false in at least one world in the system.*

The system $\{n, k\}$ above is a counter-example to:

$(p \supset q)$ (because it is false in n)
$\Box(p \supset q)$ (because it is false in every world)

But it is not a counter-example to:

$(p \lor q)$ (because it is not false in any world)
$\Diamond(p \lor q)$ (because it is not false in any world)

We have already seen that $\Box p$ is false in n. But p is true in n. So the truth value of $(p \supset \Box p)$ in n will be false. This means that the system above is a counter-example to:

$(p \supset \Box p)$ (because it is false in n)

Consider the more complex formula

$$(\Box(p \lor q) \supset (\Box p \lor \Box q))$$

in world n of the system above.

We know that:

$\Box(p \lor q)$	$(n) = 1$
$\Box p$	$(n) = 0$
$\Box q$	$(n) = 0$

So $(\Box(p \lor q) \supset (\Box p \lor \Box q))$ $(n) = 0$

The system above is a counter-example to the S5-Validity of:

$$(\Box(p \lor q) \supset (\Box p \lor \Box q))$$

Truth trees are, essentially, a diagrammatic way of searching for counter-examples. In trees for S5 we begin with the assumption that the formula is false in some arbitrary world. If this assumption is inconsistent then the tree closes. If the assumption is consistent then the tree remains open and a counter-example can be retrieved.

Consider the formula $(\Box(p \supset q) \supset (p \supset \Box q))$.

1.	$\sim(\Box(p \supset q) \supset (p \supset \Box q))$	(n)	NTF
2.	$\Box(p \supset q)$	(n)	1
3.	$\sim(p \supset \Box q)$	(n)	1
4.	p	(n)	3
5.	$\sim\Box q$	(n)	3
6.	$\Diamond\sim q$	(n)	5, MN
7.	$(p \supset q)$	(n)	2, $\Box$T

8.	$\sim p \; (n)$ $q \; (n)$		7
9.	$\times$ $\sim q$	(k)	6, $\Diamond$S5
10.	$(p \supset q)$	(k)	2, $\Box$S5
11.	$\sim p \;\; (k)$ $q \;\; (k)$		10
	$\uparrow$ $\times$		

Given the open path marked with the arrow, we can extract the following system:

	n	k
p	1	0
q	1	0

So the modal values are:

	n	k
p	1	0
q	1	0
$(p \supset q)$	1	1

	n	k
$\Box p$	0	0
$\Box q$	0	0
$\Box(p \supset q)$	1	1

So $\Box(p \supset q)$ $(n) = 1$
     $\Box q$ $(n) = 0$
     p $(n) = 1$

So $(\Box(p \supset q) \supset (p \supset \Box q))$ $(n) = 0$

So the tree has given a system of worlds which is a counter-example.
Consider now the translated argument [A''].

$$(N \supset \Box S)$$
$$(S \supset \Box D)$$
$$(D \supset \Box W)$$
$$\underline{\sim\Diamond W}$$
$$\therefore \quad\quad \sim\Diamond N$$

The tree is:

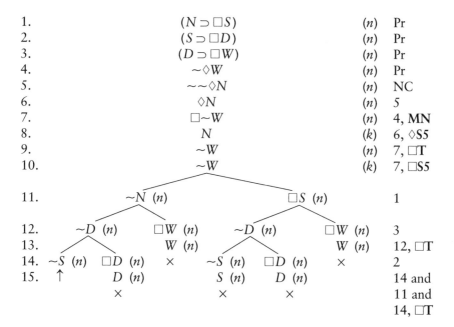

1.	$(N \supset \Box S)$	(n)	Pr
2.	$(S \supset \Box D)$	(n)	Pr
3.	$(D \supset \Box W)$	(n)	Pr
4.	$\sim\Diamond W$	(n)	Pr
5.	$\sim\sim\Diamond N$	(n)	NC
6.	$\Diamond N$	(n)	5
7.	$\Box\sim W$	(n)	4, MN
8.	N	(k)	6, $\Diamond$S5
9.	$\sim W$	(n)	7, $\Box$T
10.	$\sim W$	(k)	7, $\Box$S5

The left-most path will not close. The argument translation [A''] is not valid. This is in direct contrast to [A'].

A counter-example can be drawn from the left path.

	n	k
S	0	
D	0	
W	0	0
N	0	1

Since S, D and N are false in n, the first three premises are true in n. Since W is false in both n and k, the fourth premise is true (it is not possible for W to be true). Since N is true in k, it is possible for N to be true, and the conclusion is false.

Consider argument [B'']:

$$\frac{\begin{array}{c} (C \supset M) \\ C \end{array}}{\therefore \quad \Box M}$$

A tree for this would be:

1.	$(C \supset M)$	(n)	Pr
2.	C	(n)	Pr
3.	$\sim\Box M$	(n)	NC
4.	$\Diamond\sim M$	(n)	3, **MN**
5.	$\sim M$	(k)	4, $\Diamond$S5
6.	$\sim C$ (n) M (n)		1
7.	$\times$ $\uparrow$		

A counter-example is easily drawn from the open path:

	n	k
T	1	
M	1	0

The premises are true in n, but the conclusion, $\Box M$, is false in n.

2.4 Exercises

1. Test the following formulas for S5-Validity. Where necessary, unabbreviate the defined operators. If any formula is not S5-Valid, provide a counter-example with a test to show that it is such.

a. $(p \supset \Box\Diamond p)$
b. $(\Box\Diamond p \supset \Diamond\Box p)$

c. $\square(\square p \supset \square q) \vee \square(\square q \supset \square p)$
d. $(p \supset \lozenge q) \supset (\lozenge q \supset \sim p)$ (sceptic's thesis)
e. $(p \supset q) \supset \sim \lozenge(p \;\&\; \sim q)$
f. $(\sim \lozenge p \supset (p \prec q))$ (a paradox of strict implication)
g. $(\sim \lozenge p \supset (p \ominus q))$
h. $(p \circ q) \ominus (p \ominus q)$
i. $\nabla p \equiv \nabla \sim p$
j. $\Delta p \equiv \sim \Delta \sim p$

2.5 Concluding remarks

We now have a basic modal logic. It is propositional S5. For the time being we shall concentrate on propositional modal logic. S5 is just one of many modal logics. It is a central logic in a group of modal logics known as the *normal modal logics*. In Chapter 3 I will turn my attention to several normal modal logics.

References and further reading

Hintikka, J. K. 1957. "A New Approach to Sentential Logic". *Societas Scientarium Fennica Commentationes Physico-Mathematicae* **17**.
Hintikka, J. K. 1969. *Models for Modalities*. Dordrecht: Reidel.
Hughes, G. E & M. J. Cresswell 1996. *A New Introduction to Modal Logic*. London & New York: Routledge.
Kripke, S. A. 1959. "A Completeness Theorem in Modal Logic". *Journal of Symbolic Logic* **24**: 1–14.
Kripke, S. A. 1963. "Semantical Analysis of Modal Logic I, Normal Propositional Calculi". *Zeitschrift für mathematische Logik und Grundlagen der Mathematik* **9**: 67–96.

CHAPTER 3

The normal modal logics

3.1 Introduction

If you look at the modal rules for trees you will see that they are of three kinds. First, the **MN** (modal negation) rules simply show the inter-definability of box and diamond. Second, the ◊S5 rule is a **world generator** rule. Each time it is used in a tree another world is added to the system that, we hope, will result in a counter-example. Third, the □S5 rule is a **world filler** rule. After worlds are generated by the ◊S5 rule, the □S5 rule fills the new world (or worlds) with various formulas.

3.2 Accessibility

Consider the world generator rule. Let us add to it a condition that enables us to keep track of which worlds were generated from which worlds. Look at the S5 tree:

1.	$\sim((\Diamond p \;\&\; \Diamond q) \supset \Diamond(p \;\&\; q))$	(n)	NTF
2.	$(\Diamond p \;\&\; \Diamond q)$	(n)	1
3.	$\sim\Diamond(p \;\&\; q)$	(n)	1
4.	$\Box\sim(p \;\&\; q)$	(n)	3, MN
5.	$\Diamond p$	(n)	2
6.	$\Diamond q$	(n)	2
7.	p	(k)	5, ◊S5
8.	q	(l)	6, ◊S5
9.	$\sim(p \;\&\; q)$	(k)	4, □S5

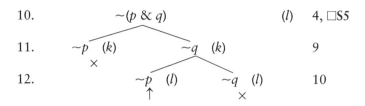

10. $\sim(p \,\&\, q)$ (l)   4, □S5

11. $\sim p$ (k) $\sim q$ (k)   9
          ×

12. $\sim p$ (l) $\sim q$ (l)   10
                 ↑   ×

Note carefully how the worlds k and l are *generated from* world n. When this happens we say:

    n has *generated k*
and n has *generated l*

One way of changing the logic is to *restrict* the world filler rule. The restriction can work so that filling only happens *to* worlds generated *from* the world in which the □α formulas occur:

If the value of □α in ω = 1 and ω *generated* υ, then the value of α in υ = 1

When one world generates another then it has *access* to the world it generated. We write "ωAυ" for "ω *has access to* υ". The *accessibility* relation between worlds is very important in possible world semantics. Accessibility is a *binary* or *dyadic* relation between pairs of worlds.

    If ω *generated* υ, then ωAυ

If we write "the value of α in ω = 1" as "α(ω) = 1" and "the value of α in ω = 0" as "α(ω) = 0", then we have:

    If □α(ω) = 1 and ωAυ, then α(υ) = 1

We have a new rule for diamond in which generating accessibility is explicit:

    If ◇α(ω) = 1 then there is at least one world, υ, such that ωAυ and α(υ) = 1

These are both strengthened to and rewritten as two logically equivalent principles:

    □α(ω) = 1 ⇔ (∀υ)(ωAυ ⇒ α(υ) = 1)

    ◇α(ω) = 1 ⇔ (∃υ)(ωAυ & α(υ) = 1)

In the tree above the generated access can be represented by the diagram:

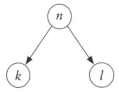

We can see that there is no generated access from k to l.

The world filler rules are quite unrestricted in S5. If $\Box\alpha$ is in a world, then α can be put into any world whatsoever. This can be described as: In S5 every world has access to every world (including itself).

To keep track of access, and to apply the restriction to the $\Box$S5 rule, we have to modify the modal tree rules so as to write in the accessibility generated by the diamond principle. We get:

$$(\Diamond R) \qquad \Diamond\alpha \quad (\omega)$$
$$\vdots$$
$$\omega A\upsilon$$
$$\alpha \quad (\upsilon)$$
where υ is NEW *to this path of the tree*

$$(\Box R) \qquad \Box\alpha \quad (\omega)$$
$$\omega A\upsilon$$
$$\vdots$$
$$\alpha \quad (\upsilon)$$

The accessibility generated by $\Diamond R$ is entered into the tree. The generated world must be new just as the constant used in the existential instantiation rule for predicate logic must be new. The new necessity rule, $\Box R$, can work only if there is accessibility. That means that we have removed the condition that was in the old rule, $\Box$S5: υ *is* ANY *world*.

We can't even assume that a world has access to itself, a fact that followed from the $\Box$S5 rule. This self-access in S5 is expressed in the $\Box$T rule. But in the restricted logic we are looking at, we do not have $\Box$T. Self-access is not generated, and is not guaranteed by any other stipulation.

If you completed the exercises in Chapter 2 you will have tested $(\Box p \supset \Box\Box p)$ and found it S5-Valid. We now test it with the new restricted rules above:

1. $\sim(\Box p \supset \Box\Box p)$ (n) NTF
2. $\Box p$ (n) 1
3. $\sim\Box\Box p$ (n) 1
4. $\Diamond \sim \Box p$ (n) 3, **MN**
5. nAk 4, $\Diamond R$ (to keep track of accessibility)
6. $\sim\Box p$ (k) 4, $\Diamond R$
7. $\Diamond \sim p$ (k) 6, **MN**
8. p (k) 2, 5, $\Box R$ (*two* entries are needed to justify this)

9.   *kAl*   7, ◊R (see line 5 above)

10.   ~ *p*   (*l*)   7, ◊R
         ↑

The tree will not close. *n* does not have access to *l*, so there is no way of getting the *p* in □*p* in *n* into *l* for tree closure. We can use a diagram to show the access in the tree above: *nAk, kAl*

There is no arrow from *n* to *l*,
because there is no access *nAl*

Unless there is some other stipulation, we just do not have *nAl*. We shall see in the next section that it is possible to put additional conditions onto accessability, conditions other than purely generated access.

3.3 K to S5

We know that the tree rules for **S5** are the possible world propositional logic rules, the modal negation rules and the two simple modality rules: ◊S5 and □S5. The rule □T is also an **S5** rule.

Let **PTr** stand for the set of propositional logic tree rules.
Let **MN** stand for the set of modal negation tree rules.
Since **PTr** and **MN** are single world rules let **SW** = **PTr** ∪ **MN**
Let **S5Tr** stand for the set of **S5** tree rules for modal propositional logic.

So: **S5Tr** =**SW** ∪ {◊S5, □S5}
or: **S5Tr** =**SW** ∪ {◊S5, □S5, □T}

The new logic we get with the more restricted rules, ◊R and □R, and without □T, is the logic **K**.

Let **KTr** stand for the set of **K** tree rules for modal propositional logic.

So: **KTr** =**SW** ∪ {◊R, □R}

We apply the **K** rules.

Consider the formula $(p \supset \Box \Diamond p)$. Its tree is:

1.	$\sim(p \supset \Box \Diamond p)$	(n)	NTF
2.	p	(n)	1
3.	$\sim \Box \Diamond p$	(n)	1
4.	$\Diamond \sim \Diamond p$	(n)	3, MN
5.	nAk		4, $\Diamond$R
6.	$\sim \Diamond p$	(k)	4, $\Diamond$R
7.	$\Box \sim p$	(k)	6, MN
	$\uparrow$		

We can go no further. The access diagram is:

The logics **K** and **S5** are two **normal** modal logics. There are several well known normal modal logics. We shall consider **K, T, S4, Br** and **S5**. In many texts the modal logic **T** is called "M" and **Br** is called "B". These logics can all be constructed by various modifications to **K**. Even **S5** can be constructed from **K**, as we shall see.

There are two strategies for constructing the normal modal logics from **K**. They are the *orthodox* and the *Hintikka* strategies. The Hintikka strategy is, in many ways, the simpler of the two. So we begin with the Hintikka strategy. We shall look at the orthodox strategy later.

The Hintikka strategy

The Hintikka strategy is to add additional filler rules besides the rule $\Box$R. To get the system **T** from the system **K**, the rule $\Box$T is added. The Hintikka **T** tree rules are set out below the **K** rules to show the addition:

$$\mathbf{KTr} = \mathbf{SW} \cup \{\Diamond R, \Box R\}$$
$$\mathbf{HTTr} = \mathbf{SW} \cup \{\Diamond R, \Box R, \Box T\}$$

Consider the tree for: $(\Box p \supset p)$ in **K**.

1.	$\sim(\Box p \supset p)$	(n)	NTF
2.	$\Box p$	(n)	1
3.	$\sim p$	(n)	1

At this point we can go no further in **K**. The tree will be open. But in a **T** tree we can use □T to get:

4.	p	(n)	2, □T
	×		

So, T-Valid $((□p \supset p))$
but: not K-Valid $((□p \supset p))$

$(□p \supset p)$ is a crucial formula for indicating the difference between **K** and **T**.

The system **S4** is gained by adding yet another filler rule to the rules for **T**. The new **S4** rule is:

$$(□□R) \qquad □\alpha \quad (\omega)$$
$$\omega A \upsilon$$
$$\vdots$$
$$□\alpha \quad (\upsilon)$$

So we set out the Hintikka **S4** tree rules as:

$$\textbf{HS4Tr} = \textbf{SW} \cup \{◇R, □R, □T, □□R\}$$

The crucial formula here, which distinguishes **S4** from **T** is $(□p \supset □□p)$. Consider the tree:

1.	$\sim(□p \supset □□p)$	(n)	NTF
2.	$□p$	(n)	1
3.	$\sim□□p$	(n)	1
4.	$◇\sim□p$	(n)	3, MN
5.	nAk		4, ◇R
6.	$\sim□p$	(k)	4, ◇R
7.	$◇\sim p$	(k)	6, MN
8.	p	(k)	2, 5, □R
9.	kAl		7, ◇R
10.	$\sim p$	(l)	7, ◇R

At this point in either **K** or **T** we can go no further. The tree remains open. But in **S4** with the new rule □□R, we can get line 11. The new rule allows the whole formula □p to be moved to k rather than just the p.

11.	$□p$	(k)	2, 5, □□R
12.	p	(l)	9, 11, □R
	×		

So: S4-Valid$((\Box p \supset \Box\Box p))$
But: not T-Valid$((\Box p \supset \Box\Box p))$
and: not K-Valid$((\Box p \supset \Box\Box p))$

The next logic of interest is **Br**. The system **Br** is gained by adding yet another filler rule to the rules for **T**. Note that this is an addition to **T**, not to **S4**. The new **Br** rule is:

($\Box$SymR) $\Box\alpha$ (υ)
                                 $\omega A \upsilon$
                                    $\vdots$

                                 α (ω)

So if υ was generated by ω and $\Box p$ is in υ, p can be put in ω. So if there is access from ω to υ then there will be access from υ to ω.

The Hintikka **Br** tree rules are:

$$\textbf{HBrTr} = \textbf{SW} \cup \{\Diamond \textbf{R}, \Box \textbf{R}, \Box \textbf{T}, \Box\Box \textbf{R}, \Box \textbf{SymR}\}$$

The crucial formula that distinguishes **Br** from all the others so far is:

$(p \supset \Box\Diamond p)$

Its tree is:

1.	$\sim(p \supset \Box\Diamond p)$	(n)	NTF
2.	p	(n)	1
3.	$\sim \Box\Diamond p$	(n)	1
4.	$\Diamond\sim\Diamond p$	(n)	3, **MN**
5.	nAk		4, $\Diamond$**R**
6.	$\sim\Diamond p$	(k)	4, $\Diamond$**R**
7.	$\Box\sim p$	(k)	6, **MN**
8.	$\sim p$	(k)	7, $\Box$**T**

At this point in either **K**, **T** or **S4** we can go no further. The tree remains open. We need the **Br** rule:

9.	$\sim p$	(n)	5, 7, $\Box$**SymR**

The next logic of interest is **S5**. To get the tree system for **S5** there are two options available. The first was set out in Chapter 2.

The other option is to add yet another filler rule to the rules for **K**. We do this by adding to the rules for **S4**. It is like the $\Box\Box$**R** rule, but "backwards" from υ to ω.

$(\Box\Box\mathrm{SymR})$ $\qquad\qquad \Box\alpha$ (υ)

$\qquad\qquad\qquad\quad \omega A\upsilon$

$\qquad\qquad\qquad\quad \vdots$

$\qquad\qquad\qquad \Box\alpha$ (ω)

So we set out the Hintikka S5 tree rules as:

$$\mathbf{HS5Tr} = \mathbf{SW} \cup \{\Diamond\mathbf{R}, \Box\mathbf{R}, \Box\mathbf{T}, \Box\Box\mathbf{R}, \Box\Box\mathbf{SymR}\}$$

The crucial formula that distinguishes S5 from all the others is:

$$(\Diamond p \supset \Box\Diamond p)$$

Its tree is:

1.	$\sim(\Diamond p \supset \Box\Diamond p)$	(n)	NTF
2.	$\Diamond p$	(n)	1
3.	$\sim\Box\Diamond p$	(n)	1
4.	$\Diamond\sim\Diamond p$	(n)	3, MN
5.	nAk		4, $\Diamond$R
6.	$\sim\Diamond p$	(k)	4, $\Diamond$R
7.	nAl		2, $\Diamond$R
8.	p	(l)	2, $\Diamond$R
9.	$\Box\sim p$	(k)	6, MN

At this point in either **K**, **T** or **S4** we can go no further. In those systems the tree remains open. What of **Br**? We can go a little further. We get:

10.	$\sim p$	(n)	5, 9, $\Box$SymR

But the tree still remains open. We need the S5 rule to get not just $\sim p$ into n, but also $\Box\sim p$ into n:

11.	$\Box\sim p$	(n)	5, 9, $\Box\Box$SymR
12.	$\sim p$	(l)	5, 11, $\Box$R
	$\times$		

So: S5-Valid$((\Diamond p \supset \Box\Diamond p))$

There are many other normal modal logics, but we shall not concern ourselves with them just yet. We turn now to the orthodox strategy for trees for **K** to **S5**.

The orthodox strategy

The orthodox strategy stipulates *properties* for the accessibility relation. For example, we can guarantee the worlds have self-access just by stipulating that the accessibility relation is *reflexive: Refl(A)*. A tree rule for reflexivity is:

(Refl)   ⋮

$\qquad\qquad$ $\omega A \omega$

$\qquad$ *for* ANY ω *in this path*

If we stipulate that *Refl(A)* and add the **Refl** rule to the tree rules for **K**, then we have an alternative set of rules for **T**. The orthodox tree rules for **T, TTr,** are:

$$\textbf{TTr} = \textbf{SW} \cup \{\Diamond\textbf{R}, \Box\textbf{R}, \textbf{Refl}\}$$

Consider the tree for $(\Box p \supset p)$.

1.	$\sim(\Box p \supset p)$	(n) NTF
2.	$\Box p$	(n) 1
3.	$\sim p$	(n) 1

At this point we can go no further in **K**. The tree is open. But, if we have the **Refl** rule, we get *nAn*. So, in a **T** tree we get:

4.	nAn	**Refl**
5.	p	(n) 2, 4, $\Box$**R**
	$\times$	

So,$\qquad$ **T**-Valid$((\Box p \supset p))$
but:$\qquad$ not **K**-Valid$((\Box p \supset p))$

If we stipulate that accessibility is *transitive, Trans(A),* as well as *reflexive,* then we have tree rules for the logic **S4**. A tree rule for transitivity is:

(Trans)$\qquad$ $\omega A \upsilon$
$\qquad\qquad\quad$ $\upsilon A \tau$
$\qquad\qquad\quad$ ⋮
$\qquad\qquad\quad$ $\omega A \tau$

The orthodox tree rules for **S4, S4Tr,** are:

$$\textbf{S4Tr} = \textbf{SW} \cup \{\Diamond\textbf{R}, \Box\textbf{R}, \textbf{Refl}, \textbf{Trans}\}$$

The crucial formula that distinguishes **S4** from **T**, as we have seen above, is:

$$(\Box p \supset \Box\Box p)$$

Consider the tree:

1.	$\sim(\Box p \supset \Box\Box p)$	(n)	NTF
2.	$\Box p$	(n)	1
3.	$\sim\Box\Box p$	(n)	1
4.	$\Diamond\sim\Box p$	(n)	3, **MN**
5.	nAk		4, $\Diamond$**R**
6.	$\sim\Box p$	(k)	4, $\Diamond$**R**
7.	$\Diamond\sim p$	(k)	6, **MN**
8.	p	(k)	2, 5, $\Box$**R**
9.	kAl		7, $\Diamond$**R**
10.	$\sim p$	(l)	7, $\Diamond$**R**

At this point in either **K** or **T** we can go no further. The tree remains open. But, in **S4**, since we have **Trans**, we can derive *nAl* from 5 and 9.

11.	nAl		5, 9, **Trans**
12.	p	(l)	2, 11, $\Box$**R**
	$\times$		

So: **S4**-Valid $((\Box p \supset \Box\Box p))$
But: not **T**-Valid $((\Box p \supset \Box\Box p))$
and: not **K**-Valid $((\Box p \supset \Box\Box p))$

If we stipulate that accessibility is *symmetric*, *Sym(A)*, as well as *reflexive*, then we have tree rules for the logic **Br**. A tree rule for symmetry is:

(**Sym**) $\omega A \upsilon$
                     $\vdots$
              $\upsilon A \omega$

The orthodox tree rules for **Br**, **BrTr**, are:

BrTr = SW $\cup$ {$\Diamond$**R**, $\Box$**R**, **Refl**, **Sym**}

The crucial formula that distinguishes **Br** from **T** and **S4** is:

$$(p \supset \Box\Diamond p)$$

If we stipulate that accessibility has all three properties mentioned above, *reflexive*, *transitive*, and *symmetric*, then we have the logic we started with: **S5**.

The orthodox S5 tree rules, **S5Tr**, are:

S5Tr = PTr ∪ MN ∪ {◇R, □R, Refl, Trans, Sym}

The crucial formula that distinguishes **S5** from all the others is $(◇p ⊃ □◇p)$. Its tree is:

1.	$\sim(◇p ⊃ □◇p)$	(*n*)	NTF
2.	$◇p$	(*n*)	1
3.	$\sim□◇p$	(*n*)	1
4.	$◇\sim◇p$	(*n*)	3, **MN**
5.	*nAk*		4, ◇R
6.	$\sim◇p$	(*k*)	4, ◇R
7.	*nAl*		2, ◇R
8.	*p*	(*l*)	2, ◇R
9.	$□\sim p$	(*k*)	6, **MN**

At this point in either **K**, **T** or **S4** we can go no further. Although **S4** gives us **Trans**, there is no way to apply it. The tree remains open. In **S5**, where we have both **Sym** and **Trans**, we use **Sym** to derive *kAn* from *nAk* at 5.

10.	*kAn*	5, **Sym**

Then we can derive *kAl* from *kAn* and *nAl*.

11.	*kAl*	10, 7, **Trans**
12.	$\sim p$	(*l*) 11, 9, □R
	×	

So: S5-Valid $((◇p ⊃ □◇p))$

In the tree above, the generated access up to line 10 can be represented by the diagrams below.

The arrow from *k* to *n* was generated by **Sym**, but we need **Trans** to get all the way from *k* to *l*:

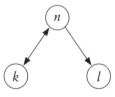

The final accessibility for the three worlds and **S5** will be (assuming reflexive access as well):

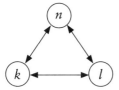

So, we have access from every world to every world, the real mark of **S5**.

The systems of worlds related by the appropriate accessibility relations with the properties set out above are known as "frames". So a **T** frame is a reflexive frame. And **S4** frame is a transitive reflexive frame, and so on. We have been using the term "system" for a set of worlds with values assigned to propositional letters in the worlds. Such a system is often called a "model". When treated as a counter-example it is sometimes called a "counter-model".

We set out the orthodox tree rules for the logics above as:

> **KTr** = SW ∪ {◇R, □R}
> **TTr** = SW ∪ {◇R, □R, Refl}
> **S4Tr** = SW ∪ {◇R, □R, Refl, Trans}
> **BrTr** = SW ∪ {◇R, □R, Refl, Sym}
> **S5Tr** = SW ∪ {◇R, □R, Refl, Sym, Trans}

You can see that the tree rules for **S4** and those for **Br**, when put together, give the tree rules for **S5**.

> **S5Tr** = **S4Tr** ∪ **BrTr**

We set out the Hintikka tree rules for the logics above as:

> **KTr** = SW ∪ {◇R, □R}
> **HTTr** = SW ∪ {◇R, □R, □T}
> **HS4Tr** = SW ∪ {◇R, □R, □T, □□R}
> **HBrTr** = SW ∪ {◇R, □R, □T, □□R, □SymR}
> **HS5Tr** = SW ∪ {◇R, □R, □T, □□R, □□SymR}

With the Hintikka strategy it is not true that the simple union of the **S4** and **Br** rules give the rules for **S5** trees. The additional □□SymR rule has to be added.

Both sets of rules for each logic yield the same valid formulas and arguments for that logic.

The normal modal logics are related in the following ways:

> All the **K**-Valid formulas are **T**-Valid formulas.
> All the **T**-Valid formulas are **S4**-Valid formulas.

All the **T**-Valid formulas are **Br**-Valid formulas.
All the **S4**-Valid formulas are **S5**-Valid formulas.
All the **Br**-Valid formulas are **S5**-Valid formulas.

This can be represented in a diagram where "**X** → **Y**" means "All **X**-Valid formulas are **Y**-Valid".

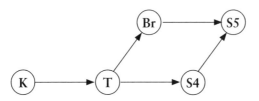

All the valid formulas of all the systems are **S5**-Valid. So, **S5** is said to be the *strongest* normal modal logic. The arrow in "**X** → **Y**" can be read as "**Y** is stronger than **X**", or "**X** is weaker than **Y**". It then follows that **K** is the *weakest* of the systems above.

3.3 Exercises

1. Show that each of the following formulas is valid in **K**.

a. $(\Diamond(p \vee q) \supset (\Diamond p \vee \Diamond q))$
b. $(\Box \sim p \supset \Box(p \supset \sim p))$
c. $(\Box \sim p \supset \Box(p \supset q))$
d. $(\Box p \supset (\Diamond q \supset \Diamond(p \,\&\, q)))$
e. $(\Diamond(p \supset q) \equiv (\Box p \supset \Diamond q))$

2. Each of the following formulas is valid in at least one of **T**, **S4** and **S5**. What is the weakest logic in which each is valid? Show this with a truth tree.

a. $(\Box(\Box(p \supset \Box p) \supset \Box p) \supset (\Diamond \Box p \supset \Box p))$
b. $(\Box(\Box p \vee \Box q) \equiv (\Box p \vee \Box q))$
c. $(\Diamond \Box p \supset p)$
d. $(\Box(p \equiv q) \supset \Box(\Box p \equiv \Box q))$
e. $(\Diamond(\Diamond p \,\&\, \sim q) \vee \Box(p \supset \Box q))$
f. $\Box(p \supset \Box \Diamond p)$
g. $((\Diamond \sim p \vee \Diamond \sim q) \vee \Diamond(p \vee q))$
h. $(p \supset (\Diamond \Box \Box p \supset \Box p))$
i. $(\Box(\Box p \supset q) \vee \Box(\Box q \supset p))$
j. $(\Box \Diamond p \equiv \Box \Diamond \Box \Diamond p)$

3.4 Counter-examples

The way of showing that a system of worlds provided a counter-example in S5 will continue to work for that logic, but not for the others. For example, consider the formula $(\Box p \supset p)$ in the system **K**.

If you look at the open tree earlier, you will see that the system of worlds is just one world: $\{n\}$. This world has access to no worlds, not even itself.

We have: $p(n) = 0$

How can we calculate the value of $\Box p(n)$?

The tree has $\Box p(n) = 1$

The calculation is based on the principle already set out, that:

$$\Box\alpha(\omega) = 1 \Leftrightarrow (\forall\upsilon)(\omega A\upsilon \Rightarrow \alpha(\upsilon) = 1)$$

That is, $\Box\alpha$ is true in ω iff α is true in every world to which ω has access. This gives us the following surprising fact:

If ω has access to *no world* then $\Box\alpha$ is at once true in ω.

If you find this difficult to believe then test the validity of the argument:

Premise: $\Box\alpha(\omega) = 1 \Leftrightarrow (\forall\upsilon)(\omega A\upsilon \Rightarrow \alpha(\upsilon) = 1)$
Premise: ω *has access to nothing.*
Conclusion: $\Box\alpha(\omega) = 1$

This argument is definitely valid in ordinary predicate logic.

So the system $\{n\}$ in which we have $p(n) = 0$, and in which n has access to nothing, is a system in which $\Box p(n) = 1$. So, the system $\{n\}$ is a counter-example to the formula $(\Box p \supset p)$ in **K**. This is set out more formally in the table below. All the sub-formulas of the formula are in the left column. The values for each world are in the columns with the world index at the top.

	n
p	0
$\Box p$	1

So: $(\Box p \supset p)\,(n) = 0$

The definition of a counter-example is the same as it was for **S5**:

A system is a counter-example to a formula's being K-Valid iff the formula is false in at least one world in the system.

Consider the first tree in this chapter. It is, as it happens, a tree which could have been constructed with the rules for **K**. It has an open path from which we can construct a system of worlds: $\{n, k, l\}$ in which n has access to k and to l. Note that k and l have no access to any world, not even to themselves.

The calculation for the value of $\Diamond\alpha$ is based on the principle:

$$\Diamond\alpha(\omega) = 1 \Leftrightarrow (\exists\upsilon)(\omega A\upsilon \text{ and } \alpha(\upsilon) = 1)$$

That is, $\Diamond\alpha$ is true in ω iff α is true in at least one world to which ω has access.

If ω has access to no world then $\Diamond\alpha$ is at once false in ω.

We now set out the facts from the open path in the tree.

	n	k	l
p	0	1	0
q	0	0	1

These facts can be represented clearly in a table for all the sub-formulas of the formula being tested. The values of the formulas in the worlds are entered in each column in the obvious way:

	nAk		nAl
	n	k	l
p	0	1	0
q	0	0	1
$(p \,\&\, q)$	0	0	0
$\Diamond p$	1	0	0
$\Diamond q$	1	0	0
$\Diamond(p \,\&\, q)$	0	0	0

We can calculate the value of the formula from the values of its sub-formulas in world n:

$$((\Diamond p \,\&\, \Diamond q) \supset \Diamond(p \,\&\, q)) \quad (n)$$
$$= ((1 \,\&\, 1) \supset 0) \quad (n)$$
$$= (1 \supset 0) \quad (n)$$
$$= 0 \quad (n)$$

THE NORMAL MODAL LOGICS

So the system does give a counter-example to the formula in **K**.

For a counter-example in **T** we retrieve a system of worlds from the open **T** tree for $(\Diamond p \supset \Box \Diamond p)$. That is, the tree for this formula ending at line 9.

	n	k	l
p	0	1	0

These facts, and some more, can be tabularized as

		nAk	nAl	nAn	kAk	lAl
		n	k	l		
p		0	1	0		
$\Diamond p$		1	1	0		
$\Box \Diamond p$		0	1	0		

Note that the values for $\Diamond p$ in k and l must be worked out in the knowledge that these worlds do have access to themselves. So the value of $\Diamond p$ in k will be 1, but in l will be 0.

We can calculate the value of the formula from the values of its subformulas in world n:

$$(\Diamond p \supset \Box \Diamond p) \quad (n)$$
$$= (1 \supset 0) \quad (n)$$
$$= 0 \quad (n)$$

So the system of worlds and values for p does give a counter-example in **T**.

Now consider whether or not this same system of worlds is an **S4** counter-example, as well as being a **T** counter-example. The system will be an **S4** system so long as the accessibility relation is both reflexive and transitive.

Given the facts that nAk and nAl, what follows from **Trans**(A)? In fact, nothing does. So, the system of worlds above is also an **S4** counter-example to the formula $(\Diamond p \supset \Box \Diamond p)$.

Consider the formula $(\Box \Diamond p \supset \Diamond \Box p)$. Its tree is:

1.	$\sim(\Box \Diamond p \supset \Diamond \Box p)$	(n) NTF
2.	$\Box \Diamond p$	(n) 1
3.	$\sim \Diamond \Box p$	(n) 1
4.	$\Box \sim \Box p$	(n) 3, **MN**

At this point in **K** we can go no further. The tree remains open in **K**. We can go on with **T** rules, especially with $\Box$**T**.

5.	$\Diamond p$	(n) 2, $\Box$**T**
6.	$\sim \Box p$	(n) 4, $\Box$**T**
7.	$\Diamond \sim p$	(n) 6, **MN**

43

8.	nAk		7, $\Diamond$R
9.	$\sim p$	(k)	7, $\Diamond$R
10.	$\Diamond p$	(k)	2, 8, $\Box$R
11.	$\sim\Box p$	(k)	4, 8, $\Box$R
12.	$\Diamond\sim p$	(k)	11, MN
13.	kAl		12, $\Diamond$R
14.	$\sim p$	(l)	12, $\Diamond$R
15.	kAj		10, $\Diamond$R
16.	p	(j)	10, $\Diamond$R
17.	nAi		5, $\Diamond$R
18.	p	(i)	5, $\Diamond$R
19.	$\Diamond p$	(i)	2, 17, $\Box$R
20.	$\sim\Box p$	(i)	4, 17, $\Box$R
21.	$\Diamond\sim p$	(i)	20, MN
22.	iAm		21, $\Diamond$R
23.	$\sim p$	(m)	21, $\Diamond$R
24.	iAx		19, $\Diamond$R
25.	p	(x)	19, $\Diamond$R

With **T** rules we can go no further. The tree remains open in **T**.

There are many worlds in the tree. The accessibility relations are also quite complex. It is useful to draw a diagram of all the worlds and their relations. Just such a diagram is set out below. Before you look at it, try to draw your own diagram.

The worlds could be diagrammed as:

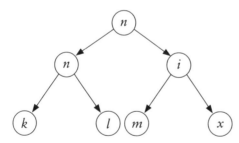

Before going on to consider the **S4** tree we can draw out the **K** and **T** counter-examples. The **K** counter-example is simple. World n has no access to any world. So, in n the formula $\Box\Diamond p$ is 1, and the formula $\Diamond\Box p$ is 0:

$$(\Box\Diamond p \supset \Diamond\Box p)\ (n) = (1 \supset 0)\ (n) = 0\ (n)$$

The case of the **T** counter-example is far more interesting. We could extract a seven world system from the tree:

$$\{n, k, i, l, j, m, x\}$$

But this is not necessary. The fact that the tree is not going to close means that there is a counter-example. We can fairly easily produce a two-world system for the counter-example.

Consider starting with the following table. In it we make the antecedent of the formula true in n, and we make the consequent false in n. We also set out an accessibility diagram:

	nAk n	nAn k	kAk
p			
$\Diamond p$			
$\Box\Diamond p$	1		
$\Box p$			
$\Diamond\Box p$	0		

We need $\Diamond p$ to be true in both worlds for $\Box\Diamond p$ to be true in n. We also need $\Box p$ to be false in both worlds for $\Diamond\Box p$ to be false in n. We make it so:

	nAk n	nAn k	kAk
p			
$\Diamond p$	1	1	
$\Box\Diamond p$	1		
$\Box p$	0	0	
$\Diamond\Box p$	0		

This value of $\Box p$ in k requires that p be false in k, because it has access only to itself. It follows that, no matter what the value of p in n, the value of $\Box p$ in n will be false, because n has access to both n and k. We make it so:

	nAk n	nAn k	kAk
p		0	
$\Diamond p$	1	1	
$\Box\Diamond p$	1		
$\Box p$	0	0	
$\Diamond\Box p$	0		

This means that the value of $\Diamond p$ in k will be false, because it has access only to itself. This makes it look impossible to set up a counter-example. But we can complete the counter-example. We make the accessibility relation more elaborate than we would normally expect in a system of worlds for **T**. We add kAn. Then we make p true in n.

	nAk	kAn	nAn	kAk
	n	k		
p	1	0		
$\Diamond p$	1	1		
$\Box \Diamond p$	1			
$\Box p$	0	0		
$\Diamond \Box p$	0			

The values are all now correct for a counter-example in two worlds.

This manipulation of the accessibility relation might seem quite illicit, especially since it makes the system of worlds look like a *symmetric* or **Br** system, and we are constructing a counter-example in **T**. But although it is *not mandatory* for the accessibility relation to be symmetric in **T**, it is *permissible* for it to be so for any given system of worlds. The only thing that is mandatory for **T** is that accessibility be reflexive.

Also, the counter-example satisfies any requirement that the accessibility relation be transitive. So it is a counter-example in **S4**. Since it satisfies any requirement that the accessibility be reflexive, transitive and symmetric, it is also an **S5** counter-example.

The moral of this story is that it sometimes better to *construct* a counter-example from the formula itself and a small number of worlds than to get the counter-example from the truth tree. It is simply the application of the method of assigning values in a modal context.

An open tree that involves more than three worlds should be viewed with some scepticism when one is trying to produce a counter-example.

3.4 Exercises

1. Provide **S5** counter-examples for each of the following formulas.

a. $\Box(p \vee (q \,\&\, (r \vee \Box s)))$
b. $(\Box(\Box(p \equiv q) \supset \Diamond q) \supset \Box(\Box(p \equiv q) \supset q))$
c. $((\Box\Diamond p \,\&\, \Box\Diamond q) \supset \Diamond(p \,\&\, q))$

2. Provide **S4** counter-examples for each of the following formulas.

a. $(\Diamond(\Diamond p \,\&\, {\sim}q) \vee \Box(p \,\&\, \Box q))$
b. $(\Box(\Box p \supset q) \vee \Box(\Box q \supset p))$
c. $(\Box(\Box(p \supset \Box p) \supset \Box p) \supset (\Diamond\Box p \supset \Box p))$

3. Provide **T** counter-examples for each of the following formulas.

a. $(\Box(\Box p \vee \Box q) \equiv (\Box p \vee \Box q))$
b. $(\Box(p \equiv q) \supset \Box(\Box p \equiv \Box q))$
c. $(\Box\Diamond p \equiv \Box\Diamond\Box\Diamond p)$

3.5 Finite modalities

Say there is a formula of the form:

O...Oα

where **O...O** is a sequence of boxes and diamonds such as:

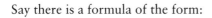

There are interesting logical equivalences in **S4** that mean that any such sequence of modal operators can be reduced to one of the following seven sequences or its negation, where "–" means "no operators at all":

   –   □   ◊   □◊   ◊□   □◊□   ◊□◊

It is often said, as a result of this, that there are only *fourteen modalities* in **S4**. The equivalences are:

$$□□p ≡ □p$$
$$◊◊p ≡ ◊p$$
$$□◊□◊p ≡ □◊p$$
$$◊□◊□p ≡ ◊□p$$

If these equivalences are applied we have the following:

- If we add one modality to -α we get either □α or ◊α.
- If we add ◊ to □α we get ◊□α, which is one of the fourteen.
- If we add □ to □α we get □□α, which is equivalent to □α.
- If we add ◊ to ◊α we get ◊◊α, which is equivalent to ◊α.
- If we add □ to ◊α we get □◊α, which is one of the fourteen. .
- If we add ◊ to □◊α we get ◊□◊α, which is one of the fourteen.
- If we add □ to □◊α we get □□◊α, which is equivalent to □◊α.
- If we add ◊ to ◊□α we get ◊◊□α, which is equivalent to ◊□α.
- If we add □ to ◊□α we get □◊□α, which is equivalent to □◊α.
- If we add ◊ to □◊□α we get ◊□◊□α, which is equivalent to ◊□α.
- If we add □ to □◊□α we get □□◊□α, which is equivalent to □◊□α.

So, for every formula of the form **O...O**α there is an equivalent formula where the sequence **O...O** is replaced by one of the fourteen modalities.

In **S5** sequences of modalities can always be reduced to one of the following or its negation:

   –   □   ◊

There are *six* modalities in S5.

For S5 there is the following rule:

> *In any sequence of modal operators we may delete all but the last to gain an equivalent formula.*

So $\Box\Diamond\Box\Box\Diamond\Box\Diamond\Box\Diamond\alpha$ is equivalent to $\Diamond\alpha$.

3.6 The non-reflexive normal modal logics

The system **K** is unlike all the other normal modal logics in this chapter so far, because accessibility is not reflexive in **K**. What would happen if we dropped reflexivity from the other logics as well? The simple answer is that for every other normal modal logic there is a similar but non-reflexive logic. We would get a group of **K** logics: **K, KB, K4** and **K5**.

If we simply leave out reflexivity then not only is ($\Box p \supset p$) not valid, but ($\Box p \supset \Diamond p$) is also not valid. Indeed, it is not valid in **K**. Consider the tree:

1.	$\sim(\Box p \supset \Diamond p)$	(n)	NTF
2.	$\Box p$	(n)	1
3.	$\sim\Diamond p$	(n)	1
4.	$\Box\sim p$	(n)	3, MN
	$\uparrow$		

Since n does not have access to any world we cannot get closure of the tree.

This formula is important for some applications of non-reflexive systems, so it is worth while seeing how we can get logics which are non-reflexive but contain ($\Box p \supset \Diamond p$) as a valid formula.

If we were to add the following Hintikka strategy $\Box$D rule, we could close the tree above.

($\Box$D)

$$\Box\alpha \quad (\omega)$$
$$\vdots$$
$$\Diamond\alpha \quad (\omega)$$

If we add this rule to the tree rules for each of the **K** systems above we get the D logics: **DT, D4, DBr** and **D5**.

If we use the rule $\Box$D, then we follow the Hintikka strategy. The orthodox addition would be to modify the accessibility relation so that it is a *serial* relation: $(\forall x)(\exists y)xAy$ (every world has access to at least one world). An orthodox tree rule for *Serial(A)* is:

(Serial) $\Box\alpha$ (ω)
                              $\vdots$
                            $\omega A\upsilon$
                            α (υ)
                    where υ is NEW *to*
                    this path of the tree

It should be obvious that **Serial** is virtually the same as $\Box$**D** in its effect on the tree.

The following map tells the story of the system relationships:

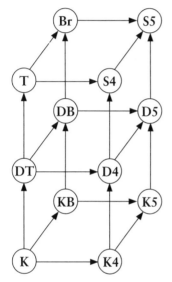

If **KTr** is the set of tree rules for **K**, and so on, then, on the orthodox strategy we have the sets of rules below:

$\quad$**KTr** = SW $\cup$ {$\Diamond$R, $\Box$R}
$\quad$**K4Tr** = SW $\cup$ {$\Diamond$R, $\Box$R, Trans}
$\quad$**KBTr** = SW $\cup$ {$\Diamond$R, $\Box$R, Sym}
$\quad$**K5Tr** = SW $\cup$ {$\Diamond$R, $\Box$R, Trans, Sym}
$\quad\;$**DTr** = SW $\cup$ {$\Diamond$R, $\Box$R, Serial}
$\quad$**D4Tr** = SW $\cup$ {$\Diamond$R, $\Box$R, Serial, Trans}
$\quad$**DBTr** = SW $\cup$ {$\Diamond$R, $\Box$R, Serial, Sym}
$\quad$**D5Tr** = SW $\cup$ {$\Diamond$R, $\Box$R, Serial, Trans, Sym}

On Hintikka's strategy we have the sets of tree rules:

$\quad$**HK4Tr** = SW $\cup$ {$\Diamond$R, $\Box$R, $\Box\Box$R}
$\quad$**HK5Tr** = SW $\cup$ {$\Diamond$R, $\Box$R, $\Box\Box$R, $\Box\Box$SymR}

HDTr = SW ∪ {◇R, □R, □D}
HD4Tr = SW ∪ {◇R, □R, □D, □□R}
HD5Tr = SW ∪ {◇R, □R, □D, □□R, □□SymR}

It is useful to set out rules for these logics with □D replacing **Serial**. We then get sets of "mixed" strategy rules.

MDTr = SW ∪ {◇R, □R, □D}
MD4Tr = SW ∪ {◇R, □R, □D, **Trans**}
MD5Tr = SW ∪ {◇R, □R, □D, **Trans**, **Sym**}

Notice that neither □T nor **Refl** are in the sets of rules for the **D** systems. This means that ($\Box p \supset p$) is not **DT**-Valid. It is not valid in any of the non-reflexive systems.

3.7 Valid and invalid

We begin this section by noting that if a formula or argument is valid in **K**, then it is valid in all the modal logics we have looked at. But also, if a formula or argument is invalid in **S5**, then it is invalid in all the modal logics we have looked at.

If we look back at the arguments we considered in Chapter 2, then we shall see that the arguments which were invalid in **S5** will be invalid in all the logics so far considered. So, A″ and B″ are quite conclusively invalid.

But, what are we to say about A′? It is valid in **S5**. What is its status in the weaker systems? The tree with explicit accessibility relations is:

1.	$\Box(N \supset S)$	(n)	Pr
2.	$\Box(S \supset D)$	(n)	Pr
3.	$\Box(D \supset W)$	(n)	Pr
4.	$\sim\!\Diamond W$	(n)	Pr
5.	$\sim\!\sim\!\Diamond N$	(n)	NC
6.	$\Diamond N$	(n)	5
7.	$\Box\!\sim\!W$	(n)	4, MN
8.	nAk		6, ◇R
9.	N	(k)	6, ◇R
10.	$\sim\!W$	(k)	7, 8 □R
11.	$(N \supset S)$	(k)	1, 8 □R
12.	$(S \supset D)$	(k)	2, 8 □R

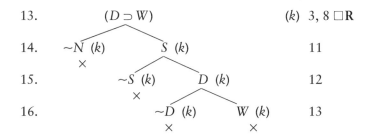

13. $(D \supset W)$ (k) 3, 8 $\square$**R**

14. ~N (k) S (k) 11
        ×

15.   ~S (k) D (k) 12
            ×

16.   ~D (k) W (k) 13
               ×   ×

This is somewhat surprising, but it does mean that A' is valid in *all* the normal modal logics.

Further reading

Chellas, B. F. 1980. *Modal Logic: An Introduction*. London: Cambridge University Press.

Hughes, G. E. & M. J. Cresswell 1996. *A New Introduction to Modal Logic*. London & New York: Routledge.

Kripke, S. A. 1963. "Semantical Analysis of Modal Logic I, Normal Propositional Calculi". *Zeitschrift für mathematische Logik und Grundlagen der Mathematik* **9**: 67–96.

CHAPTER 4

The non-normal modal logics

4.1 Introduction

Two of the normal modal logics are **S4** and **S5**. These logics were created by C. I. Lewis (1883–1964) as part of a sequence of modal logics. The logics started with System 1, **S1**, and go on to **S2**, **S3**, **S4**, and **S5**. The first three of these are not normal modal logics, and are referred to as either non-normal or sub-normal. We shall use the term "non-normal" to refer to them, and to other such logics.

There are various ways in which the distinction between the normal and the non-normal logics can be described or defined. Some descriptions focus on the differences between the sets of valid formulas. Some focus on differences in the logic apparatus. In our case we shall focus on systematic differences in the tree rules.

The tree rules we have given so far are rules that apply to formulas in all worlds. The definition of validity applies across all worlds. In non-normal logics we depart from this uniformity. We need different modal rules depending on the world the formula is in. The definition of validity is also qualified.

4.2 Two sorts of worlds

In any tree for modal logic the tree begins at some arbitrary world. We have always begun with n. This world can be any world in a system of worlds for a normal modal logic. But, in the non-normal modal logics the worlds are divided into two sets. One set is the set of *normal* worlds. The remainder are the *non-normal* worlds. The non-normal worlds are sometimes called the "sub-normal" worlds.

If a system of worlds is Ω, then the set of normal worlds will be **N** such that $\mathbf{N} \subseteq \Omega$. The set of sub-normal worlds will be **S**, all the worlds in Ω that are not normal. We can define **N** and **S** as follows:

$$\mathbf{N} \cup \mathbf{S} = \Omega \qquad \text{and} \qquad \mathbf{N} \cap \mathbf{S} = \varnothing$$

In truth-tree systems we distinguish between normal and non-normal worlds in a way that is slightly different from the standard way. We use the Hintikka strategy. A normal world is one *to which there is no generated, or outside, access*. So, standardly, the world at the start of a tree is normal. A non-normal world in a tree is a world to which there is access from outside. A non-normal world in a tree is a generated world.

$$\omega \in \mathbf{N} \Leftrightarrow \sim(\exists \upsilon)(\upsilon \neq \omega \text{ and } \upsilon A \omega)$$
$$\omega \in \mathbf{S} \Leftrightarrow (\exists \upsilon)(\upsilon \neq \omega \text{ and } \upsilon A \omega)$$

In non-normal truth trees we have two sets of tree rules, one for the **N** worlds, and one for **S** worlds. One of the simplest of the non-normal modal logics is Lemmon's favourite, **S0.5** ("S zero point five"). We now look at how the trees for **S0.5** work.

4.3 The system S0.5

For **S0.5** we have the following tree rules. The **SW** rules remain the same and apply across all worlds. These include the modal negation rules. They apply uniformly to both **N** and **S** worlds, because they can be seen simply as rules for the interdefinability of $\Diamond$ and $\Box$:

$$\sim\Diamond\alpha =_{df} \Box\sim\alpha \qquad \text{or} \qquad \sim\Box\alpha =_{df} \Diamond\sim\alpha$$

(MN) $\qquad \sim\Diamond\alpha \quad (\omega)$ $\qquad\qquad\qquad\qquad \sim\Box\alpha \quad (\omega)$
$$\vdots \qquad\qquad\qquad\qquad\qquad\qquad \vdots$$
$\qquad\qquad \Box\sim\alpha \quad (\omega)$ $\qquad\qquad\qquad\qquad \Diamond\sim\alpha \quad (\omega)$

The real difference is found in the rules for box and diamond. In **N** worlds:

($\Diamond$RN) $\qquad \Diamond\alpha \quad (\omega) \quad \omega \in \mathbf{N}$ $\qquad$ ($\Box$RN) $\qquad \Box\alpha \quad (\omega) \quad \omega \in \mathbf{N}$
$$\vdots \qquad\qquad\qquad\qquad\qquad\qquad\qquad \omega A \upsilon$$
$\qquad\qquad \omega A \upsilon \qquad\qquad \upsilon \in \mathbf{S}$ $\qquad\qquad\qquad\qquad\qquad \vdots$
$\qquad\qquad\quad \alpha \quad (\upsilon)$ $\qquad\qquad\qquad\qquad\qquad\qquad \alpha \quad (\upsilon)$
$\qquad$ *where υ is* NEW *to this*
$\qquad\qquad$ *path of the tree*

(□TN)   □α (ω)   ω ∈ N
          ⋮

          α (ω)

For all practical purposes these rules are the same as the rules for normal systems in the previous chapter. For normal worlds, ◊RN is ◊R, and □RN is □R and □TN is □T. The additional notation in ◊RN that υ ∈ S can also be dropped since we can work that out from the rule itself or from its application.

There are no box and diamond rules other than MN is S0.5 for S worlds, that is, for generated worlds. In S0.5, the generated worlds are, in essence, non-modal.

The starting world for an S0.5 tree has to be a normal world. This is because the definition of S0.5-Validity is:

S0.5-Valid($α$) ⇔ for every ω ∈ N, ~α ∉ ω

That is, the negation of a valid formula is not a member of any N world. We shall designate n to be an N world.

Consider the tree to test: $□(p ⊃ p)$

1.	~□(p ⊃ p)	(n)	NTF n ∈ N
2.	◊~(p ⊃ p)	(n)	1, MN
3.	nAk		2, ◊RN k ∈ S
4.	~(p ⊃ p)	(k)	2, ◊RN
5.	p	(k)	4
6.	~p	(k)	5
	×		

So: S0.5-Valid($□(p ⊃ p)$)

Consider the tree to test: $□□(p ⊃ p)$

1.	~□□(p ⊃ p)	(n)	NTF n ∈ N
2.	◊~□(p ⊃ p)	(n)	1, MN
3.	nAk		2, ◊RN k ∈ S
4.	~□(p ⊃ p)	(k)	2, ◊RN
6.	◊~(p ⊃ p)	(k)	4, MN
	↑		

The tree is open because, apart from the interdefinability of ◊ and □ in the modal negation rules, no other modal tree rule can be used in world k. k is an S world.

If we take a counter-example from the last tree we get:

nAk	$n \in \mathbf{N}$		$k \in \mathbf{S}$
		n	k
p		1	0
$\Box(p \supset p)$		1	0
$\Box\Box(p \supset p)$		0	0

We know from the previous tree that $\Box(p \supset p)$ is true in every $\mathbf{N}$ world. So $\Box(p \supset p)$ is true in n. But, in world k, the $\Box$ effectively renders the rest of the formula into an atomic formula or an undifferentiated blob.

So, since we have $\sim\Box(p \supset p)$ (k), the value of $\Box(p \supset p)$ in k is false, no matter what the value of p is. So:

S0.5-Invalid($\Box\Box(p \supset p)$)

even though:

S0.5-Valid($\Box(p \supset p)$)

If τ is a tautology, then S0.5-Valid(τ). But no formula of the form $\Box\Box\alpha$ is S0.5-Valid. You can see why if you look back to the last tree.

Let the set of tree rules for S0.5 be TrS0.5.

$$\text{TrS0.5} = \text{SW} \cup \{\Diamond\text{RN}, \Box\text{RN}, \Box\text{TN}\}$$

The truth-trees of S0.5 are the same as the trees for T for the root world of the tree, and then the same as for propositional logic (with MN) in all the other worlds.

4.4 The Lewis systems S2 and S3

We now look at the two Lewis systems, S2 and S3. We skip across S1 for the moment because the semantics for S1 are fiendishly complex.

The trees for S2 contain exactly the same rules as S0.5 for $\mathbf{N}$ worlds. There are additional rules for diamond and box in S worlds:

$(\Diamond RS2)$ $\quad \Diamond\alpha \quad (\omega) \qquad \omega \in \mathbf{S}$
$\qquad\qquad \Box\beta \quad (\omega)$
$\qquad\qquad \vdots$
$\qquad\qquad \omega A\upsilon \qquad\qquad \upsilon \in \mathbf{S}$
$\qquad\qquad\quad \alpha \quad (\upsilon)$
$\qquad$ *where υ is* NEW *to this*
$\qquad\quad$ *path of the tree*

$(\Box RS2)$ $\quad \Box\alpha \quad (\omega) \qquad \omega \in \mathbf{S}$
$\qquad\qquad \omega A\upsilon$
$\qquad\qquad \vdots$
$\qquad\qquad\quad \alpha \quad (\upsilon)$

The new rule for diamond effectively extends the $\mathbf{N}$ world rules to every $\mathbf{S}$

world which contains a formula of the form $\Box\beta$. The reflexive rule, $\Box$T, is extended to all worlds.

$$(\Box\text{T}) \qquad \Box\alpha \quad (\omega)$$
$$\vdots$$
$$\alpha \ (\omega)$$

Consider an S2 tree for the formula: $\Box(\Box(p \supset q) \supset (\Box p \supset \Box q))$

1.	$\sim\Box(\Box(p \supset q) \supset (\Box p \supset \Box q))$	(n)	NTF, $n \in$ N
2.	$\Diamond\sim(\Box(p \supset q) \supset (\Box p \supset \Box q))$	(n)	1, MN
3.	nAk		2, $\Diamond$RN, $k \in$ S
4.	$\sim(\Box(p \supset q) \supset (\Box p \supset \Box q))$	(k)	2, $\Diamond$NN
5.	$\Box(p \supset q)$	(k)	4
6.	$\sim(\Box p \supset \Box q))$	(k)	4
7.	$\Box p$	(k)	6
8.	$\sim\Box q$	(k)	6
9.	$\Diamond\sim q$	(k)	8, MN
10.	kAl		9, 5, $\Diamond$RS2 (a formula of form $\Box\beta$ is in k)
11.	$\sim q$	(l)	9, 5, $\Diamond$RS2
12.	$(p \supset q)$	(l)	5, 10, $\Box$RS2
13.	p	(l)	7, 10, $\Box$RS2

14. $\sim p$ (l) q (l) 12
      ×   ×

So: $\Box(\Box(p \supset q) \supset (\Box p \supset \Box q))$ is S2-Valid.

Inspect the tree and you will see that the tree could not continue beyond line 9 in S0.5. But the presence of $\Box p(k)$ at line 7 allows for the generation of world l and the closure of the tree.

Let the set of tree rules for S2 be TrS2.

$$\text{TrS2} = \text{SW} \cup \{\Diamond\text{RN}, \Diamond\text{NS2}, \Box\text{RN}, \Box\text{RS2}, \Box\text{T}\}$$
or $\text{TrS2} = \text{TrS0.5} \cup \{\Diamond\text{NS2}, \Box\text{RS2}, \Box\text{T}\}$

The Lewis system S3 requires the accessibility relation to be *transitive* also. We add the orthodox strategy (Trans) rule:

(Trans) $\omega A\upsilon$
                 $\upsilon A\tau$
                 $\vdots$
                 $\omega A\tau$

Let the set of tree rules for S3 be TrS3.

$$\text{TrS3} = \text{SW} \cup \{\Diamond\text{RN}, \Diamond\text{RS2}, \Box\text{RN}, \Box\text{RS2}, \Box\text{T, Trans}\}$$
or $\quad$ $\text{TrS3} = \text{TrS2} \cup \{\text{Trans}\}$

The relationship between S2 and S3 is like the relationship between T and S4. To get S4 from T we make the accessibility relation transitive. To get S3 from S2 we make accessibility transitive.

Consider an S3 tree for the formula: $(\Box(p \supset q) \supset \Box(\Box p \supset \Box q))$

1.	$\sim(\Box(p \supset q) \supset \Box(\Box p \supset \Box q))$	(n)	NTF, $n \in \mathbf{N}$
2.	$\Box(p \supset q)$	(n)	1
3.	$\sim\Box(\Box p \supset \Box q)$	(n)	1
4.	$\Diamond\sim(\Box p \supset \Box q)$	(n)	3, MN
5.	nAk		4, $\Diamond$RN $\quad k \in \mathbf{S}$
6.	$\sim(\Box p \supset \Box q)$	(k)	4, $\Diamond$RN
7.	$\Box p$	(k)	6
8.	$\sim\Box q$	(k)	6
9.	$\Diamond\sim q$	(k)	8, MN
10.	kAl		9, 7, $\Diamond$RS2
11.	$\sim q$	(l)	9, 7, $\Diamond$RS2
12.	nAl		5, 10, Trans
13.	$(p \supset q)$	(l)	2, 12, $\Box$RN
14.	p	(l)	7, 12, $\Box$RS2

15. $\qquad \sim p \quad (l) \qquad\qquad q \quad (l) \qquad\qquad$ 13
$\qquad\qquad \times \qquad\qquad\qquad\quad \times$

So: $\quad (\Box(p \supset q) \supset \Box(\Box p \supset \Box q))$ is S3-Valid.

Had this been an S2 tree, we would not have been able to get line 12. Then we would not have been able to get line 13. So the tree would have remained open.

4.4 Exercises

1. Test the following formulas for validity in S0.5, S2, and S3. (Each is valid in at least one of these non-normal logics.)

a. $(\Box\Box p \supset \Box\Box(q \supset p))$
b. $(\Box\Box p \supset \Box\Box(p \supset p))$
c. $(\Box(p \supset p) \supset (\Box p \supset \Box p))$
d. $\Box(\Box(p \supset p) \supset (\Box p \supset \Box p))$
e. $(\Box p \supset p)$

4.5 S1 and neighbourhoods

We set out the tree system for **S1** in a separate section because the logic is quite different from the other non-normal logics and considerably more difficult. The possible world semantics for **S1** were developed quite some time after those for the other non-normal modal logics. This section can be skipped, but if you intend to read Chapter 6 it would be best to wrestle with the material here.

For **S1** we add to the tree rules for **S0.5** a quite different set to those added for **S2**. This is because we have to introduce a second set of relationships between worlds. It is the neighbourhood relation, *N*, which relates single worlds to sets of worlds. The sets of worlds are *neighbourhoods*. In each world in a neighbourhood some key formula is true. So, for example, the α neighbourhood is all the worlds in which α is true. The α neighbourhood is often called the α *truth-set*. We use $|\alpha|$ for the α neighbourhood or truth-set. The definition of the α neighbourhood is:

$$|\alpha| \ =\ _{df}\{\omega \in \Omega : \alpha(\omega)\}$$

Clearly $|\alpha| \subset \Omega$ (the α neighbourhood is a subset of the worlds in Ω).

The introduction of neighbourhoods and the neighbourhood relation, N, takes **S1** into quite another realm of non-normal modal logics. Each neighbourhood gives us a kind of restricted non-normal necessity.

Accessibility is still retained. So there are two relations, A and N. To get the semantics for **S1** we add to **S0.5** the following truth-tree rules for non-normal worlds:

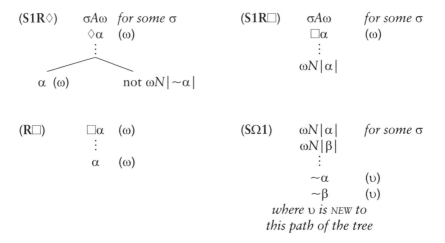

We also need rules with which to manipulate truth-sets.

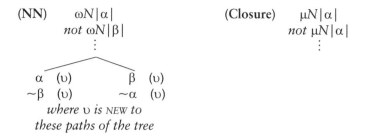

(NN) $\omega N|\alpha|$
       not $\omega N|\beta|$
       $\vdots$

(Closure) $\mu N|\alpha|$
            not $\mu N|\alpha|$
            $\vdots$

α (υ) β (υ)
$\sim\beta$ (υ) $\sim\alpha$ (υ)
where υ *is* NEW *to*
these paths of the tree

We also need a set of tree rules, (NPL), by means of which truth-set equivalences can be dealt with:

$\omega N|\sim\sim\alpha|$
$\vdots$
$\omega N|\alpha|$

$\omega N|\sim(\alpha\supset\beta)|$
$\vdots$
$\omega N|\alpha|$
$\omega N|\sim\beta|$

$\omega N|(\alpha\supset\beta)|$
$\vdots$
$\omega N|\sim\alpha|$ $\omega N|\beta|$

Because of the interdefinability of $\Diamond$ and $\Box$, we need neighbourhood versions of **MN**:

$\omega N|\sim\Diamond\alpha|$
$\vdots$
$\omega N|\Box\sim\alpha|$

$\omega N|\sim\Box\alpha|$
$\vdots$
$\omega N|\Diamond\sim\alpha|$

We look first at a tree for the key **S1** formula:

$$\Box((\Box(p\supset q)\ \&\ \Box(q\supset r))\supset\Box(p\supset r))$$

1.	$\sim\Box((\Box(p\supset q)\ \&\ \Box(q\supset r))\supset\Box(p\supset r))$	(*n*)	NTF
2.	$\Diamond\sim((\Box(p\supset q)\ \&\ \Box(q\supset r))\supset\Box(p\supset r))$	(*n*)	
3.	*nAk*		
4.	$\sim((\Box(p\supset q)\ \&\ \Box(q\supset r))\supset\Box(p\supset r))$	(*k*)	
5.	$(\Box(p\supset q)\ \&\ \Box(q\supset r))$	(*k*)	
6.	$\sim\Box(p\supset r)$	(*k*)	
7.	$\Diamond\sim(p\supset r)$	(*k*)	
8.	$\Box(p\supset q)$	(*k*)	
9.	$\Box(q\supset r)$	(*k*)	
10.	$(p\supset q)$	(*k*)	8, R$\Box$
11.	$(q\supset r)$	(*k*)	9, R$\Box$

12. $\sim(p\supset r)$ (*k*)   *not* $kN|\sim\sim(p\supset r)|$ 7, S1R$\Diamond$
13. p (*k*) $kN|(p\supset q)|$ 8, S1R$\Box$

14.	$\sim r$ (k)	$kN\,|(q \supset r)|$	9, **S1R**□
15.		$\sim (p \supset q)$ (j)	13, 14, **SΩ1**
16.	$\sim p$ (k) q (k)	$\sim (q \supset r)$ (j)	13, 14, **SΩ1**
17.	×	p (j)	15, **PL**
18.	$\sim q$ (k) r (k)	$\sim q$ (j)	15, **PL**
19.	× ×	q (j)	16, **PL**
20.		$\sim r$ (j)	16, **PL**
21.		×	18, 19

We turn next to a formula which should not be valid in **S1** but which is valid in a semantics which for some time was thought to be the semantics for **S1** but was not.

$$\Box((\Box p \,\&\, \Box q) \supset \Box(p \,\&\, q))$$

This formula is known as the **S1⁺** formula:

1.	$\sim\Box((\Box p \,\&\, \Box q) \supset \Box(p \,\&\, q))$ (n)	NTF
2.	$\Diamond\sim((\Box p \,\&\, \Box q) \supset \Box(p \,\&\, q))$ (n)	
3.	nAk	
4.	$\sim ((\Box p \,\&\, \Box q) \supset \Box(p \,\&\, q))$ (k)	
5.	$(\Box p \,\&\, \Box q)$ (k)	
6.	$\sim\Box(p \,\&\, q)$ (k)	
7.	$\Diamond\sim (p \,\&\, q)$ (k)	
8.	$\Box p$ (k)	
9.	$\Box q$ (k)	
10.	p (k)	
11.	q (k)	
12.	$\sim (p \,\&\, q)$ (k) $not\ kN\,|\sim\sim(p \,\&\, q)|$	3, 7, **S1R**◊
13.	× 12, 10, 11 $kN\,|p|$	8, **S1R**□
14.	$kN|q|$	9, **S1R**□
15.	$\sim p(j)$	13, 14, **SΩ1**
16.	$\sim q(j)$	13, 14, **SΩ1**
17.	$\sim\sim(p \,\&\, q)$ (m) p (m)	12, 13, **NN**
18.	$\sim p$ (m) $\sim\sim\sim(p \,\&\, q)$ (m)	12, 13, **NN**
19.	$(p \,\&\, q)$ (m) $\sim(p \,\&\, q)$ (m)	
20.	p (m) $\sim p$ (m) $\sim q$ (m)	
21.	q (m) ×	
22.	× × $\sim\sim(p \,\&\, q)$ (i) q (i)	
23.	$\sim q$ (i) $\sim\sim\sim(p \,\&\, q)$ (i)	

25. $(p \mathbin{\&} q)$ (i) $\sim(p \mathbin{\&} q)$ (i)

26. p (i)

27. q (i) $\sim p$ (i) $\sim q$ (i)

                                      $\times$ $\uparrow$ $\times$

This open tree delivers an **S1** counter-example to the **S1**$^+$ formula.

Let **S** be the set of worlds in Ω which are alternate. The counter-example is:

$$\Omega = \{n, k, j, m, i\} \qquad S = \{k\}$$
$$nAk \quad \{kN \{k, i\}, kN \{k, m\}\}$$

There are several logics close to **S1** that have neighbourhood semantics. Chief among them is **S0.9**. There is also the system **S1**$^+$, which has a simpler semantics than **S1**, but its semantics is nonetheless quite strange. We shall not look at these systems in this text.

4.5 Exercises

1.   Test the formulas from 4.4 Exercises for validity in **S1**.

4.6 The E systems

Lemmon sets out a group of non-normal logics called the "E" systems. Consider again the definition above of formula validity for non-normal logics. If **L** is some non-normal logic then:

    L-Valid$(\alpha) \Leftrightarrow$ for every $\omega \in \mathbf{N}$, $\sim\alpha \notin \omega$

Formulas are tested in **N** worlds only. But, since there are two kinds of worlds, what would happen if we were to have a more general definition of formula validity? Consider what happens when the definition for normal modal logics is applied to the non-normal systems:

    L-Valid$(\alpha) \Leftrightarrow$ for every ω, $\sim\alpha \notin \omega$

To apply this definition we would have to *double test* formulas. They must be tested in both **N** and **S** worlds. A moment's reflection would reveal that any formula tested in an **S** world in **S0.5** would be valid only if it was a valid formula of non-modal logic. Consider the tree starting with an **S** world of **S0.5** for $(\Box(p \supset q) \supset (\Box p \supset \Box q))$.

1. $\sim(\Box(p \supset q) \supset (\Box p \supset \Box q))$ (n) NTF, $n \in S$
2. $\Box(p \supset q)$ (n)
3. $\sim(\Box p \supset \Box q)$ (n)
4. $\Box p$ (n)
5. $\sim\Box q$ (n)
6. $\Diamond\sim q$ (n)

Nothing more can be done. Even line 6 is merely a concession to the interdefinability of box and diamond. So, both the **K** and the **T** axioms fail. This is the system **E0.5**. Modality is not of much use here. It has no logical role.

Things are not so impoverished in **E2**. We could continue the tree above:

7. $\sim q$ (k) 6, 4, $\Diamond$**RS2**
8. nAk 6, 4, $\Diamond$**RS2**
9. p (k) 4, 8, $\Box$**RS2**
10   $(p \supset q)$ (k) 2, 8, $\Box$**RS2**
11. $\times$ (7, 9, 10 and **PTr**)

Both the **K** and the **T** axioms are valid in **E2**. But, as in **S0.5**, the necessitated versions of these are not valid. When, for example, $\sim\Box(\Box p \supset p)$ is placed in an S world of **S2**, the only rule that can be applied is **MN**.

There is a non-reflexive version of **E2**. Lemmon calls it "**C2**". The non-reflexive and serial system is called "**D2**". It would be better, given our naming conventions, to call it "**ED2**", since we would use **D2** for non-reflexive serial **S2**.

The **E** systems are interesting because they have no valid formulas of the form $\Box\alpha$.

The set of tree rules for **E2** is **TrE2**, the same as for **S2**:

TrE2 = **TrS2**

The difference is in the definition of valid formulas.

The tree rules for **ED2** and **C2** are:

TrED2 = SW ∪ {$\Diamond$**RN**, $\Diamond$**RS2**, $\Box$**RN**, $\Box$**RS2**, $\Box$**D**}
and   **TrC2** = SW ∪ {$\Diamond$**RN**, $\Diamond$**RS2**, $\Box$**RN**, $\Box$**RS2**}

In Chapter 3 there is a diagram to show how the sets of valid formulas in the normal modal logics were related. If all the valid formulas of one logic were a subset of the valid formulas of another, this was represented by an arrow meaning "included in". We now present an extended diagram.

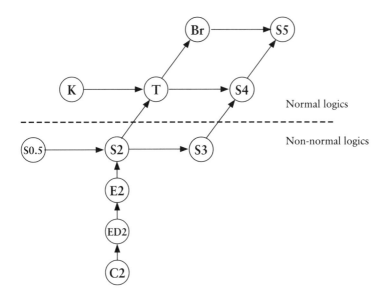

K is the weakest of the normal modal logics in the map. C2 is the weakest non-normal system. Lemmon says that C2 is a "minimal" modal logic.

4.6 Exercises

1.   Show that the following formulas are valid in E2:

a. $\Box(p \& q) \supset (\Box p \& \Box q)$
b. $(\Box p \lor \Box q) \supset \Box(p \lor q)$
c. $\Diamond(p \& q) \supset (\Diamond p \& \Diamond q)$
d. $\Box{\sim}p \supset \Box(p \supset q)$
e. $\Diamond(p \lor q) \supset (\Diamond p \lor \Diamond q)$

4.7 The pure logic of necessity

There is one more logic which we should consider before moving on. It is the system **N**, to be found in Fitting (1992). By some lights this is actually a normal modal logic. But, according to Fitting, normal modal logics have four features. They are:

1.   If α is a tautology then $\Box\alpha$ is valid.
2.   If α is valid, then so is $\Box\alpha$.

3. Any formula of the form $(\Box(\alpha \supset \beta) \supset (\Box\alpha \supset \Box\beta))$ is valid.
4. *Modus ponens* is a valid argument form.

Any logic which fails to have any one of these features is *sub-normal*.

We have seen, for example, that S0.5, S2 and S3 have feature 1, but fail to have feature 2. $\Box(p \supset p)$ is valid in all, but $\Box\Box(p \supset p)$ is valid in none.

The logic **N** fails to have the third feature. The form given in feature 3 is known as **K**, because it is **K**-Valid and **K** is the "weakest" of the normal modal logics.

Before setting out the tree rules for **N** we need to discuss the relationship between the validity of formulas and the validity of arguments. When an argument is tested for validity in a truth tree, the tree begins with the premises and the negation of the conclusion:

1.	P_1	Premise 1
	$\vdots$	$\vdots$
$n.$	P_n	Premise n
$n+1.$	$\sim C$	Negated Conclusion

The definition of an argument is often given as:

An argument is a set of premises and a conclusion.

This definition allows for the possibility of an empty set of premises. It allows for an argument with a conclusion, but no premises. The test of the validity of such an argument will be exactly the same as the test for the validity of the formula which is the conclusion of a no premise argument.

In the logic **N** all the tests are tests for the validity of arguments. The premises of arguments are indexed with (nP) to show that they are in the usual normal starting world for the tree, and are premises as well. So, the start of a tree will be:

1.	P_1	(nP)	Premise 1
	$\vdots$		$\vdots$
$n.$	P_n	(nP)	Premise n
$n+1.$	$\sim C$	(n)	Negated Conclusion

The tree rules for **N** contain all the tree rules for propositional logic and the modal negation rules. The modal rules are:

($\Diamond$**PN**)	$\Diamond\alpha$	(ω)	$\checkmark \upsilon$		(□**PN**)	α	(ρP)	$\backslash \upsilon$
	$\vdots$					$\vdots$	
	α	(υ)				α	(υ)
	where υ is NEW *to this*					*where υ is* ANY *index*
	path of the tree					

Consider the tree for the argument form:

$$(\Box p \supset q)$$
$$(\Box {\sim} \Box p \supset q)$$
$$({\sim}\Box q \vee p)$$
$$\underline{\qquad\qquad {\sim}q \qquad\qquad}$$
$$\therefore \qquad p$$

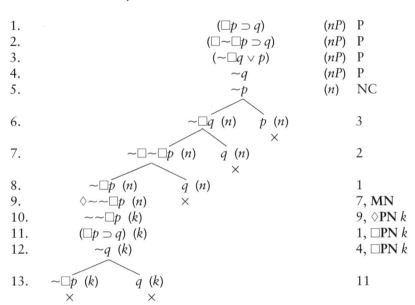

1.	$(\Box p \supset q)$	(nP)	P
2.	$(\Box {\sim} \Box p \supset q)$	(nP)	P
3.	$({\sim}\Box q \vee p)$	(nP)	P
4.	${\sim}q$	(nP)	P
5.	${\sim}p$	(n)	NC

6. ${\sim}\Box q$ (n) p (n) 3
                                ×

7. ${\sim}\Box{\sim}\Box p$ (n) q (n) 2
                               ×

8. ${\sim}\Box p$ (n) q (n) 1
9. $\Diamond{\sim}{\sim}\Box p$ (n) ×   7, **MN**
10. ${\sim}{\sim}\Box p$ (k) 9, ◊**PN** k
11. $(\Box p \supset q)$ (k) 1, □**PN** k
12. ${\sim}q$ (k) 4, □**PN** k

13. ${\sim}\Box p$ (k) q (k) 11
     ×   ×

The tree closes and the argument is valid in **N**.

Two things are clear. First, the premises are treated as if they and only they were necessarily true.

Secondly, if there are no premises, as in the test of the validity of a formula, then the rule for □ will be inoperative. It follows that the valid formulas will include all the tautologies of non-modal propositional logic. Their negations will always produce a closed tree.

If τ is a tautology, then $\Box\tau$ will be valid. The closure will be in a world other than n. It also follows that if τ is a tautology, then $\Box \ldots \Box\tau$ will be valid. The negation of the formula will, by modal negation, convert all the boxes to diamonds. This will simply generate worlds until the diamonds are all dealt with. Then we shall have a negated tautology, and that will close the tree.

But none of the "usual" modal formulas will be valid. Consider a formula of the **K** form: $(\Box(p \supset q) \supset (\Box p \supset \Box q))$.

The tree in **N** is:

1. $\sim(\Box(p \supset q) \supset (\Box p \supset \Box q))$ (n) NC
2. $\Box(p \supset q)$ (n) 1
3. $\sim(\Box p \supset \Box q)$ (n) 1
4. $\Box p$ (n) 3
5. $\sim\Box q$ (n) 3
6. $\Diamond\sim q$ (n) 5, **MN**
7. $\sim q$ (k) 6, $\Diamond$**PN** k
                    $\uparrow$

The tree will not close. Note that the tree began with the negation of the conclusion of a no premise argument.

4.7 Exercises

1.   Test the following arguments for validity in both **T** and **N**.

a. $\Box(p \supset q), \Box p \; / \therefore \; \Box q$
b. $\Box(p \vee p) \; / \therefore \; \Box p$
c. $\Box p \; / \therefore \; \Box\Box p$
d. $\Box p \; / \therefore \; p$
e. $p \; / \therefore \; \Box p$

4.8 Validity of arguments

The arguments to which we have returned, A′ and A″, are worth considering in terms of the non-normal modal systems. The first of these, A′, is valid in all the reflexive non-normal modal logics we have been looking at. You can check this by going back to the tree for **K** in the last chapter. This tree is easily converted to a tree for **N** as well as for the systems **S0.5**, **S2**, **E2** and **S3**.

You will also discover that there will be a counter-example for A″ in all these systems.

Further reading

Chellas, B. F. & K. Segerberg 1996. "Modal Logics in the Vicinity of S1". *Notre Dame Journal of Formal Logic* 37: 1–24.
Cresswell, M. J. 1995. "S1 is Not So Simple". In *Modality, Morality and Belief: Essays*

in Honour of Ruth Barcan Marcus, W. Sinnott-Armstrong, D. Raffman & N. Asher (eds), 29–40. Cambridge: Cambridge University Press.

Fitting, M. C., V. W. Marek & M. Truszczynski 1992. "The Pure Logic of Necessitation". *Journal of Logic and Computation* 2(3): 349–73.

Girle, R. A. 1975. "S1 ≠ S0.9". *Notre Dame Journal of Formal Logic* 16(3): 339–44.

Girle, R. A. 2007. "The Neighbourhood of S1 and S0.9". In *Automated Reasoning with Analytic Tableaux and Related Methods*, N. Olivetti (ed.). Berlin: Springer.

Hughes, G. E. & M. J. Cresswell 1996. *A New Introduction to Modal Logic*. London & New York: Routledge.

Kripke, S. A. 1965. "Semantical Analysis of Modal Logic II, Non-normal Propositional Calculi". In *The Theory of Models*, J. W. Addison, L. Henkin & A. Tarski (eds). Amsterdam: North Holland.

Lemmon, E. J. 1966. "Algebraic Semantics for Modal Logics I". *Journal of Symbolic Logic* 31: 46–65.

Lemmon, E. J. 1966. "Algebraic Semantics for Modal Logics II". *Journal of Symbolic Logic* 31: 191–218.

CHAPTER 5

Natural deduction and axiomatics

5.1 Introduction

Modal logic has long been studied from a proof theoretic perspective. The three main kinds of proof theory are well represented in the literature: natural deduction, sequent systems, and axiomatic systems. We shall set out both natural deduction systems and axiomatic systems for propositional modal logics.

Since most of you will have met some sort of natural deduction system in introductory logic, we begin with natural deduction. We set out a Fitch style system. His are in *Symbolic Logic: An Introduction* (Fitch 1952). We then move to axiomatic systems.

5.2 Natural deduction

We assume that you are already familiar with a natural deduction system for propositional logic. There are several well known systems. Fitch's and Lemmon's are two of the most well known. We base our exposition on Fitch and Hughes and Cresswell. An introductory exposition is to be found in Fitch, Copi or Kahane.

We take it that we have the standard set of replacement rules. These include the commutativity, associativity and idempotence for both & and ∨; double negation and DeMorgan's laws; contraposition and exportation/importation for ⊃; and the interdefinability of ⊃ and ∨, often called *material implication*.

We assume that there are at least the following inference rules: simplification, conjunction, disjunctive addition, disjunctive syllogism, *modus ponens*, *modus tollens*, hypothetical syllogism, conditional proof, and some form of *reductio ad absurdum*. A summary of these is to be found at the end of this chapter.

These replacement and inference rules will contain enough redundancy to make proof and validation relatively easy in classical propositional logic.

We now have to consider the replacement and inference rules that have to be added for modal logic. We shall set out the rules for **T**, **S4** and **S5**. We begin with some fairly obvious modal replacement rules. They are, first, the modal negation rules:

$$\sim\Diamond\sim\alpha \quad :: \quad \Box\alpha$$
$$\sim\Box\sim\alpha \quad :: \quad \Diamond\alpha$$
$$\sim\Box\alpha \quad :: \quad \Diamond\sim\alpha$$
$$\sim\Diamond\alpha \quad :: \quad \Box\sim\alpha$$

The inference rules are of two kinds. The first kind is the *categorical* rule of inference. Such rules are like simplification and *modus ponens*. They have one or more premises, and a conclusion is drawn in a simple and unqualified way. The second kind of rule is the assumption based rule of inference. These are like conditional proof and *reductio ad absurdum*.

For modal logic we have five new categorical rules of inference. The first is the proof version of the reflexivity rule. It is called *necessity elimination*. In natural deduction form it is:

$$\frac{\Box\alpha}{\therefore \quad \alpha} \quad \text{Necessity Elimination (NE)}$$

The second is, in a sense, the contrapositive of **NE**:

$$\frac{\alpha}{\therefore \quad \Diamond\alpha} \quad \text{Possibility Introduction (PI)}$$

The next three are *modal reiteration rules*. Although the first of these is exactly the same as **NE**, it is simpler for our purposes in the long run to repeat it with a new name:

$$\frac{\Box\alpha}{\therefore \quad \alpha} \quad \text{Modal Reiteration T (MRT)}$$

$$\frac{\Box\alpha}{\therefore \quad \Box\alpha} \quad \text{Modal Reiteration S4 (MRS4)}$$

$$\frac{\Diamond\alpha}{\therefore \quad \Diamond\alpha} \quad \text{Modal Reiteration S5 (MRS5)}$$

5.3 Null assumption proof

We now turn to assumption based proof rules. It is here that we see something quite new. We begin by setting out conditional proof and drawing attention to some of its features, and some of the terminology that is used for features of conditional proof.

Conditional proof begins with an assumption. This is displayed by the horizontal line to the left of α above. When there are justification annotations, the annotation to the right of α is **Ass**. The β below the three dots is the last formula before the long horizontal line, and is the *intermediate conclusion* of the conditional proof. The vertical line to the left of the proof shows the *scope* of the assumption. The horizontal line below the intermediate conclusion *discharges the assumption* and allows the conclusion, (α ⊃ β), to be entered. Once the assumption has been discharged, then the formulas within the scope of the assumption are not to be used in the remainder of the deduction. They become inaccessible for proof beyond the conclusion of the conditional proof.

The new assumption based proof rules are *null assumption* rules. Null assumption proofs have the following features:

1. There is *no assumption* (or a *null assumption*).
2. Every formula inside the scope of a null assumption is to be deduced from preceeding formulas *inside the scope* of that null assumption unless it is deduced by *modal reiteration* for the appropriate modal logic.
3. The proof ends with a horizontal *discharge of null assumption* line.
4. After the discharge of the null assumption line, where the formula immediately before the discharge line is β, the next formula is □β.

The general format of a null assumption proof is:

The null assumption is registered by a double horizontal assumption line in place of the usual single line and assumption formula. The vertical line marks the *scope* of the assumption, even though it is a null assumption.

A null assumption proof together with the **MRT** rule gives us the rule of necessity introduction (**NI**) for **T**.

We now set out a deduction in **T** of the validity of argument A' in Chapter 1.

1.	$\Box(N \supset S)$	Premise
2.	$\Box(S \supset D)$	Premise
3.	$\Box(D \supset W)$	Premise
4.	$\sim\Diamond W$	Premise / $\therefore \sim\Diamond N$
5.	$\Box\sim W$	4, **MN**
6.		**Null Ass**
7.	$(N \supset S)$	1, **MRT**
8.	$(S \supset D)$	2, **MRT**
9.	$(D \supset W)$	3, **MRT**
10.	$\sim W$	5, **MRT**
11.	$(N \supset D)$	7, 8, **HS**
12.	$(N \supset W)$	9, 11, **HS**
13.	$\sim N$	10, 12, **MT**
14.	$\Box\sim N$	6–13, **NI**
15.	$\sim\Diamond N$	14, **MN**

We note that, apart from **MRT**, the null assumption proof is almost a separate deduction. Natural deduction rules are used within the proof, but there is no non-**MRT** reference to earlier formulas outside the scope of the null assumption.

There is an interesting similarity between this sort of deduction and the possible world semantics. The null assumption proof is almost like a deduction in a separate "world", a world different from the main deduction's world. The only "access" from the main deduction to the null assumption proof is by means of necessity formulas in the main deduction at lines 1, 2, 3 and 5: lines before the null assumption.

We now set out a deduction for a theorem of **T**.

The theorem is: $(\Box p \, \& \, \Box q) \supset \Box(p \, \& \, q)$.

1.	$(\Box p \, \& \, \Box q)$	**Assumption**
2.	$\Box p$	1, **Simp**
3.	$\Box q$	1, **Simp**
4.		**Null Ass**
5.	p	2, **MRT**
6.	q	3, **MRT**
7.	$(p \, \& \, q)$	5, 6, **Conj**
8.	$\Box(p \, \& \, q)$	4–7, **NI**
9.	$(\Box p \, \& \, \Box q) \supset \Box(p \, \& \, q)$	1–8, **CP**

A null assumption proof together with the **MRS4** rule gives us the rule of necessity introduction (**NI**) for S4.

The strengthening from **T** to **S4** is highly analogous to the strengthening of the world filler rule in the semantics.

We now set out the deduction of the S4 theorem: $(\Box p \supset \Box\Box p)$.

1.		$\Box p$	Assumption
2.			Null Ass
3.		$\Box p$	1, MRS4
4.		$\Box\Box p$	2–3, NI
5.		$(\Box p \supset \Box\Box p)$	1–4, CP

A null assumption proof together with the **MRS4** and **MRS5** rules gives us the rule of necessity introduction (**NI**) for S5.

We now set out the proof of the S5 theorem: $(\Diamond p \supset \Box\Diamond p)$.

1.		$\Diamond p$	Assumption
2.			Null Ass
3.		$\Diamond p$	1, MRS5
4.		$\Box\Diamond p$	2–3, NI
5.		$(\Diamond p \supset \Box\Diamond p)$	1–4, CP

5.4 Deduction and proof

We now introduce a formal definition of a deduction. Remember, a deduction is really just the list, or sequence, of formulas. The numbers, assumption scope lines, and justifications are merely devices to assist our understanding of the deduction. The definition is:

A *deduction* is a finite non-empty sequence of formulas each of which is:

(a)   a premise, or

(b)   an assumption that is discharged before the end of the sequence, or

(c)   not preceded by an undischarged null assumption and follows by replacement or inference rules from previous formulas that do not occur within the scope of a previously discharged assumption, or

(d)   is preceded by an undischarged null assumption and either

(i) follows by replacement or inference rules from previous formulas that occur after the nearest undischarged null assumption, or

(ii) follows by a modal reiteration rule from a previous formula that does not occur within the scope of a previously discharged assumption, or

(e)   follows from an immediately preceding discharge of an assumption by either the conditional proof inference rule, the *reductio ad absurdum* rule, or the necessity introduction rule.

Null assumption proofs can be nested. They can be mixed with conditional proof or *reductio ad absurdum*, as we have seen above.

5.5 Axiomatic logic

Modal logics were, for a long time, studied in terms of axiom systems. The advent of possible world semantics made it possible to study them in a semantic way as well. The Lewis systems, the first major modern modal logics, were developed as axiomatic systems, and only later were given possible world semantics.

Since the axiom systems for all the logics set out in this part of the text are well known, we shall set them out here.

Axiom systems for modal logics are a convenient way of summarizing the logics. The axiom systems also provide a neat way of comparing the many modal logics.

An axiom system for a logic contains three elements: a set of axioms; a set of inference rules; and definitions for proofs and theorems. There are also definitions for the derivation of conclusions from sets of premises. We shall concentrate most of our attention on the definitions of proofs and theorems.

Classical propositional logic (**PL**) can be described by means of the following axiom system. The axiom system is called **PS** (see Hunter 1970). We shall use *axiom schema* instead of axioms.

Where A, B and C are any formulas of **PS**, the axioms of propositional logic are:

A1: $(A \supset (B \supset A))$
A2: $((A \supset (B \supset C)) \supset ((A \supset B) \supset (A \supset C)))$
A3: $((\sim A \supset \sim B) \supset (B \supset A))$

A1, A2 and A3 are the three axiom schema for **PS**. They are *not* formulas of **PL**. We use them as follows to get actual axioms.

Given a schema, we replace A throughout with a formula of **PS**, replace B throughout with a formula of **PS**, and replace C throughout with a formula of **PS**, to get an actual axiom of **PS**. So, the following are axioms:

$(p \supset (q \supset p))$
$(\sim p \supset (p \supset \sim p))$
$((\sim(p \supset q) \supset \sim(r \supset \sim\sim s)) \supset ((r \supset \sim\sim s) \supset (p \supset q)))$

$$((\sim(p \supset q) \supset \sim\sim q) \supset (\sim q \supset (p \supset q)))$$
$$(p \supset (p \supset p))$$

The last is where p is substituted throughout A1 for both A and B.

There are infinitely many axioms in this axiomatic system. But each must have the *logical form* of one of the three axiom schema.

Now we turn to the second element in this axiom system. There is one rule of inference. It is *modus ponens*. It can be set out in several different ways. We set it out first as a definition of an immediate consequence (IC).

Where A and B are any formulas of **PS**:

*B is an **immediate consequence** of A and (A $\supset$ B)*

The third element is a set of definitions. There are definitions for proof, proof of a formula, and theorem.

We define a proof as follows:

> *A **proof** is a finite sequence of formulas such that each formula is either an axiom, or an immediate consequence of two preceding formulas.*

The following is a sample proof:

1.	$(p \supset ((p \supset p) \supset p))$	Axiom 1
2.	$((p \supset ((p \supset p) \supset p)) \supset ((p \supset (p \supset p)) \supset (p \supset p)))$	Axiom 2
3.	$((p \supset (p \supset p)) \supset (p \supset p))$	IC of 1 and 2
4.	$(p \supset (p \supset p))$	Axiom 1
5.	$(p \supset p)$	IC of 3 and 4

The proof is just the sequence of five formulas. The numbering to the left is for ease of reference. The comments to the right contain information about the proof.

We have two further definitions:

> *If $<A_1, \ldots, A_n>$ is a proof, then it is a **proof** of A_n. If there is a proof of A, then A is a **theorem** of propositional logic.*

From the proof above we see that $(p \supset p)$ is a theorem of **PS**.

We use the symbol $\vdash_S$ to mean "It is a theorem of system S that". The symbol is a *turnstile*. So we have: $\vdash_{PS} (p \supset p)$.

When it is clear what the logic is, then the system name subscript is left out: $\vdash (p \supset p)$.

But, if you look at the definitions you will see that every formula in a proof is a theorem of **PS**. So, we could have written:

1. ⊢ $(p \supset ((p \supset p) \supset p))$ Axiom 1
2. ⊢ $((p \supset ((p \supset p) \supset p)) \supset ((p \supset (p \supset p)) \supset (p \supset p)))$ Axiom 2
3. ⊢ $((p \supset (p \supset p)) \supset (p \supset p))$ IC of 1 and 2
4. ⊢ $(p \supset (p \supset p))$ Axiom 1
5. ⊢ $(p \supset p)$ IC of 3 and 4

The *modus ponens* rule of inference for proofs could be written:

R1:   ⊢ A, ⊢ $(A \supset B) \Rightarrow$ ⊢ B

The operators of **PL** such as ∨, & and ≡ are all defined. They are, in a way, abbreviations for formulas. So, given that A and B are any formulas of **PL** and $=_{df}$ means "abbreviates", we have the following definitional schemas:

Def ∨ $(A \vee B) =_{df} (\sim A \supset B)$
Def & $(A \,\&\, B) =_{df} \sim(A \supset \sim B)$
Def ≡ $(A \equiv B) =_{df} ((A \supset B) \,\&\, (B \supset A))$

It is a well established fact that all the theorems of **PS** are tautologies. This means that **PS** is *sound* with respect to the truth-table semantics for **PL**. It is also the case that all the tautologies are theorems of **PS**. This means that **PS** is *complete* with respect to the semantics. Axiomatic **PL** *completely* captures the tautologies.

So, with three axiom schema and one rule of inference we summarize the whole of standard propositional logic.

The same can be done for all the propositional modal logics to which we have been introduced.

5.6 Schematic proofs and theorem schemas

We define a proof schema as follows:

> A *proof schema* is a finite sequence of formula schemas such that each schema is either: *an axiom schema,* or *an immediate consequence of two preceding schemas.*

If we take the proof above and use the schematic letter A, where A stands for any **PS** formula, we can set out a proof schema.

1. ⊢ $(A \supset ((A \supset A) \supset A))$ Axiom 1
2. ⊢ $((A \supset ((A \supset A) \supset A)) \supset ((A \supset (A \supset A)) \supset (A \supset A)))$ Axiom 2

3.	⊢ ((A ⊃ (A ⊃ A)) ⊃ (A ⊃ A))	IC of 1 and 2
4.	⊢ (A ⊃ (A ⊃ A))	Axiom 1
5.	⊢ (A ⊃ A)	IC of 3 and 4

This sequence of schema gives us a proof of all theorems of the form $(A \supset A)$. It should be clear that schematic proofs and theorem schemas are far more useful than standard proofs and single theorems.

We shall keep a catalogue of proved theorem schemas. We start with:

TS1 $(A \supset A)$

Once a theorem schema has been proved, it can then be used in subsequent proofs. We can extend the definition of proof schema as follows:

> A **proof schema** is a finite sequence of formula schemas such that each schema is either: an axiom schema, or a theorem schema, or an immediate consequence of two preceding schemas.

For example:

1.	⊢ (~A ⊃ ~A)	TS1
2.	⊢ (A ∨ ~A)	1, Def ∨

This gives us **TS2**, commonly known as the law of excluded middle (LEM).

From a practical point of view, a theorem schema is an abbreviation for a whole proof. The whole proof of that schema could be inserted into a larger proof where the theorem schema occurs.

Here are two more proof schemas (without the turnstiles):

1.	(((A ⊃ (B ⊃ C)) ⊃ ((A ⊃ B) ⊃ (A ⊃ C))) ⊃ ((B ⊃ C) ⊃ ((A ⊃ (B ⊃ C)) ⊃ ((A ⊃ B) ⊃ (B ⊃ C)))))	Ax 1
2.	((A ⊃ (B ⊃ C)) ⊃ ((A ⊃ B) ⊃ (A ⊃ C)))	Ax 2
3.	((B ⊃ C) ⊃ ((A ⊃ (B ⊃ C)) ⊃ ((A ⊃ B) ⊃ (B ⊃ C))))	1, 2, **MP**
4.	(((B ⊃ C) ⊃ ((A ⊃ (B ⊃ C)) ⊃ ((A ⊃ B) ⊃ (B ⊃ C)))) ⊃ ((B ⊃ C) ⊃ (A ⊃ (B ⊃ C))) ⊃ ((B ⊃ C) ⊃ ((A ⊃ B) ⊃ (A ⊃ C)))))	Ax 2
5.	((B ⊃ C) ⊃ (A ⊃ (B ⊃ C))) ⊃ ((B ⊃ C) ⊃ ((A ⊃ B) ⊃ (A ⊃ C))))	3, 4, **MP**
6.	((B ⊃ C) ⊃ (A ⊃ (B ⊃ C)))	Ax 1
7.	((B ⊃ C) ⊃ ((A ⊃ B) ⊃ (A ⊃ C)))	5, 6, **MP**

1. $((\sim B \supset \sim A) \supset (A \supset B))$ Ax 3
2. $(((\sim B \supset \sim A) \supset (A \supset B)) \supset (\sim A \supset ((\sim B \supset \sim A) \supset$
   $(A \supset B))))$ Ax 1
3. $(\sim A \supset ((\sim B \supset \sim A) \supset (A \supset B)))$ 1, 2, **MP**
4. $((\sim A \supset ((\sim B \supset \sim A) \supset (A \supset B)) \supset$
   $((\sim A \supset (\sim B \supset \sim A)) \supset (\sim A \supset (A \supset B)))$ Ax 2
5. $((\sim A \supset (\sim B \supset \sim A)) \supset (\sim A \supset (A \supset B)))$ 3, 4, **MP**
6. $(\sim A \supset (\sim B \supset \sim A))$ Ax 1
7. $(\sim A \supset (A \supset B))$ 5, 6, **MP**

So we get two additional theorem schema (and first two) with common name:

TS1 $(A \supset A)$
TS2 $(A \vee \sim A)$ (law of excluded middle: LEM)
TS3 $(\sim A \supset (A \supset B))$ (Duns Scotus law)
TS4 $((B \supset C) \supset ((A \supset B) \supset (A \supset C)))$ (implicative syllogism: Imp Syl)

Proof of the following is left to the reader:

TS5 $(\sim\sim A \supset A)$ (double negation: DN)
TS6 $(A \supset \sim\sim A)$ (double negation: DN)
TS7 $\sim\sim(A \supset \sim\sim A)$ or $\sim(A \,\&\, \sim A)$ (law of non-contradiction: LNC)
TS8 $((A \,\&\, B) \supset A)$ (simplification: Simp)
TS9 $((A \,\&\, B) \supset B)$ (simplification: Simp)
TS10 $(A \supset (A \vee B))$ (addition: Add)
TS11 $(B \supset (A \vee B))$ (addition: Add)
TS12 $(\sim(A \,\&\, B) \supset (\sim A \vee \sim B))$ (DeMorgan's law: DeM)
TS13 $(\sim(A \vee B) \supset (\sim A \,\&\, \sim B))$ (DeMorgan's law: DeM)
TS14 $((\sim A \vee \sim B) \supset \sim(A \,\&\, B))$ (DeMorgan's law: DeM)
TS15 $((\sim A \,\&\, \sim B) \supset \sim(A \vee B))$ (DeMorgan's law: DeM)
TS16 $(A \supset ((A \supset B) \supset B))$ (*modus ponens*: **MP**)
TS17 $((A \supset B) \supset (\sim B \supset \sim A))$ (contraposition: Contra)
TS18 $(A \supset (B \supset (A \,\&\, B)))$
TS19 $((A \supset B) \supset ((A \supset C) \supset (A \supset (B \,\&\, C))))$
TS20 $((A \supset C) \supset ((B \supset C) \supset ((A \vee B) \supset C)))$

It can be shown that the following is also a rule of inference in **PS**. Where A and B are any formulas of **PL**, $(A \,\&\, B)$ is a *proof consequence* of A and B.
    This can be written as:

R2 $\vdash A, \vdash B \Rightarrow \vdash (A \,\&\, B)$

It is known as *Adjunction (Adj)*.

We can extend the definition of proof schema as follows:

*A **proof schema** is a finite sequence of formula schemas such that each schema is either: an axiom schema, or a theorem schema, or an immediate consequence of two preceding schemas, or a proof consequence of one or more preceding schemas.*

For example:

1.	$(\sim\sim A \supset A)$	TS5
2.	$(A \supset \sim\sim A)$	TS6
3.	$((\sim\sim A \supset A) \mathbin{\&} (A \supset \sim\sim A))$	1, 2, Adj
4.	$(\sim\sim A \equiv A)$	3, Def $\equiv$

So we have a proof of the double negation equivalence:

TS21 $(\sim\sim A \equiv A)$

Similarly, from **TS15** and A3 we get the contraposition equivalence:

TS22 $((A \supset B) \equiv (\sim B \supset \sim A))$

Theorem equivalences such as **TS21** and **TS22** can be used with the **PS** rule of inference below to make proofs much easier:
Where A, B, C and D are any formulas of **PL**:

*If $\vdash (C \equiv D)$, and C is either A or a sub-formula of A, and B is the result of replacing one or more occurrences of C with D in A, then B is a **proof consequence** of A.*

This inference rule means that we can replace formula schemas, or parts of them, with schemas which have been proved to be equivalent. **TS21** and **TS22** are two of the most useful equivalences of **PS**. The rule can be written as:

R3 $\vdash (C \equiv D), \vdash A(C) \Rightarrow \vdash A(D/C)$

where $A(\gamma)$ means A with γ as a sub-formula, and $A(\delta/\gamma)$ means A with δ replacing zero or more occurrences of γ.

R3 is known as the *rule of the substitutivity of material equivalents.*

Further important rules of inference for **PS** are set out below. Some are obviously related to theorem schemas. We omit the turnstiles:

R4	$(A \supset B), \sim B \Rightarrow \sim A$	(*modus tollens*)
R5	$A \Rightarrow (A \vee B)$	(disjunctive addition)
R6	$(A \vee B), \sim A \Rightarrow B$	(disjunctive syllogism)
R7	$(A \& B) \Rightarrow A$	(simplification)
R8	$(A \supset B), (B \supset C) \Rightarrow (A \supset C)$	(chain argument)
R9	$\sim(A \& B), A \Rightarrow \sim B$	(affirm the negadjunct)
R10	$\sim\sim A \Rightarrow A$	(double negation)
R11	$((A \& B) \supset C) \Rightarrow (A \supset (B \supset C))$	(exportation)
R12	$(A \supset (B \supset C)) \Rightarrow ((A \& B) \supset C)$	(importation)
R13	$(A \& (B \vee C)) \Rightarrow ((A \& B) \vee (A \& C))$	(distribution &$\vee$)
R14	$(A \vee (B \& C)) \Rightarrow ((A \vee B) \& (A \vee C))$	(distribution $\vee$&)
R15	$(A \vee B), (A \supset C), (B \supset D) \Rightarrow (C \vee D)$	(complex dilemma)

5.7 Axioms for modal propositional logics

We shall set out the axioms and definitions in schematic form. Many of the axioms and rules have well established names. These are appended.

Def $\Diamond$	$\Diamond A =_{df} \sim\Box\sim A$
Def $\leftrightarrow$	$(A \leftrightarrow B) =_{df} (\Box(A \supset B) \& \Box(B \supset A))$

A1:	$(A \supset (B \supset A))$	
A2:	$((A \supset (B \supset C)) \supset ((A \supset B) \supset (A \supset C)))$	
A3:	$((\sim A \supset \sim B) \supset (B \supset A))$	(contraposition)
A4:	$(\Box A \supset A)$	(**T** or reflexivity)
A5:	$(\Box(A \supset B) \supset (\Box A \supset \Box B))$	(**K** or distribution of box over $\supset$)
A6:	$(\Box(A \supset B) \supset \Box(\Box A \supset \Box B))$	
A7:	$(\Box A \supset \Box\Box A)$	(**S4** or *KK*-Thesis or positive introspection)
A8:	$(A \supset \Box\Diamond A)$	(the Platonic thesis)
A9:	$(\Diamond A \supset \Box\Diamond A)$	(**S5** or negative introspection)
A10:	$(\Box A \supset \sim\Box\sim A)$	(*D* or consistency)
A11:	$(\Box(A \supset B) \supset (\Box(B \supset C) \supset \Box(A \supset C)))$	

The rules of inference are:

R1:	$\vdash A, \vdash (A \supset B) \Rightarrow \vdash B$	(*modus ponens*)
MR1:	$\vdash A \Rightarrow \vdash \Box A$	(necessitation)
MR2:	$\vdash_{ps} A \Rightarrow \vdash \Box A$	(Descartes)
MR3:	$\vdash \Box(A \supset B) \Rightarrow \vdash \Box(\Box A \supset \Box B)$	

MR4: $\vdash \Box(A \supset B) \Rightarrow \vdash (\Box A \supset \Box B)$
MR5: $\vdash (A \leftrightarrow B) \Rightarrow \vdash (\Box A \leftrightarrow \Box B)$
MR6: *If A differs from B only in having a formula C*
   in some places where B has D, then:
   $\vdash (C \leftrightarrow D) \Rightarrow \vdash (A \leftrightarrow B)$ (substitution of strict
                                                                                   equivalents)

The minimal sets of axioms and inference rules for each system are set out in the next section. For the moment we look at the sets for the five key normal modal logics. They can be set out as:

K = {A1, A2, A3, A5, **R1, MR1**}
T = {A1, A2, A3, A4, A5, **R1, MR1**}   **K** ∪ {A4}
S4 = {A1, A2, A3, A4, A5, A5, **R1, MR1**}   **T** ∪ {A5}
Br = {A1, A2, A3, A4, A5, A8, **R1, MR1**}   **T** ∪ {A8}
S5 = {A1, A2, A3, A4, A5, A9, **R1, MR1**}   **T** ∪ {A9}

The axiom system for **T** is simply **K** with A4 added. The other three systems, **S4, Br** and **S5**, can all be axiomatized by simply adding just one axiom schema to **T**. This approach is a "minimalist" approach to the three systems. For the minimalist approach to the five key logics we need only A1 to A5, A5, A8, and A9. What then of the other axiom schemas?

   The 11 schema above all belong to **S5**. That is, they are all axiom schema or theorem schema of **S5**. The axiom schemas which we have listed above are valid in the five logics as follows:

Axioms	K	T	S4	Br	S5
A1 – A3	Yes	Yes	Yes	Yes	Yes
A4 Refl	NO	Yes	Yes	Yes	Yes
A5 *K*	Yes	Yes	Yes	Yes	Yes
A6 *S3*	NO	NO	Yes	NO	Yes
A7 *KK*	NO	NO	Yes	NO	Yes
A8 *Plato*	NO	NO	NO	Yes	Yes
A9 Neg. Int.	NO	NO	NO	NO	Yes
A10 *D*	NO	Yes	Yes	Yes	Yes
A11	Yes	Yes	Yes	Yes	Yes

Given the minimal sets for each system, the reader is invited to prove that the additionally valid schemas are theorem schemas of the appropriate logics.

The following are theorem schemas of **T**. We number them as modal theorem schemas (MTS). Proof is left to the reader.

MTS1	$(\Box(A \equiv B) \supset (\Box A \equiv \Box B))$
MTS2	$(\Box(A \ \& \ B) \equiv (\Box A \ \& \ \Box B))$
MTS3	$(\Box A \equiv \sim\Diamond\sim A)$
MTS4	$(\Box\sim A \equiv \sim\Diamond A)$
MTS5	$(\sim\Diamond(A \vee B) \equiv (\sim\Diamond A \ \& \ \sim\Diamond B))$
MTS6	$(\Diamond(A \vee B) \equiv (\Diamond A \vee \Diamond B))$
MTS7	$(\Box(A \supset B) \supset (\Diamond A \supset \Diamond B))$
MTS8	$((\Box A \vee \Box B) \supset \Box(A \vee B))$
MTS9	$(\Diamond(A \ \& \ B) \supset (\Diamond A \ \& \ \Diamond B))$

There are also the following additional rules for inference for all five logics.

MR7	$(A \supset B) \ \Rightarrow \ (\Box A \supset \Box B)$
MR8	$(A \equiv B) \ \Rightarrow \ (\Box A \equiv \Box B)$
MR9	$(A \supset B) \ \Rightarrow \ (\Diamond A \supset \Diamond B)$

5.8 Axiom systems

We now set out minimal sets of axiom schemas and rules of inference for a wide range of logics.

The normal modal logics

K = {A1, A2, A3, A5, **R1**, **MR1**}	
T = {A1, A2, A3, A4, A5, **R1**, **MR1**}	**K** ∪ {A4}
S4 = {A1, A2, A3, A4, A5, A7, **R1**, **MR1**}	**T** ∪ {A5}
Br = {A1, A2, A3, A4, A5, A8, **R1**, **MR1**}	**T** ∪ {A8}
S5 = {A1, A2, A3, A4, A5, A9, **R1**, **MR1**}	**T** ∪ {A9}
K4 = {A1, A2, A3, A5, A7, **R1**, **MR1**}	**K** ∪ {A7}
KBr = {A1, A2, A3, A5, A8, **R1**, **MR1**}	**K** ∪ {A8}
K5 = {A1, A2, A3, A5, A9, **R1**, **MR1**}	**K** ∪ {A9}
DT = {A1, A2, A3, A5, A7, **R1**, **MR1**}	**K** ∪ {A10}
D4 = {A1, A2, A3, A5, A7, **R1**, **MR1**}	**DT** ∪ {A5}
DBr = {A1, A2, A3, A5, A8, **R1**, **MR1**}	**DT** ∪ {A8}
D5 = {A1, A2, A3, A5, A9, **R1**, **MR1**}	**DT** ∪ {A9}

The non-normal modal logics

S0.5 = {A1, A2, A3, A4, A5, **R1, MR2**}
S2 = {A1, A2, A3, A4, A5, **R1, MR2, MR3**}
S3 = {A1, A2, A3, A4, A6, **R1, MR2**}

E2 = {A1, A2, A3, A4, A5, R1, **MR4**}
ED2 = {A1, A2, A3, A5, A10, R1, **MR4**}
C2 = {A1, A2, A3, A5, R1, **MR4**}

Lemmon short circuits the need for rule **MR2** in the following way.
First, he defines:

If axiom schema A_i (0<i≤10) is α *, then* □A_i *is* □α

He then defines the systems (equivalent to) **S0.5** to **S3** as follows:

S0.5 = {□A1, □A2, □A3, A4, A5, R1}
S0.9 = {□A1, □A2, □A3, A4, A5, R1, **MR5**}
S1 = {□A1, □A2, □A3, A4, A11, **R1, MR6**}
S2 = {□A1, □A2, □A3, A4, A5, **R1, MR3**}
S3 = {□A1, □A2, □A3, A4, A6, R1}

If we use Lemmon style definitions we can rewrite them.
Let: □**PL** = {□A1, □A2, □A3, **R1**}. Then:

S0.5 = □**PL** ∪ {A4}
S0.9 = □**PL** ∪ {A4, A5, **MR5**}
S2 = □**PL** ∪ {A4, A5, **MR3**}
S3 = □**PL** ∪ {A4, A6}
S1 = □**PL** ∪ {A4, A11, **MR6**}

It now becomes clearer as to why people have felt that **S0.9** comes more
"naturally" in the sequence from **S0.5** to **S2** than does **S1**. The A11 axiom
seems to be quite out of place in the sequence of increasingly stronger axiomatic systems.

Summary of rules

Replacement rules

$\sim\sim\alpha \ :: \ \alpha$	double negation (**DN**)
$(\alpha \vee \beta) \ :: \ (\beta \vee \alpha)$	commutation for $\vee$ (**Com**)
$(\alpha \ \& \ \beta) \ :: \ (\beta \ \& \ \alpha)$	commutation for $\&$ (**Com**)
$(\alpha \vee (\beta \vee \delta)) \ :: \ ((\alpha \vee \beta) \vee \delta)$	association (**Assoc**)
$(\alpha \ \& \ (\beta \ \& \ \delta)) \ :: \ ((\alpha \ \& \ \beta) \ \& \ \delta)$	association (**Assoc**)
$(\alpha \vee (\beta \ \& \ \delta)) \ :: \ ((\alpha \vee \beta) \ \& \ (\alpha \vee \delta))$	distribution (**Dist**)
$(\alpha \ \& \ (\beta \vee \delta)) \ :: \ ((\alpha \ \& \ \beta) \vee (\alpha \ \& \ \delta))$	distribution (**Dist**)
$(\sim\alpha \vee \sim\beta) \ :: \ \sim(\alpha \ \& \ \beta)$	DeMorgan (**DeM**)
$(\sim\alpha \ \& \ \sim\beta) \ :: \ \sim(\alpha \vee \beta)$	DeMorgan (**DeM**)
$(\alpha \vee \alpha) \ :: \ \alpha$	idempotence (**Idem**)
$(\alpha \ \& \ \alpha) \ :: \ \alpha$	idempotence (**Idem**)
$(\alpha \supset \beta) \ :: \ (\sim\alpha \vee \beta)$	material implication (**IMP**)
$(\alpha \supset \beta) \ :: \ (\sim\beta \supset \sim\alpha)$	contraposition (**Cont**)
$((\alpha \ \& \ \beta) \supset \delta) \ :: \ (\alpha \supset (\beta \supset \delta))$	exportation (**Exp**)
$(\alpha \supset (\beta \supset \delta)) \ :: \ (\beta \supset (\alpha \supset \delta))$	permutation (**Per**)
$(\alpha \equiv \beta) \ :: \ ((\alpha \supset \beta) \ \& \ (\beta \supset \alpha))$	equivalence (**Equiv**)
$(\alpha \equiv \beta) \ :: \ ((\alpha \ \& \ \beta) \vee (\sim\alpha \ \& \ \sim\beta))$	equivalence (**Equiv**)
$\alpha \ :: \ (\alpha \ \& \ (\beta \vee \sim\beta))$	taut. conj. (**TConj**)
$\alpha \ :: \ (\alpha \vee (\beta \ \& \ \sim\beta))$	contr. disj. (**CDisj**)
$\sim\Box\alpha \ :: \ \Diamond\sim\alpha$	modal negation **MN**
$\sim\Diamond\alpha \ :: \ \Box\sim\alpha$	modal negation **MN**
$\sim\Box\sim\alpha \ :: \ \Diamond\alpha$	modal negation **MN**
$\sim\Diamond\sim\alpha \ :: \ \Box\alpha$	modal negation **MN**

Inference rules

$$\frac{(\alpha \ \& \ \beta)}{\therefore \quad \alpha}$$

Simplification (**Simp**)

$$\begin{array}{c} \alpha \\ \vdots \\ \beta \\ \hline \therefore \quad (\alpha \ \& \ \beta) \end{array}$$

Conjunction (**Conj**)

$$\frac{\begin{array}{c} (\alpha \vee \beta) \\ \sim\alpha \end{array}}{\therefore \quad \beta}$$

Disjunctive syllogism (**DS**) or
denying a disjunct (**DD**)

$$\frac{\alpha}{\therefore \quad (\alpha \vee \beta)}$$

Addition (**Add**) or
disjunctive addition (**DA**)

$$\frac{\begin{array}{c}(\alpha \supset \beta)\\ \alpha\end{array}}{\therefore \quad \beta}$$

$$\frac{\begin{array}{c}(\alpha \supset \beta)\\ \sim\beta\end{array}}{\therefore \quad \sim\alpha}$$

Modus ponens (**MP**) or affirming the antecedent (**AA**)

Modus tollens (**MT**) or denying the consequent (**DC**)

$$\frac{\begin{array}{c}(\alpha \supset \beta)\\ (\beta \supset \delta)\end{array}}{\therefore \quad (\alpha \supset \delta)}$$

$$\frac{\begin{array}{c}(\alpha \supset \beta)\\ (\gamma \supset \delta)\\ (\alpha \vee \gamma)\end{array}}{\therefore \quad (\beta \vee \delta)}$$

Hypothetical syllogism (**HS**) or chain argument (**ChArg**)

Constructive dilemma (**CD**)

Conditional proof (**CP**) is :

Reductio ad absurdum (**RAA**) is :

$$\frac{\begin{array}{c}\quad\quad \alpha\\ \vdots\\ \quad\quad \beta\end{array}}{\therefore \quad (\alpha \supset \beta)}$$

$$\frac{\begin{array}{c}\quad\quad \sim\alpha\\ \vdots\\ \quad (\beta\ \&\ \sim\beta)\end{array}}{\therefore \quad\quad \alpha}$$

Modal rules of inference

$$\frac{\Box\alpha}{\therefore \quad \alpha}$$

Necessity elimination (**NE**) or modal reiteration T (**MRT**)

$$\frac{\alpha}{\therefore \quad \Diamond\,\alpha}$$

Possibility introduction (**PI**)

$$\frac{\Box\,\alpha}{\therefore \quad \Box\,\alpha}$$

Modal reiteration S4 (**MRS4**)

$$\frac{\Diamond\,\alpha}{\therefore \quad \Diamond\,\alpha}$$

Modal reiteration S5 (**MRS5**)

Necessity introduction (**NI**)

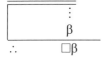

$$\therefore \quad \Box\beta$$

Every formula inside the scope of the null assumption is to be deduced from preceeding formulas *inside the scope* of that null assumption but not within the scope of a discharged assumption, unless it is deduced by *modal reiteration* (for the appropriate modal logic) from a formula outside the scope of every previously discharged assumption.

Definition of a deduction

A deduction is a finite non-empty sequence of formulas, each of which is either:

(a) a premise, or
(b) an assumption which is discharged before the end of the sequence, or
(c) not preceeded by an undischarged null assumption and follows by replacement or inference rules from previous formulas which do not occur within the scope of a previously discharged assumption, or
(d) is preceeded by an undischarged null assumption and either
  (i) follows by replacement or inference rules from previous formulas which occur after the nearest undischarged null assumption, or
  (ii) follows by a modal reiteration rule from a previous formula which does not occur within the scope of a previously discharged assumption, or
(e) follows from an immediately preceeding discharge of an assumption by either the conditional proof inference rule, the *reductio ad absurdum* rule, or the necessity introduction rule.

5.8 Exercises

Some of the exercises in previous chapters can be repeated using the modal natural deduction systems. In particular, the valid arguments and formulas can be shown valid. Remember, the axioms of a logic can also be deduced as zero premise conclusions of a natural deduction logic.

1. Valid formulas in 2.3, 2.4, 3.3 Q2 and modal theorem schemas 1–9 in this chapter.
2. Valid arguments in 2.3 and MR7–9 in this chapter.

References and further reading

Fitch, F. 1952. *Symbolic Logic: An Introduction*. New York: Ronald Press.

Hughes, G. E. & M. J. Cresswell 1968. *An Introduction to Modal Logic*. London: Methuen.

Hunter, G. G. B. 1950. *Metalogic*. London: Macmillan.

Lemmon, E. J. 1966. "Algebraic Semantics for Modal Logics I". *Journal of Symbolic Logic* **31**: 46–65.

Lemmon, E. J. 1966. "Algebraic Semantics for Modal Logics II". *Journal of Symbolic Logic* **31**: 191–218.

CHAPTER 6
Conditional logic

6.1 Introduction

Modal logic has been used for purposes other than providing formal languages for necessity and possibility. In fact, at the very beginning of the creation of modern modal logic one of the main aims was to provide a formal language for *conditional* propositions, the propositions usually expressed by "If … then …" sentences. The major systematic development of early modal logic resulted in the five Lewis systems: S1 to S5. These were first developed as *conditional logics*. The whole enterprise grew out of a dissatisfaction with the use of the material conditional as the standard translation for "If … then …" and "… only if …".

One early alternative idea was that "If p then q" should be understood not as "Either not p or q" but as "p is *incompatible* with not q" or as "It is *not possible* that p and not q". Modal logic enters at once.

In this chapter we focus on a few of the formal systems of *conditional logic*. We shall look at a range of conditional logics and see what distinguishes one from the other. We shall not discuss directly the merits of any of the logics but simply note which formulas are theorems and which argument forms are valid. The question of which logic, if any, might be better than which will be discussed in Chapter 14 as part of a general philosophical discussion of conditionals. In this chapter we shall just look at formal features.

6.2 Formal issues

There are many features that distinguish one logic from another. Some are general features, such as whether a logic is classical or paraconsistent, or whether it is monotonic or non-monotonic. Some of these features have a conditional dimension; some are best seen in terms of arguments.

In what follows we consider differences between logics in terms of differences of interpretation of $(p \Rightarrow q)$. The $\Rightarrow$ arrow can be interpreted as either a material conditional hook ($\supset$), or a strict conditional fish-hook ($\prec$), or a conditional implies ($>$), or a semi-classical arrow ($\rightarrow$). We shall list eleven key formulas and nine key argument forms as a basis for comparison. The nine argument forms are premise–conclusion versions of nine of the formulas.

The first two cases for comparison are cases of negated conditionals. The first case is Jackson's *uncontested principle* (UP) (1987: 4):

UP $\quad ((p \ \& \ {\sim}q) \Rightarrow {\sim}(p \Rightarrow q))$

$$\textbf{UP'} \qquad\qquad \frac{\begin{array}{c} p \\ {\sim}q \end{array}}{\therefore \quad {\sim}(p \Rightarrow q)}$$

Next is the converse of **UP**, (**UPCon**) and its allied argument form:

UPCon $\ ({\sim}(p \Rightarrow q) \Rightarrow (p \ \& \ {\sim}q))$

$$\textbf{UPCon'} \qquad \frac{{\sim}(p \Rightarrow q)}{\therefore \quad (p \ \& \ {\sim}q)}$$

If the arrow is the material conditional $\supset$, **UPCon** is a tautology and **UPCon'** is valid. **UPCon** is seen by many as quite unacceptable, as we shall see in Chapter 14.

In both of these we have generated the argument form from the formula by making the consequent of a main operator $\Rightarrow$ into the conclusion, and the antecedent into the premise or premises. If the antecedent of the $\Rightarrow$ is a conjunction then each conjunct is a premise as in **UP'**; otherwise the whole antecedent is a single premise as in **UPCon'**. If the main operator of the formula is not $\Rightarrow$ then there will be no related argument form. In what follows we simply set out the formulas. The related argument form will be easy to construct. If the formula is designated by "**X**", then the related argument form will be "**X'**".

The second two cases are the formulas of *modus ponens* (**MP**) and *modus tollens* (**MT**) and the related argument forms **MP'** and **MT'**.

MP. $\quad ((p \ \& \ (p \Rightarrow q)) \Rightarrow q)$
MT. $\quad (({\sim}q \ \& \ (p \Rightarrow q)) \Rightarrow {\sim}p)$

The fifth case is the formula known as *Weakening* (**Wk**):

Wk. $((p \Rightarrow q) \Rightarrow ((p \, \& \, r) \Rightarrow q))$

Logics in which the argument form **Wk'** is not valid are known as *non-monotonic* logics, and those in which **Wk'** is valid are *monotonic* logics.

The sixth and seventh cases are *Contraposition* (**Contra**) and *Hypothetical Syllogism* (**HS**):

Contra. $((p \Rightarrow q) \Rightarrow (\sim q \Rightarrow \sim p)$
HS. $(((p \Rightarrow q) \, \& \, (q \Rightarrow r)) \Rightarrow (p \Rightarrow r))$

The next four cases are the *paradox* cases. Only the first two have related argument forms:

Para1. $(p \Rightarrow (q \Rightarrow p))$
Para2. $(\sim p \Rightarrow (p \Rightarrow q))$
Para3. $((p \Rightarrow q) \vee (q \Rightarrow p))$
Para4. $((p \Rightarrow q) \vee (q \Rightarrow r))$

All the formulas above are tautologies of classical logic, that is, when the arrow is uniformly interpreted as the material conditional $\supset$. The last four in material conditional interpretation are known as *paradoxes of material implication*. It is important to recognize that none of these "paradoxes" are problematic in and of themselves. The description of these four formulas as *paradoxes* has been somewhat misleading, to say the least. They are not contradictory or logically paradoxical.

We shall consider three groups of logics. The first group is the logics of C. I. Lewis: S1 to S5. These are the logics of the strict conditional or of *strict implication*. We met this sequence in the earlier chapters as modal logics. But they were originally conceived of as logics for "If … then …". Lewis's own preference was for S2.

The second group is simply known as the *conditional logics*. These are derived from the work of Stalnaker and David Lewis (not C. I. Lewis). We shall not consider their logics specifically, but the logics we consider are weaker, and whatever is valid in them will be valid in Stalnaker's and Lewis's systems.

The third group will be represented by one semi-classical relevant logic, **RM**. This logic is chosen because its semantics and truth-trees are easily manageable. But it gives some idea of other alternatives to classical logic.

6.3 The axiomatic approach

C. I. Lewis tried the strategy of defining a new connective for "If p then q" by the use of the $\Diamond$ for possibility. But he did not have the idea of possible worlds on which to base a semantics. He was part of a logic ethos in which axiomatic systems dominated the approach to logic and there was virtually no coherent semantics for modal logic. We have met all five of his systems in modal logic guise, and we have seen them through the lens of possible worlds semantics. But this is not how the five were originally set out.

Lewis began by taking negation, conjunction and possibility, and created a new system, **S1**, in axiomatic form. The strict implication fish-hooks connective, $\prec$, was the new connective for "If … then …".

Lewis defined:

$$(p \prec q) =_{df} \sim\Diamond(p \;\&\; \sim q)$$

Then he set out conditional logics in axiomatic form.

If you have skipped over Chapter 5 and the details of axiomatic systems of logic, then the next three sections might not make much sense. It would be best to revise the axiomatic sections of Chapter 5 before reading the Lewis's systems sections below. Otherwise skip forward to the sections on other approaches to conditional logic.

The Lewis system S1

The primitive symbols of **S1** were propositional letters, tilde $\sim$, ampersand & (Lewis actually used dot, $\bullet$, instead of ampersand) and diamond $\Diamond$.

We already have the definition of fish-hooks, and add the following definitions for *vel* , $\vee$, and the strict equivalence *quodbar* $\equiv$ (Lewis used = instead of *quodbar*, but = can cause confusion if the logic is extended to predicate logic with identity.):

$$(\alpha \vee \beta) =_{df} \sim(\sim\alpha \;\&\; \sim\beta)$$
$$(\alpha \equiv \beta) =_{df} ((\alpha \prec \beta) \;\&\; (\beta \prec \alpha))$$

We can also define *hook* and *tribar* in terms of & and $\sim$.

$$(\alpha \supset \beta) =_{df} \sim(\alpha \;\&\; \sim\beta)$$
$$(\alpha \equiv \beta) =_{df} (\sim(\alpha \;\&\; \sim\beta) \;\&\; \sim(\beta \;\&\; \sim\alpha))$$

This means that all the formulas of **PC** are in **S1**.

S1 has the following seven axioms and four rules of inference:

S1.1 $((p \;\&\; q) \prec (q \;\&\; p))$

S1.2 $((p \,\&\, q) \prec p)$
S1.3 $(p \prec (p \,\&\, p))$
S1.4 $(((p \,\&\, q) \,\&\, r) \prec (p \,\&\, (q \,\&\, r)))$
S1.5 $(p \prec {\sim}{\sim}p)$
S1.6 $(((p \prec q) \,\&\, (q \prec r)) \prec (p \prec r))$
S1.7 $((p \,\&\, (p \prec q)) \prec q)$

It was later shown that the fifth axiom was redundant because it could be derived from the other six. So it is usually left out of Lewis style axiomatic **S1**, but it is given here for historical accuracy.

Lewis gives four rules of inference, where "⊢α" means "α is a theorem of **S1**":

S1.R1   If ⊢α and π is a propositional letter in α and β is the result of replacing every occurrence of π in α with any formula γ, then ⊢β (*uniform substitution*)

S1.R2   If ⊢α and β is the result of replacing γ in α with δ at one or more places, then if ⊢(γ ≡ δ), then ⊢β (*substitution of strict equivalents*)

S1.R3   If ⊢α and ⊢β then ⊢(α & β) (*adjunction*)

S1.R4   If ⊢α and ⊢(α ≺ β) then ⊢β (*strict modus ponens*)

These rules above are not literally the same as Lewis's, but they function in exactly the same way.

We now set out two proofs of theorems to show how the system functions. Remember, a proof is a list of formulas each of which is either an axiom or follows from previous formulas in the list by a rule of inference.

To prove theorem 1:

T1. $(p \prec p)$

1.	$((p \,\&\, q) \prec p)$	Axiom S1.2 (or just S1.2)
2.	$((p \,\&\, p) \prec p)$	*Uniform substitution* in 1 of p for q (This can be shortened to: 1, (p/q))
3.	$(((p \prec q) \,\&\, (q \prec r)) \prec (p \prec r))$	S1.6
4.	$(((p \prec (p \,\&\, p)) \,\&\, ((p \,\&\, p) \prec r)) \prec (p \prec r))$	3, $((p \,\&\, p)/q)$
5.	$(((p \prec (p \,\&\, p)) \,\&\, ((p \,\&\, p) \prec p)) \prec (p \prec p))$	4, (p/r)
6.	$(p \prec (p \,\&\, p))$	S1.3
7.	$((p \prec (p \,\&\, p)) \,\&\, ((p \,\&\, p) \prec p))$	2, 6, S1.R3 (*Adjunction*)
8.	$(p \prec p)$	5, 7, *Strict MP*

Once we have proved a theorem we can use it as if it were an axiom, because we could insert its proof in subsequent proofs. Also, a definition can be used in much the same way as a rule of inference to replace a formula or one of its sub-formulas in a previous line of a proof.

To prove theorem 2 we begin with T1.

T2. $((p \equiv q) \equiv ((p \prec q) \,\&\, (q \prec p)))$

1.	$(p \prec p)$	T1.
2.	$((p \equiv q) \prec (p \equiv q))$	1, $((p \equiv q)/p)$
3.	$(p \prec (p \,\&\, p))$	S1.3
4.	$(((p \equiv q) \prec (p \equiv q)) \prec$	
	$\quad (((p \equiv q) \prec (p \equiv q)) \,\&\, ((p \equiv q) \prec (p \equiv q))))$	3, $(((p \equiv q) \prec (p \equiv q))/p)$
5.	$(((p \equiv q) \prec (p \equiv q)) \,\&\, ((p \equiv q) \prec (p \equiv q)))$	2, 4, *Strict MP*
6.	$((p \equiv q) \equiv (p \equiv q))$	5, Def. $\equiv$
7.	$((p \equiv q) \equiv ((p \prec q) \,\&\, (q \prec p)))$	6, Def. $\equiv$

One important theorem is:

T3. $((p \prec q) \prec (p \supset q))$

Given the definition of $\supset$ it follows that:

T3′. $((p \prec q) \prec \sim(p \,\&\, \sim q))$

The converse is not a theorem, and this is one important distinction between $\prec$ and $\supset$.

The proof of T3 is no simple matter, but we leave it as a challenge for the reader. Once this is proved the first five axioms will swiftly yield theorems that are pure propositional logic theorems with no modality at all.

One thing to notice about Lewis's S1 is that it is not set out like the axiomatic modal logics in Chapter 5. Those axiom systems begin with three axiom schema and one rule of inference for propositional logic with the material conditional and without modality. Modal axioms and modal rules of inference are then added. But Lewis's axioms for S1 are all modal. The material conditional does not appear at all.

The second is that even though Lewis defines $\prec$ in terms of $\Diamond$, $\sim$ and &, he does not explicitly use $\Diamond$ in the axiom system. In his original work he proceeds for thirty pages without $\Diamond$ appearing in any of the theorems, even though it does appear in three proofs. He says, "We have proceeded, so far as possible, in the same manner as if **p** $\prec$ **q** had been taken as a primitive idea, instead of $\Diamond$ *p*" (Lewis & Langford 1932: 163).

It is this emphasis on $\prec$ that allows us to see S1 as a conditional logic, rather than as a modal logic.

The third thing has to do with the eleven formulas and nine argument forms. Because Lewis defines $\prec$ the way he does and makes $p \prec q$ the translation of "If p then q", we can replace the $\Rightarrow$ by $\prec$ in all the formulas and argument forms and see how they fare in S1. The first three formulas are all theorems of **S1**. The allied argument forms are valid. **MP′** is one of the rules of inference, and is known as *strict MP*.

Now for the rest of the cases:

UPCon $_\prec$. $(\sim(p \prec q) \prec (p \;\&\; \sim q))$

is not a theorem. This also means that the negation of the conditional "If p then q" is not equivalent to "p and not q".

But what of the other formulas? If we transpose them to formulas with $\prec$ for $\Rightarrow$, we get:

Wk $_\prec$. $((p \prec q) \prec ((p \;\&\; r) \prec q))$
Contra $_\prec$. $((p \prec q) \prec (\sim q \prec \sim p))$
HS $_\prec$. $((p \prec q) \;\&\; (q \prec r)) \prec (p \prec r)))$
Para1 $_\prec$. $(p \prec (q \prec p))$
Para2 $_\prec$. $(\sim p \prec (p \prec q))$
Para3 $_\prec$. $((p \prec q) \vee (q \prec p))$
Para4 $_\prec$. $((p \prec q) \vee (q \prec r))$

We shall not consider mixed operator formulas such as $(p \supset (q \prec p))$ because our concern is with uniform interpretation and not for finer logical points.

Wk $_\prec$, **Contra** $_\prec$ and **HS** $_\prec$ are theorems of **S1**. Indeed, **HS** $_\prec$ is an axiom. The last four, the paradoxes, are not theorems of **S1**.

Since all the theorems of **S1** are also theorems of **S2** to **S5**, it follows that **Wk** $_\prec$ to **HS** $_\prec$ are all theorems of **S2** to **S5**. It then follows that the Lewis systems are all *monotonic*. And they validate *weakening, contraposition* and *hypothetical syllogism*. The paradoxes of implication, **Para1** $_\prec$ to **Para4** $_\prec$, turn out not to be theorems. They are not theorems of **S5** and hence are not of any of the sequence **S1** to **S4** either. The argument forms **Para1′** $_\prec$ and **Para2′** $_\prec$ are invalid in **S5** and hence in **S1** to **S4**.

The use of strict implication was not successful in the ways Lewis had hoped. We shall see later in Chapter 14 whether he should have been so pessimistic. Nevertheless, Lewis's disappointment prevailed at the time and attention turned away from the conditional logic interpretation of the Lewis systems. The emphasis shifted to the possibility/necessity interpretation of the Lewis system and other closely related systems such as **K** and **T**. Some logicians continued the search for a conditional logic in other directions. They turned to other alternatives in the search for a logic for conditionals: to logics that were specifically *conditional logics*. We consider some of these systems in the next section.

6.3 Exercises

1.   Prove the following theorems of S1.

    a. $((\sim p \prec q) \prec (\sim q \prec p))$
    b. $(\sim\sim p \prec p)$
    c. $((p \prec q) \prec ((p \ \& \ r) \prec q))$
    d. $((p \prec q) \prec (\sim q \prec \sim p))$
    e. $((p \prec q) \prec ((q \prec r) \prec (p \prec r)))$

6.4 Conditional logics

We now turn to logics that use possible world semantics but not quite in the way in which we have seen in previous chapters. The first of these is known as **C**, for conditional logic. We more or less follow the treatment given for these logics in Graham Priest's *An Introduction to Non-Classical Logic* (2008; hereafter *INCL*).

A new operator is introduced for "If … then …" It is > The logic of > is the second interpretation for ⇨. So we have the clause added to propositional logic:

If α and β are formulas then so is $(\alpha > \beta)$.

This operator is used to set up a sequence of **C** logics. These logic all include standard propositional logic. Priest develops them as extensions of the normal modal logics. But the material conditional is not used to translate "If … then …". Just as there are a range of normal modal logics, each built on the previous ones like **K**, **T**, **S4** and **S5**, by varying the accessibility relation, so we have a sequence of **C** logics.

6.4.1 The conditional logic C

How are we to get an intuitive grip on the logic for the new operator? One way is to see it as a variation on necessity and possibility. Just for the moment we introduce two new variations on box and diamond. Where α and β are formulas we have $[\alpha]$ and $\langle\alpha\rangle$ In each case the α is a formula which is the *index* for the box or diamond operator. Then, there is a sense in which $(\alpha > \beta)$ is treated as $[\alpha]\beta$ in the **C** logics. The index is the antecedent of the conditional. The conditional $(p > q)$ is being read as "In all the worlds in which p is true so is q". This is not the same as $(p \prec q)$. Since $(p \prec q)$ is equivalent to $\Box(p \supset q)$, it's reading is "In all accessible worlds, either p is false or q is true."

In the normal modal logics the diamond generates new worlds. Plain box and diamond are inter-definable, and so are indexed box and diamond. $\langle\alpha\rangle\,\beta$ is similarly equivalent to $\sim[\alpha]\sim\beta$.

If indexed diamond is like diamond, and indexed box is like box, then indexed diamond will generate worlds in truth-trees and indexed box will fill them. Each indexed diamond not only generates a world, but also sets up an indexed accessibility relation.

More importantly, if $(\alpha > \beta)$ is treated like $[\alpha]\beta$, then $\sim(\alpha > \beta)$ is treated like $\sim[\alpha]\beta$, and this is equivalent to $\langle\alpha\rangle\sim\beta$. Diamonds generate new worlds in trees, so negated conditionals generate new worlds and set up indexed accessibility relations. Since the index in the operator is the antecedent of the conditional, the index for the accessibility relation, A, will be indexed.

Each A is subscripted with the *antecedent* of the conditional that generates a new world. So when $\sim(\alpha > \beta)$ generates a new world the accessibility will be A_α. This gives us the following principle:

> If $\sim(\alpha > \beta)(\omega)$, then there is at least one world, υ, such that $\omega A\alpha\upsilon$ and $\sim\beta(\upsilon)$

This gives the tree rule for negated $>$:

$(\sim\!\!>\!\mathbf{R})$ $\sim(\alpha > \beta)$ (ω)
                     ⋮

               $\omega A_\alpha\upsilon$
               $\sim\beta$ (υ)
          where υ is NEW to
          this path of the tree

The rule for positive $>$ is restricted so that only an accessibility relation indexed with the antecedent can enable the consequent to fill the accessible world:

$(>\!\mathbf{R})$ $(\alpha > \beta)$ (ω)
                $\omega A_\alpha\upsilon$
                 ⋮

               β (υ)

Antecedent and accessibilty index must match.

The principles for these rules can be set out as:

$$\sim(\alpha > \beta)(\omega) = 1 \Leftrightarrow (\exists\upsilon)(\omega A_\alpha\upsilon \,\&\, \beta(\upsilon) = 0)$$

$$(\alpha > \beta)(\omega) = 1 \Leftrightarrow (\forall\upsilon)(\omega A_\alpha\upsilon \Rightarrow \beta(\upsilon) = 1)$$

The set of tree rules is **TrC**

$$\text{TrC} = \text{PTr} \cup \{\sim{>}R, >R\}$$

We set out a sample tree in which we test the argument form:

$$\begin{array}{c} (p > q) \\ (p > r) \\ \hline \therefore \quad (p > (q\ \&\ r)) \end{array}$$

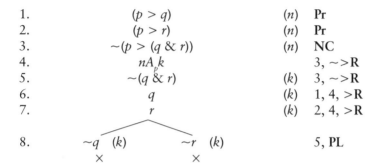

1.	$(p > q)$	(n)	**Pr**
2.	$(p > r)$	(n)	**Pr**
3.	$\sim(p > (q\ \&\ r))$	(n)	**NC**
4.	$nA_p k$		$3, \sim{>}R$
5.	$\sim(q\ \&\ r)$	(k)	$3, \sim{>}R$
6.	q	(k)	$1, 4, >R$
7.	r	(k)	$2, 4, >R$
8.	$\sim q$ (k) $\sim r$ (k)		$5,$ **PL**

The argument form is valid.
   Consider the argument form **UP′**:

$$\begin{array}{c} p \\ \sim q \\ \hline \therefore \quad \sim(p > q) \end{array}$$

The tree is:

1.	p	(n)	**Pr**
2.	$\sim q$	(n)	**Pr**
3.	$\sim(p > q)$	(n)	**NC**
4.	$nA_p k$		$3, \sim{>}R$
5.	$\sim q$	(k)	$3, \sim{>}R$
	$\uparrow$		

The tree does not close and **UP′** is invalid, which is a somewhat surprising result.
   We consider **UPCon** where $>$ replaces $\Rightarrow$:

UPCon$_>$. $(\sim(p > q) > (p\ \&\ \sim q))$

The tree is:

1. $\sim(\sim(p > q) > (p \,\&\, \sim q))$ (n)   NTF
2. $nA_{\sim(p > q)}k$ 1, $\sim$>R
3. $\sim(p \,\&\, \sim q)$ (k)   1, $\sim$>R

4. $\sim p$ (k) $\sim\sim q$ (k)
        ↑   ↑

As might be expected, **UPCon$_>$** is not a tautology of **C**.

We now turn to the argument form for *weakening*, the second case.

Wk'$_>$. $\dfrac{(p > q)}{\therefore \quad ((p \,\&\, r) > q)}$

The tree is:

1. $(p > q)$ (n)   **Pr**
2. $\sim((p \,\&\, r) > q)$ (n)   **NC**
3. $nA_{(p \,\&\, r)}k$ 2, $\sim$>R
4. $\sim q$ (k)   2, $\sim$>R
        ↑

Nothing more can be done in this tree because the antecedent of the first premise does not match the index of the accessibility relation. So the rule for positive > cannot be applied. The premise is true because there is no accessibility indexed with just p, and the conclusion is false because q is false in the world, k, to which n has access indexed with $(p \,\&\, r)$.

The formulas and the argument forms for *contraposition* (**Contra** and **Contra'**) and *hypothetical syllogism* (**HS** and **HS'**) are transposed. The formulas, for example, are set out as follows:

Contra$_>$. $((p > q) > (\sim q > \sim p))$
HS$_>$. $(((p > q) \,\&\, (q > r)) > (p > r))$

These or their related argument forms with **Para1$_>$** to **Para4$_>$** are set as exercises below.

6.4.1 Exercises

1. Use trees to test the argument forms **MP'$_>$**, **MT'$_>$**, **Contra'$_>$**, and **HS'$_>$** in **C** to show which, if any, are valid.
2. Use trees to test the formulas **Para1$_>$**, **Para2$_>$**, **Para3$_>$**, and **Para4$_>$** in **C** to discover which, if any, are theorems.

6.4.2 The conditional logic C⁺

The logic **C** is somewhat like **K** in the sequence of normal modal logics. In **C** there are no conditions such as reflexivity or transitivity placed on the accessibility relation.

If you look at the rules and conditions then you will see that although the antecedent indexed accessibility is supposed to be to worlds where the antecedent is true, there is no explicitly true antecedent in the generated worlds. This can be amended with the following three rules. The first extends the generation of accessibility by adding that the antecedent is true in the generated world:

$(\sim > R^+)$ $\sim (\alpha > \beta)$ (ω)
$\vdots$

$\omega A_\alpha \upsilon$
α (υ)
$\sim\beta$ (υ)
where υ is NEW to
this path of the tree

This rule seems far more intuitively correct than the $(\sim > R)$ rule.

The next two rules introduce a version of reflexivity appropriate to both the positive and negative >:

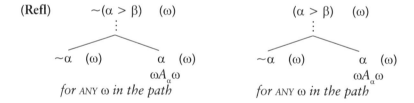

(Refl) $\sim(\alpha > \beta)$ (ω) $(\alpha > \beta)$ (ω)
                  $\vdots$ $\vdots$

$\sim\alpha$ (ω) α (ω) $\sim\alpha$ (ω) α (ω)
                          $\omega A_\alpha \omega$ $\omega A_\alpha \omega$
for ANY ω in the path   *for ANY ω in the path*

With these three new rules added to **C** we get the system **C⁺**. The set of tree rules is Tr **C⁺**. We can replace $\sim > R$ with $\sim > R^+$ since inspection will show that the first is included in the second.

$$\text{Tr}\mathbf{C}^+ = \text{PTr} \cup \{\sim>R, >R, \sim>R^+, \text{Refl}\}$$

Consider now the tree for *modus tollens* for > in **C⁺**:

$(p > q)$
$\underline{\sim q}$
$\therefore$ $\sim p$

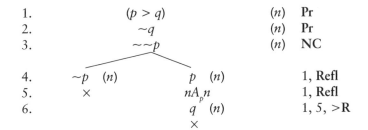

1.	$(p > q)$		(n)	**Pr**
2.	$\sim q$		(n)	**Pr**
3.	$\sim\sim p$		(n)	**NC**

	$\sim p$ (n)	p (n)	1, Refl
4.			
5.	$\times$	$nA_p n$	1, Refl
6.		q (n)	1, 5, >**R**
		$\times$	

So **MT′**$_>$ is valid in **C$^+$**. You can also see that without **Refl** the tree would not close, because world n would have no access to any world, not even itself, and >**R** could not be applied to the first premise. So **MT′**$_>$ is valid in **C$^+$** although it is invalid in **C**.

6.4.2 Exercises

1. Use trees to test the argument forms **UP′**$_>$, **UPCon′**$_>$, **MP′**$_>$, **Wk′**$_>$, **Contra′**$_>$, and **HS′**$_>$ to show which, if any, are valid in **C$^+$**.
2. Use trees to test formulas **Para1**$_>$, **Para2**$_>$, **Para3**$_>$ and **Para4**$_>$ in **C$^+$** to discover which, if any, are theorems.

6.5 Semi-classical logic

We consider the semi-classical logics, which have all the formulas of propositional logic together with a new operator: →, *arrow*, for "If ... then ...". We now interpret ⇨ with the logic for →. So we have the clause added to the formation rules for propositional logic:

If α and β are formulas then so is $(\alpha \to \beta)$.

Semi-classical logics have possible worlds semantics. But, instead of the classical logic semantics with the two truth values *true* and *false*, semi-classical logics have values from the four values, *null*, *just true*, *just false*, and *both true and false*.

Classical logic takes values from the set $\{1, 0\}$.

Semi-classical logic takes values from the set $\{\{\}, \{1\}, \{0\}, \{1, 0\}\}$.

In what follows we intoduce flagged formulas for truth-trees. There are four flags. They are **t**, **nt**, **f** and **nf**. The flags mean **at least true**, **not true**, **at least false**, and **not false** respectively. Flagged formulas cannot themselves be flagged. When "F α (ω)" occurs in a tree then it means that α is F in world ω. Since there are four flags, there will be four rules for each operator. The tree rules for the classical propositional logic connectives are very much as one might expect.

6.5.1 Flagged tree rules for classical connectives

Neg

t $\sim p$ (ω)	f $\sim p$ (ω)	nt $\sim p$ (ω)	nf $\sim p$ (ω)
$\vdots$	$\vdots$	$\vdots$	$\vdots$
f p (ω)	t p (ω)	nf p (ω)	nt p (ω)

Amp

t (p & q) (ω)
$\vdots$
t p (ω)
t q (ω)

f (p & q) (ω)
$\vdots$

f p (ω)   f q (ω)

nf (p & q) (ω)
$\vdots$
nf p (ω)
nf q (ω)

nt (p & q) (ω)
$\vdots$

nt p (ω)   nt q (ω)

Vel

f ($p \vee q$) (ω)
$\vdots$
f p (ω)
f q (ω)

t ($p \vee q$) (ω)
$\vdots$

t p (ω)   t q (ω)

nt ($p \vee q$) (ω)
$\vdots$
nt p (ω)
nt q (ω)

nf ($p \vee q$) (ω)
$\vdots$

nf p (ω)   nf q (ω)

If we were to take just the rules for t and **nt**, then we would have the tree rules for *classical flagged formula* trees. Up to this point the rules for the other flags are just simple mirrors of the rules for t and **nt**.

We go on to set out the **classical closure** rules (**CC**).

(CC)

t α (ω)	f α (ω)	nt α (ω)	t α (ω)
$\vdots$	$\vdots$	$\vdots$	$\vdots$
nt α (ω)	nf α (ω)	nf α (ω)	f α (ω)
$\times$	$\times$	$\times$	$\times$

If we used these rules and started each tree to test α with fα, then we would have flagged formula trees for ordinary propositional logic.

6.5.2 The system RM

We need to add additional rules for *arrow* and non-classical closure. These will give us a logic called **RM**. This logic does not allow formulas to have the null value. So, the closure rules are:

(NCC)

t α (ω)	f α (ω)	nt α (ω)
⋮	⋮	⋮
nt α (ω)	nf α (ω)	nf α (ω)
×	×	×

The third closure rule prevents any formula having the null value. The rules do not give closure when a formula is both true and false.

The expected four rules for → are best set out as five rules. There is one rule for a *not true arrow*, and two rules for *true arrow*

(nt→)

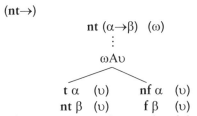

where υ is NEW *to these paths of the tree*

(t→)

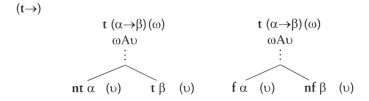

The rules for **not true** and **true** for arrow are like the modal rules for diamond and box in modal logic. The **not true** rule is a world generator rule, and the **true** rules are world filler rules. This makes the → analogous to strict implication in the $\Box(p \supset q)$ form. It would generate a new world if not true, and fill worlds if true.

If you look at the (nt→) rule you will notice two things. First, the rule generates a new world. Secondly, in that world either the antecedent is true and the consequent is not true, or the consequent is false and the antecedent is not false. If the former is the case then it is as if *modus ponens* fails for truth. If it is the latter then it is as if *modus tollens* fails for falsehood.

We now turn to the tree rules for **not false** and **false** *arrow*.

$(f{\rightarrow})$ **nf** $(\alpha{\rightarrow}\beta)$ (ω) **f** $(\alpha{\rightarrow}\beta)$ (ω)

                    ⋮   ⋮

                                          t α (ω)

nt α (ω) **nf** β (ω) **f** β (ω)

These two rules are just like the rules for material implication. If the *arrow* is **false** then the antecedent is **true** and the consequent is **false**. A **false** *arrow* has an immediate counter-example in the same world.

There are some other world-filling rules, known as **hereditary conditions (HC)**. These rules guarantee, in a way, that once a formula gets to be **true** or **false**, it remains so from world to accessible world. The rules are:

(HC)

       t α (ω) **f** α (ω) **nt** α (ω) **nf** α (ω)

       $\omega A\upsilon$ $\omega A\upsilon$ ⋮   ⋮

       ⋮   ⋮   **f** α (ω) **t** α (ω)

       t α (υ) **f** α (υ)

The third and fourth rules follow from there being no **null** valued formulas in **RM**.

The accessibility relation is also reflexive and linear, that is, it is reflexive, anti-symmetric and connected. This gives the tree rules:

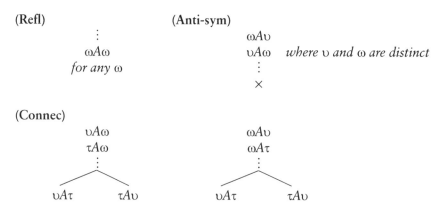

(Refl)   **(Anti-sym)**

            ⋮ $\omega A\upsilon$

       $\omega A\omega$ $\upsilon A\omega$ *where υ and ω are distinct*

     for any ω ⋮

                               ×

(Connec)

          $\upsilon A\omega$ $\omega A\upsilon$

          $\tau A\omega$ $\omega A\tau$

            ⋮   ⋮

   $\upsilon A\tau$ $\tau A\upsilon$ $\upsilon A\tau$ $\tau A\upsilon$

The definition of **RM**-Valid is:

     RM-Valid(α) iff **nt** α is not in ρ (where ρ is the *root world* of the tree)

We turn now to some of the cases set out at the beginning of the chapter. Consider:

UPCon.→ $(\sim(p \to q) \to (p \,\&\, \sim q))$

1.   nt $(\sim (p \to q) \to (p \,\&\, \sim q))$ (n) NTF
2. nAk 1, nt →

3.   t $\sim (p \to q)$ (k) nf $\sim (p \to q)$ (k) 1, nt →
4.   nt $(p \,\&\, \sim q)$ (k) f $(p \,\&\, \sim q)$ (k) 1, nt →
5.   f $(p \to q)$ (k) 3   nt $(p \to q)$ (k) 3
6.   t p (k) 5, f → kAm 5, nt →
7.   f q (k) 5, f →
8.   t p (m) nf p (m) 5
9.   nt p (k) 4   nt $\sim q$ (k) 4   nt q (m) f q (m) 5
10.   X   nf q (k) 9   ⋮

11.   X   f p (k) f $\sim q$ (k) 4
12.   f p (m) 11, 6 HC   t q (k) 11
13.   ↑   t q (m) 12, HC
14.   X

There is an open path, and **UPCon.→** is not a theorem. Note that once there is an open path there is no need to complete the unfinished path to the right at line 9. The reader might finish it, but it will not change the outcome.

We now set out a tree for the argument form for the first paradox:

Para1.→′.

1.   t p (n) P
2.   nt $(q \to p)$ (n) NC
3. nAk 2, nt→

4.   t q (k) nf q (k) 2, nt→
5.   nt p (k) f p (k) 2, nt→
6.   t p (k) t p (k) 1, 3, HC
7.   X   t q (k) 4, HC
8.   ↑

The argument form is not valid in **RM**. The counter-example gives a system of worlds, Ω, such that:

Ω = {n, k}   n = {t p, nt (q → p)}
k = {t p, f p, nf q, t q}   nAk

It is "surprising" that we see:

$$\{\mathbf{t}\,p, \mathbf{f}\,p\} \subseteq k$$

The key is that we have *separate conditions* for truth and falsehood. Falsehood is classical in some sense, but truth is modal.

Despite the outcome for the first paradox, the third paradox is a theorem of **RM**.

Para3.→. $((p \to q) \vee (q \to p))$

1.	**nt** $((p \to q) \vee (q \to p))$	(n)	NTF
2.	**nt** $(p \to q)$	(n)	
3.	**nt** $(q \to p)$	(n)	
4.	nAk		2, nt→

5.　　　　　　**t** p (k)　　　　　　　**nf** p (k)　　　　2, nt→
6.　　　　　　**nt** q (k)　　　　　　**f** q (k)　　　　2, nt→
7.　　　　　　nAm　　　　　　　　　nAm　　　　3, nt→

8.　**t** q (m)　**nf** q (m)　　**t** q (m)　**nf** q (m)　3, nt→
9.　**nt** p (m)　**f** p (m)　　**nt** p (m)　**f** p (m)　3, nt→
10.　　　　　　**t** q (m)　　**t** p (k)
11.　kAm　mAk　**f** q (k)　　**f** p (m)　kAm　mAk　Connec
12.　**t** p (m)　**t** q (k)　　　　　　　　　**f** q (m)　**f** p (k)
13.　× 　　 × 　　 kAm　mAk　　　　　　×　　 ×
14.　　　　**f** q (m)　**t** q (k)
15.　　　　　　 × 　　 × 　　kAm　mAk
16.　　　　　　　　　　　　**t** p (m)　**f** p (k)
17.　　　　　　　　　　　　　 × 　　 ×

Since the tree closes, the formula is **RM** valid. The **hereditary condition** together with the linear nature of the accessibility relation are crucial for the closure of the tree. The theoremhood of **Para3.→** is what puts **RM** in the semi-classical category.

6.5.2 Exercises

1. Use trees to test the argument forms **UP′→**, **MP′→**, **MT′→**, **Wk′→**, **Contra′→**, and **HS′→** in **RM** to discover which, if any, are Valid.
2. Use trees to test formulas **Para2→**, and **Para4→** in **RM** to discover which, if either, are theorems in **RM**.

6.5.3 Systems near RM

Clearly, we can generate other logics of the **RM** genre by variations on the allowable value combinations. **RM** allows **just true, just false** and **both true and false**. If **null** is also allowed then we have the logic **RM-all**. There will also be the logic in which the values are **just true, just false** and **null**. The logic is **RMØ**.

There are clearly a whole range of systems near **RM** that it would be interesting to explore. But that is outside our self-imposed remit. Further exploration of the systems around **RM** is left to the reader.

6.6 Relevant logic

The logic **RM** is a "relevant logic" with the addition of semi-classical theorems. From an axiomatic point of view, **RM** is the relevant logic **R** with the addition of the mingle axiom:

Mingle: $(p \to (p \to p))$

Proof of the Mingle axiom is left to the reader. Mingle has a certain air of classicality about it, and brings considerable change to **R** in the classical direction of **RM**.

We are not going to explore the **R** system because the semantics are very complex and difficult to turn into a truth-tree system. The propositional logic is also undecidable, and that is an indication of the complexity of **R**. The system **R** and logics near it are left for the reader's separate attention.

References and further reading

Anderson, A. R. & N. D. Belnap 1975. *Entailment: The Logic of Relevance and Necessity*. Princeton, NJ: Princeton University Press.

Dunn, J. M. 1976. "A Kripke-Style Semantics for R-Mingle Using a Binary Accessibility Relation". *Studia Logica* 35: 163–72.

Hughes, G. E. & M. J. Cresswell 1968. *An Introduction to Modal Logic*. London: Methuen [esp. Ch. 12].

Jackson, F. 1987. *Conditionals*. Oxford: Oxford University Press.

Lewis, C. I. & C. H. Langford 1932. *Symbolic Logic*. New York: Dover.

Lewis, D. 1973. *Counterfactuals*. Oxford: Blackwell.

Nute, D. 1980. *Conditional Logic*. Dordrecht: Reidel.

Priest, G. 2008. *An Introduction to Non-Classical Logic*, 2nd edn. Cambridge: Cambridge University Press [esp. Ch. 5].

Stalnaker, R. 1968. "A Theory of Conditionals". In *Studies in Logical Theory*, N. Rescher (ed.), 98–112. Oxford: Blackwell.

CHAPTER 7

Modal predicate logics

7.1 Introduction

In this chapter we consider modal predicate S5. We could have modal predicate logics based on any of the systems from **K** to **S5**. But we shall focus on S5.
We extend the language of propositional S5 to modal predicate logic by simply
adding the predicate logic symbols and formation rules to what has been set
out. The formulas of modal predicate logic, or the well-formed formulas of
modal quantification theory (WMQL), include formulas such as:

$$\Box(\forall x)(Ax \supset Bx), \quad (\forall x)\Box(Ax \supset Bx), \quad (\exists x)(Ax \ \& \ \Diamond Bx)$$

The addition of identity as a predicate constant will give the formulas of modal
quantification theory with identity (WMQL=). The formulas include:

$$\Box(a = b), \quad \Diamond\sim(\exists x)(x = a), \quad (\forall x)(\forall y)(xRy \supset (x = y))$$

Given the language of modal predicate logic with identity, there are many
modal predicate S5s with identity. We shall start with two of the simplest
modal predicate S5s with identity. We take the tree rules for predicate logic
and add them to S5 without any qualification at all. We shall then consider
two ways of adding the standard tree rules for identity. This gives us **S5QT**,
and **S5QT=** in two forms.

Modal predicate logics carry with them, in the eyes of many philosophers,
a great number of problems. There are problems to do with translation,
and problems to do with the way the instantiation rules work from world
to world. There are also problems about whether or not there are ontologi-
cal assumptions built into predicate logic, and if there are, what are they?
The discussion of these problems results in suggestions about modifications
to modal predicate logic. We consider some of the modifications and their

impact on the status of certain key formulas. Depending on the actual logics, some formulas will be valid in one logic and invalid in another.

We shall consider some of these issues later in this chapter. We begin with the formal operation of a truth-tree system for **S5QT**.

7.2 Modal predicate S5

We begin with a definition of the formulas of modal quantification theory. The definition of the WML in Chapter 2 is extended as follows:

Symbols

Propositional letters operators and parentheses plus:

individual constants: $a, b, c, d, \ldots$

individual variables: $w, x, y, z, \ldots$

predicate letters (n ≥ 1): $F^n, G^n, H^n, J^n, \ldots$

quantifiers: $\forall, \exists$

Formation rules for the well-formed formulas of modal quantification logic (WMQL):

B1: Any propositional letter standing alone is a WMQL.

B2: Any predicate letter, Φ^n, immediately followed by n individual constants not necessarily distinct is a WMQL.

R~: If α is a WMQL then so is $\sim \alpha$.

R◊: If α is a WMQL then so is $\Diamond \alpha$.

R□: If α is a WMQL then so is $\Box \alpha$.

R*: If * is any dyadic operator and α and β are WMQL, then so is $(\alpha * \beta)$.

RQ: If Φ is a WMQL, then if Q is either $\forall$ or $\exists$ and η is any individual variable and κ is any individual constant in Φ and $\Phi(\eta/\kappa)$ is the result of substituting η for one or more occurrences of κ in Φ, then $(Q\eta)\Phi(\eta/\kappa)$ is a WMQL

T: Nothing else is a WMQL.

The clause **RQ** in this definition ensures that there are no free occurrences of individual variables and no vacuous quantifiers in the formulas. Standard abbreviations are used. The superscript on predicate letters is left off, and dyadic predicate formulas such as R^2ab are written in *infix* form as aRb.

We now proceed to a straightforward modalization of standard predicate logic trees. We add the rules to the orthodox S5 rules from Chapter 3 to get S5QT. All the formal machinery for this S5QT is straightforward.

The old predicate logic truth-tree rules are modified to give the new one world rules:

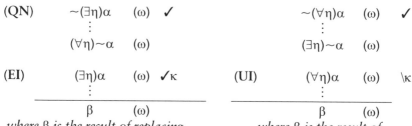

(QN)	$\sim(\exists\eta)\alpha$	(ω)	✓		$\sim(\forall\eta)\alpha$	(ω)	✓
	$\vdots$				$\vdots$		
	$(\forall\eta)\sim\alpha$	(ω)			$(\exists\eta)\sim\alpha$	(ω)	

(EI) $(\exists\eta)\alpha \quad (\omega) \quad ✓\kappa$ (UI) $(\forall\eta)\alpha \quad (\omega) \quad \backslash\kappa$
          $\vdots$ $\vdots$

              $\beta \qquad (\omega)$ $\beta \qquad (\omega)$

where β is the result of replacing every free occurrence of η in α with an individual constant, say κ, where κ is NEW to this path of tree

where β is the result of replacing every free occurrence of η in α with ANY individual constant, say κ

We can test $((\forall x) \square Fx \supset \square (\forall x)Fx)$. This formula is the simplest instance of a formula known as the **Barcan formula**. It is one of the formulas that will feature in our later discussions. The formula is named after Ruth Barcan, one of the key figures in modal logic in the late twentieth century. The tree is:

1.	$\sim((\forall x) \square Fx \supset \square(\forall x)Fx)$		(n)	NTF
2.	$(\forall x) \square Fx$	$\backslash a$	(n)	1
3.	$\sim\square(\forall x)Fx$		(n)	1
4.	$\lozenge\sim(\forall x)Fx$		(n)	3 MN
5.	nAk			4, $\lozenge$R
6.	$\sim(\forall x)Fx$		(k)	4, $\lozenge$R
7.	$(\exists x)\sim Fx$		(k) ✓ a	5, QN
8.	$\sim Fa$		(k)	7, EI a
9.	$\square Fa$		(n)	2, UI a
10.	Fa		(k)	9, 5, $\square$R

It is S5QT-Valid.

In what follows we adopt the standard abbreviation of the universal quantification: $(\forall\eta)\Phi$ is abbreviated to $(\eta)\Phi$.

7.2 Exercises

1.   Show the following to be **S5QT**-Valid.

a. $(x) \square Fx \supset \square (x)Fx$
b. $(\exists x) \square Fx \supset \square (\exists x)Fx$
c. $\square(x)Fx \supset (x) \square Fx$
d. $\lozenge(\exists x)Fx \equiv (\exists x)\lozenge Fx$
e. $\square(x)(Fx \supset Gx) \supset ((x)Fx \supset (x)Gx)$
f. $(x)(Fx \supset \square Gx) \supset ((x)Fx \supset \square(x)Gx)$
g. $(x) \square (Fx \supset Gx) \supset \square((x)Fx \supset (x)Gx)$
h. $\lozenge(x)Fx \supset (x)\lozenge Fx$
i. $(x)(\square Fx \vee \square \sim Fx) \supset \square(\square Fa \equiv Fa)$
j. $(x)(\lozenge Fx \ \& \ \lozenge \sim Fx) \supset \square(\square Fa \equiv (p \ \& \ \sim p))$

7.3 Counter-examples for modal predicate logic

Counter-examples for **S5QT** are based on the same principles as those for propositional **S5**. Values are worked out within worlds first, then they are applied across worlds in accordance with the same principles as for propositional logic.

Consider the formula $(x)\lozenge Fx \supset \lozenge(x)Fx$. The tree is:

1.	$\sim((x)\lozenge Fx \supset \lozenge(x)Fx)$	(n)	NTF
2.	$(x)\lozenge Fx$	$(n) \setminus a \ b$	1
3.	$\sim\lozenge(x)Fx$	(n)	1
4.	$\square\sim(x)Fx$	(n)	3, **MN**
5.	$\lozenge Fa$	(n)	2, **UI** a
6.	nAk		5, $\lozenge$**R**
7.	Fa	(k)	5, $\lozenge$**R**
8.	$\sim(x)Fx$	(k)	2, 6, $\square$**R**
9.	$(\exists x)\sim Fx$	(k) ✓ b	8, **QN**
10.	$\sim Fb$	(k)	8, **EI** b
11.	$\lozenge Fb$	(n)	2, **UI** b
12.	nAm		11, $\lozenge$**R**
13.	Fb	(m)	11, $\lozenge$**R**
	$\uparrow$		

It is clear that the tree will not close.

We set out a counter-example. The system will be $\{n, k, m\}$.

	n	k	m
Fa	0	1	0
Fb	0	0	1

Where values are missing from the tree we assume *false*. So the modal values are:

	n	k	m
Fa	0	1	0
Fb	0	0	1
$(Fa \,\&\, Fb)$	0	0	0
$\Diamond Fa$	1	1	1
$\Diamond Fb$	1	1	1
$\Diamond(Fa \,\&\, Fb)$	0	0	0

We expand the formula (eliminate quantifiers) for two constants, a and b:

$$((\Diamond Fa \,\&\, \Diamond Fb) \supset \Diamond(Fa \,\&\, Fb))$$

and assign values in n to get:

$$
\begin{aligned}
&((\Diamond Fa \,\&\, \Diamond Fb) \supset \Diamond(Fa \,\&\, Fb)) \quad (n) \\
&= ((1 \,\&\, 1) \supset 0) \quad (n) \\
&= (1 \supset 0) \quad (n) \\
&= 0 \quad \text{in } n
\end{aligned}
$$

So we do have a counter-example and the original formula is not valid. You will see that worlds k and m without n would provide a counter-example.

7.3 Exercises

1. Test the following formulas for S5QT-Validity. If any are not valid, provide a counter-example with the calculations to show it is so.

a. $(\Box(\exists x)Fx \supset (\exists x)\Box Fx)$
b. $((x)(\Box Fx \vee \Box \sim Fx) \vee (x)(\Diamond Fx \,\&\, \Diamond \sim Fx))$
c. $\Box(\Diamond(\exists x)Fx \supset (\exists x)\Diamond Fx)$ (the original Barcan formula)
d. $((x)(Fx \supset \Box Gx) \,\&\, (x)(Gx \supset \Box Hx)) \supset (x)(Fx \supset \Box Hx)$
e. $(\Box(x)(Gx \supset Fx) \equiv (x)(\Box Gx \supset \Diamond Fx))$

7.4 Identity and modal predicate logic

We add identity to modal predicate logic to give the well-formed formulas of modal quantification logic with identity (WMQL). Identity is a dyadic (two-place) predicate with its own specific additional logic reflected in special truth-tree rules. We shall discuss the issues that arise from the combination of identity and modality in a later section.

We add $=$ to the symbols and add to the formation rules:

B=:   If κ and ι are individual constants κ $=$ ι is a WMQLI

Negations of identities, $\sim a = b$, are often written with a slashed equals as in $a \neq b$.

In order to set out tree rules for identity we first need to make an important distinction: we need to define *atomic formulas* and *literals*.

> An *atomic formula* is one that contains no propositional operators nor any quantifiers.

Examples are: p, q, Fa, aRb, $a=b$. These conform to above definitions **B1**, **B2** and **B=**.

> A *literal* is an atomic formula or the negation of an atomic formula.

Note that the negation of a literal might not be a literal. For example, p is a literal and its negation is a literal. So $\sim p$ is a literal. But the negation of $\sim p$ is not a literal.

The following two tree rules for identity are added for **S5QT=**. The first is the rule for **substitutivity of identicals**. The second is the **closure rule for negated identity**.

(CSI)   κ $=$ ι   (ω)
              Φ   (ω)   (Closure)   κ $\neq$ κ   (ω)
              ⋮   ⋮
              Ψ   (ω)   ×

where Φ is a literal and where Ψ is the result of either replacing one or more occurrences of κ in Φ with ι or replacing one or more occurrences of ι in Φ with κ

When the substitution of identicals rule is indexed as above we have *contingent* identity. Hence the **SI** rule is labelled **CSI**.

A simple example of the application of **CSI** in a tree would be:

1.	Fa	(n)	P
2.	$a = b$	(n)	P
3.	$\sim Fb$	(n)	NC
4.	Fb	(n)	1, 2, **CSI**

The closure rule for trees makes it clear that closure depends on a formula and its negation being in the same world. So, with the rules we already have, the following would not close:

n.	$a = b$	(n)
$n+1$.	$a \neq b$	(k)

But if the substitution of identities rule is not restricted to within one world, but can be "trans-world" substitution, then we could substitute a for b in line $n+1$ to get closure:

n.	$a = b$	(n)	
$n+1$.	$a \neq b$	(k)	
$n+2$.	$a \neq a$	(k)	$n, n+1$, substitution of identicals

$$\times$$

In order to allow for trans-world substitution of identicals we would have to alter **CSI** to give **NSI**, necessary SI. We would then have a rule for identity which treated every identity as a necessary identity. Such a rule is:

(**NSI**) $\kappa = \iota$ (υ)
Φ (ω)
$\vdots$
Ψ (ω)

where υ is ANY index and Ψ is the
result of either replacing one or more
occurrences of κ in Φ with ι or replacing
one or more occurrences of ι in Φ with κ

We assume contingent identity, (CSI), for the time being in our S5QT=. The modal predicate logic with necessary identity will be S5QT □ =.

7.4 Exercises

1. Test the following formulas for both **S5QT**=-Validity and
    S5QT □ =-Validity. If any are not valid, provide a counter-
    example with a test to show invalidity.

    a. $(a = b \supset \Box(a = b))$
    b. $(a \neq b \supset \Box(a \neq b))$
    c. $(a = b \supset (\Box Fa \supset \Box Fb))$
    d. $(a = b \supset (Fa \supset \Box Fb))$
    e. $(\Box(a = b) \supset (Fa \supset Fb))$

7.5 The Barcan formula and its converse

We now have a full modal predicate S5 with identity. But we have paid no
attention to many of the points which are considered to be interesting and
controversial with our version of **S5QT**=.

In order to understand some of these problems, a range of modal predicate logics, beyond the logics set out above, have been created by logicians.
As we discuss these problems we shall set out some of the alternative modal
predicate logics. For us, this means looking at ways in which the **UI** and **EI**
rules might be modified. We shall set out some of the modifications as we
discuss the issues.

There are a set of formulas which seem to be at the centre of discussions
in this area. We begin with them.

If you have completed the exercises so far you will know that the four
following formulas are **S5QT**=-Valid.

1. $(\Diamond(\exists x)Fx \supset (\exists x)\Diamond Fx)$ (Barcan formula (BF))
2. $((\exists x)\Diamond Fx \supset \Diamond(\exists x)Fx)$ (converse of the BF (CBF))
3. $((x)\Box Fx \supset \Box(x)Fx)$ (BF)
4. $(\Box(x)Fx \supset (x)\Box Fx)$ (converse of the BF)

All four of these will also be **KQT**=-Valid given the unqualified predicate
logic truth-tree rules we have been using. Check the trees to be sure. Taken
together these mean that the universal quantifier and □ are commutative in
all the normal modal predicate logics with unqualified predicate logic truth-
tree rules. They also entail that the existential quantifier and ◊ are commutative in all normal modal predicate logics:

$((x)\Box Fx \equiv \Box(x)Fx)$
$((\exists x)\Diamond Fx \equiv \Diamond(\exists x)Fx)$

There are two issues that have a strong bearing on these results. The first concerns whether the domain of quantification is the same from possible world to possible world or not. The second concerns whether or not the quantifiers and individual constants carry existential import. We turn to a discussion of the first of these problems. The second will be discussed in Chapter 8.

7.6 The domains of quantification

When we use quantifiers in predicate logic we assume that there is a domain of quantification. When we say that $(\exists x)Fx$ is true, we claim that there is at least one item *in the domain* which has the property F. When we say that $(x)Fx$ is true, we claim that every item *in the domain* has the property F.

In modal predicate logic there is a domain of quantification for each possible world. It might or might not contain the same items from world to world. It is important to see that truth in a world requires a domain for that world. So, we have the possibility of multiple domains of quantification, one for each possible world.

If the quantifiers have existential import, then the domain of quantification is a set of existing items. In what follows we shall assume that the domains of quantification are domains of existing things. Although it might at first look as if this is going to restrict us from quantifying over any domain of items including fictional or mythological entities such as Pegasus, Pickwick or Cair Paravel, this does not necessarily follow. Each of these might exist in a possible world other than the actual world.

Our assumption does not necessarily restrict us to the things existing in the actual world. It just means that the domains are domains of the things that exist in each possible world. If we want quantification to be restricted to only those things that exist in the actual world, we have to do more than just assume that the quantifiers have domains of things that exist in the world to which the domain belongs. Restrictions have to be applied.

In quantified modal logic we need to be clear about whether the domain remains constant from world to world or varies from world to world. There are essentially three options for the domains of quantification from world to world. The first is that each world domain is completely distinct from every other. We might diagram this option as **AE**, where "E" is for "existing":

(**AE**)

The second option is where the domain is the same from world to world. It is the domain, **D**, of existing things in the actual world.

(BE)

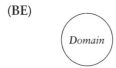

So each possible world is just a way in which the things in **D**, *the* domain of quantification, could be. This is known as the **constant domain** option. All and only these entities that exist in the actual world exist in every world. Pegasus, Pickwick and Cair Paravel are left out completely. Whatever they are, they do not exist in any possible world.

The third option is where the domains vary from world to world in quite arbitrary ways. We would have some variation on:

(CE)

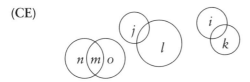

Here, the entities in one world, say *k*, might not exist in another, say *n*. But the domain of *m* might be same as that of *o*. This is known as the **variable domain** option.

There are two variations on **CE** that are of particular interest. We define $D(\delta)$ as the domain of quantification for world δ.

The first variation is where the following holds:

(D1)   If $\omega A\upsilon$ then $D(\omega) \subseteq D(\upsilon)$

This says that if a world has access to another, then the domain of the first is a subset of the domain of the second. In the simplest case this would give us the map for **CEA**, an ascending chain.

There will be a descending chain case as well. The following holds:

(D2)   If $\omega A\upsilon$ then $D(\upsilon) \subseteq D(\omega)$

If a world has access to another, then the domain of the second is a subset of the domain of the first.

In the simplest case this would give us the map for **CED** a descending chain.

(CEA)   (CED)

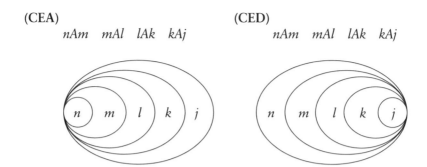

In both these diagrams the worlds are in a strict sequence of accessibility. But the cases could be far more complicated with several diverging or converging chains.

If we insist that the domains of quantification are related in terms of accessibility, then it must be noted that for **S5QT=**, where every world has access to every world, the **CEA** and **CED** cases will collapse into the **BE** case. If we add that the quantifiers are to have existential import, then there is only one of the three options where the picture is clear. It is **BE**. In the **BE** option we see that the quantifiers have the one fixed domain of existing items for every possible world, because there is one domain for all. So, $\exists$ and $\forall$ quantify over the same domain no matter what.

If we consider the ascending and descending chain cases for normal modal logics such as **S4** or **K**, then the domains do not collapse into the **BE** case. But there are so many possibilities here that we begin with the **S5** case with a constant domain.

There is no problem with $(\exists x)\Diamond Fx$. It translates as:

There exists, in some possible world, an F

This is clearly equivalent to $\Diamond(\exists x)Fx$

In some possible world there exists an F

This is the **constant domain** option, **BE**, with which the truth trees so far agree. The key truth-tree rule is **UI**. **EI** will remain the same no matter what. **EI** simply generates a new individual constant in the same world in which the existentially quantified formula occurs. **UI** "links" formulas to individual terms by instantiation. If the domain is constant across all worlds, then there is no problem. Every item in any world will be in every other world. If $(x)Fx$ is true in world n, then since a is in every world, a will be in n, and Fa will be true in n. So it is no wonder that the BF and its converse are valid in constant domain semantics, especially for **S5**.

Obviously it is not possible with a constant domain and existential import to say that some of the entities that do exist in one world do not exist in another. A formula such as:

$$\Diamond \sim (\exists x)(x = a)$$

translated as:

> *It is possible for* a *not to exist.*

Or as: *In at least one possible world* a *does not exist.*

is contradictory in **S5QT=**, and always false. The tree to show it is contradictory begins with the formula *simpliciter*:

1.	$\Diamond \sim (\exists x)(x = a)$	(n)	*Formula*
2.	nAk		1, $\Diamond$**R**
3.	$\sim(\exists x)(x = a)$	(k)	1, $\Diamond$**R**
4.	$(x) \sim (x = a)$	$(k) \setminus a$	
5.	$\sim(a = a)$	(k)	

If we want to be able to say that some of the things that do not exist in one world do exist in some other, and vice versa, then we shall have to use a variable domain semantics. We need a logic where the domains fall under either **AE** or **CE**. There are a variety of logics which agree with **AE**. Some are known as counterpart logics. We shall not deal with them in this book. We turn to **CF**.

7.7 Quantification and worlds

A logic to agree with **CE**, the variable domain option, is available. In truth-tree form the logic is one in which restrictions must be placed on the instantiation of quantifiers. Although domains are allowed to overlap, we cannot assume that they do. There is no inclusion provision or descending chain of domains.

Let **S5DRQT=** (S5 domain-relative **QT=**) be our logic to match **CE**. First we must introduce an additional feature into the formulas. We have to expand WMQLI to well-formed formulas of modal domain-relative quantified logic with identity (WMDRQLI). This is done by redefining the individual constants and making them domain relative, that is, relative to the world in whose quantification domain they are available to be quantified over. So we have:

Domain-relative individual constants: Where κ is a letter from $a, b, c, \ldots$ and ω is a world κ_ω is a domain-relative individual constant.

Since it will cause no confusion within the DR logics we shall refer to "domain-relative individual constants" as "individual constants".

We introduce domain-relative universal and existential instantiation rules, (DRUI) and (DREI). It will be best for our understanding of the rules if we simply set them out and then discuss them.

(DRUI) $(\forall \eta)\alpha$ $(\omega) \setminus \kappa_\omega$

                β (ω)

> where β is the result of replacing every
> free occurrence of η in α with any
> individual constant, say κ_ω

The purpose of the rules is to ensure that quantified formulas are instantiated only to individual constants that refer to items in the world domain over which the quantifier actually quantifies. **EI** always generates a formula in which the individual constant is sub-scripted to the world in which the main operator existential quantifier is true. **UI** operates to instantiate with only the individual constants, which occur in formulas that have truth-value in the world in which the universally quantified formula is true.

For example, say both $(x)Fx$ (k) and Fb (k) are in an open path. We assume that Fb (k) implies that b is an item in the domain of world k, or in other words, b exists in k and since $(x)Fx$ is true in k it can be instantiated in k to b. If no individual constant occurred in a formula indexed with the same world as the universally quantified formula, then a new constant would be used.

In what follows, for any formula α in a tree indexed with a world $\alpha(n)$ we shall say that "α is in n". So "Fb is in k" means Fb is indexed with (k) (which also means that Fb is true in k).

(RUI) $(\forall \eta)\alpha$ $(\omega) \setminus \kappa_\omega$

                β (ω)

> where β is the result of replacing every
> free occurrence of η in α with an individual
> constant, say κ, provided that, in this path
> of the tree, either κ occurs in any formula
> in ω or, if not, κ is NEW to this path of the tree

Let us now test the BF in **S5RQT=**:

1.	$\sim((x)\Box Fx \supset \Box(x)Fx)$	(n)	NTF
2.	$(x)\Box Fx$	(n)	1
3.	$\sim\Box(x)Fx$	(n)	1
4.	$\Diamond\sim(x)Fx$	(n)	3, **MN**
5.	nAk		4, $\Diamond$R
6.	$\sim(x)Fx$	(k)	4, $\Diamond$R

7.	$(\exists x)\sim Fx$	(k)	6, QN
8.	$\sim Fa$	(k)	7, EI a
9.	$\Box Fb$	(n)	2, RUI b (b is new)
10.	Fb	(n)	9, $\Box$T
11.	Fb	(k)	5, 9, $\Box$R
	$\uparrow$		

The tree is open, even in **S5RQT=**.

In this tree we were unable to use **UI** with a at line 9 to get $\Box Fa(n)$ because a does not occur in a formula in n. We have to use a new constant, b. If we had been able to use a, then with nAk at line 5 and $\Box$R we would have gained $Fa(k)$ for path closure. This all simply means that a does not exist in world n, but it does exist in world k.

When it comes to setting out a counter-example we use * for the case where the item does not exist in the world. In the case above, since a does not exist in n, the formula Fa has neither a true nor a false value in n. This leaves a *truth-value gap* in our table of counter-example values, and it makes assumptions about the truth-values of formulas in which there is reference to things that do not exist in the world in which the formula stands. It could be seen as saying that the formula is vacuous or meaningless.

We shall consider the counter-example from an **S5RQT=** point of view, because if it is a counter-example in **S5RQT=** it is a counter-example in all the normal restricted modal logics, all the way to **KRQT=**. Remember that every world has access to every world in **S5RQT=**. First we list the domains for each world, where $D(\omega)$ is the domain of ω:

$$D(n) = \{b\} \qquad\qquad D(k) = \{a, b\}$$

Note that a is not in the domain of n.

So, the modal values in **S5RQT=** are:

	n	k
Fa	*	0
Fb	1	1
$(x)Fx$	1	0
$\Box(x)Fx$	0	0
$\Box Fa$	*	0
$\Box Fb$	1	1
$(x)\Box Fx$	1	1

For the value of $(x)\Box Fx$ (n) we eliminate the quantifier for the domain of world n:

$$\Box Fb(n) = 1$$

So:

$$((x)\Box Fx \supset \Box(x)Fx) \quad (n)$$
$$= (1 \supset 0) = 0$$

In this logical system the quantifiers are relative to worlds. In any formula, all the quantifiers outside the scope of modal operators are relative to the world in which the formula is said to be true or false. For example, given a formula in a world n,

$$(x)\Box Fx \quad (n)$$

we read the formula as:

> Everything that exists in n is, in all worlds, F.

Or even: Everything that exists in n is, in all worlds to which n has access, F.

But we read

$$\Box(x)Fx \quad (n)$$

as: In all worlds everything that exists is F.
Or even: In all worlds accessible from n everything that exists is F.

So, the BF

$$((x)\Box Fx \supset \Box(x)Fx) \quad (n)$$

reads as

> If everything that exists in n is, in all worlds to which n has access, F,
> then in all worlds accessible from n everything that exists is F.

The counter-example above is where we have a system of two worlds, $\{n, k\}$. In world n we have a domain of quantification of just b. Now, b is F in world n. In world k we have a domain of quantification of both b and a. In world k item b is F, but item a is *not* F.

The BF antecedent states that everything in n, that is b, is F in every world to which n has access. n has access to both n and k in all systems other than **K**, and to just k in **K**. So the *antecedent is true* in all normal modal logics.

The BF consequent states that in every world to which n has access everything is F. But, not everything in world k is F. n has access to both n and k in all systems other than **K**, and to just k in **K**. So the *consequent is false* in all normal modal logics.

Let us now test the CBF in **S5RQT=**:

1. $\sim(\Box(x)Fx \supset (x)\Box Fx)$ (n) NTF
2. $\Box(x)Fx$ (n) 1
3. $\sim(x)\Box Fx$ (n) 1

4.	$(\exists x)\sim\Box Fx$	(n)	3, QN
5.	$\sim\Box Fa$	(n)	4, EI a
6.	$\Diamond\sim Fa$	(n)	5, MN
7.	nAk		6, $\Diamond$R
8.	$\sim Fa$	(k)	6, $\Diamond$R
9.	$(x)Fx$	(k)	2, 7, $\Box$R
10.	Fa	(k)	9, RUI a (a occurs in k at line 8)
	$\times$		

The tree closes. It will close even in **KRQT=**.

Given the way we read the BF, the CBF reads as:

If in all worlds accessible to n everything is F, then everything that exists in n will be F in every world accessible to n

This is reasonable given that, as at line 8 in the last tree, items from one world are "carried across" to another by means of the generation of the new world. a is carried across from n to k in the formula $\sim Fa$.

Let us now check with the formula $\Diamond\sim(\exists x)(x = a)$:

1.	$\Diamond\sim(\exists x)(x = a)$	(n)	*Formula*
2.	nAk		1, $\Diamond$R
3.	$\sim(\exists x)(x = a)$	(k)	1, $\Diamond$R
4.	$(x)\sim(x = a)$	$(k) \setminus a$	
5.	$\sim(a = a)$	(k)	4, UI a

It is inconsistent.

In the above trees, we have, in a sense, assumed that if a constant occurs in any formula in a world then that item exists in that world. So, since the formula $\sim Fa$ is true in k, a exists in k. This assumption of existence holds for all formulas. It is carried over to constants occurring in the scopes of modal operators. So, if $\Diamond\sim Fa$ is true in n, then a exists in n.

There is a strange self-fulfilling thing here in the last tree. We can use the constant a for the UI of 4 because a is in a formula in world k. It was brought across from n by the application of the rule for diamond to line 1 to give line 3.

This assumption does not have any impact in the tree above, but a strict and not unreasonable reading of $\Diamond\sim Fa$ (n) as:

In some possible world (accessible from n) a is not F

does not automatically carry the assumption that a exists in n, but only that it exists in some possible world or other.

We shall implement this reasonable reading with an even more restrictive **UI** rule, below. To rule out the assumption made in the tree above that validated the CBF, we would have to do as follows. The proviso that says that κ is to occur in any formula in *n* would be tightened to the proviso that κ is to occur in a formula *outside the scope of any diamond* in *n*. But since we have the modal negation equivalences, this will have to be extended to box as well.

We could have the tighter **RUI**:

(**TRUI**)   (∀η)α   (ω) \κ
                     ⋮
                     β   (ω)

where β is the result of replacing every free
occurrence of η in α with an individual constant,
say κ, provided that, in this path of the tree, either
κ occurs in a formula in ω not in the scope of a diamond,
or, if not, κ is NEW *to this path of the tree*

But, even with this tighter restriction, the CBF is valid, as one might expect. The formula $\lozenge\sim(\exists x)(x = a)$ is also still contradictory.

The CBF is a very resilient formula. It is valid in constant domain semantics, and in both the restricted modal predicate logics we have proposed above. Let us just reprise the CBF before going further. So, the BF

$$(\Box(x)Fx \supset (x)\Box Fx) \ (n)$$

reads as

> *If in all worlds (accessible from n) everything that exists is F then*
> *everything that exists in n is in all worlds (to which n has access), F.*

A moment's thought about this reading will show how to create a counter-example. To make the antecedent true, everything in all worlds is *F*. To make the consequent false, we need something in *n* that does not exist in another world, and if it does not exist there, all statements about it will be false. So the consequent will be false.

The CBF can be rendered invalid.

Consider the following rule of harshly restricted **UI**:

(**HRUI**)   (∀η)α   (ω) \κ
                     ⋮
                     β   (ω)

where β is the result of replacing every free
occurrence of η in α with an individual constant,
say κ, provided that, in this path of the tree, κ has
not been used for the **EI** *of a formula in a world*
other than ω and either κ occurs in a formula
in ω or, if not, κ is NEW *to this path of the tree*

Given this new rule there is one thing which should be borne in mind. When we have an indexed formula ~*Fa* (*n*), we have assumed that *Fa* is false in *n* because *a* exists in *n* and does not have the property *F*. But, *Fa* could be false because *a* does not exist in *n*. This will be important when we draw a counter-example from the next tree and test it.

Let's now re-test the CBF in **S5HRQT=**:

1.	~(□(*x*)*Fx* ⊃ (*x*)□*Fx*)	(*n*)	NTF
2.	□(*x*)*Fx*	(*n*)	1
3.	~(*x*)□*Fx*	(*n*)	1
4.	(*x*)*Fx*	(*n*)	2, □T
5.	(∃*x*)~□*Fx*	(*n*)	3, QN
6.	~□*Fa*	(*n*)	5, EI *a*
7.	◊~*Fa*	(*n*)	6, MN
8.	*nAk*		7, ◊R
9.	~*Fa*	(*k*)	7, ◊R
10.	(*x*)*Fx*	(*k*)	2, 8, □R
11.	*Fb*	(*k*)	10, **HRUI** *b* (*b* is new)
12.	*Fa*	(*n*)	4, **HRUI** *a*

↑

The tree is open, even in **S5HRQT=**.

It is not possible under the harshly restricted **UI** to use *a* for instantiation of the formula in *k* at line 10, because *a* was used for the **EI** of a formula in *n* at line 5. We have to use a new constant.

From the tree we have for a counter-example:

$$\mathbf{D}(n) = \{a\} \qquad \mathbf{D}(k) = \{a, b\}$$

In the counter-example we assume that *Fa* is * in *k* because *a* does not exist in *k*. So we have * for *Fa* under *k*. If *a* did exist in *k* then we would have been able to use it for universal instantiation. Similarly, since *b* does not exist in *n*, *Fb* is vacuous in *n* and *Fb* is * in *n*.

We also need to ensure that modal formulas have values in the worlds in which the formulas in the scope are vacuous. It follows then that □*Fa* is false in *k* and □*Fb* is false in *n*.

	n	*k*
Fa	1	*
Fb	*	1
(*x*)*Fx*	1	1
□(*x*)*Fx*	1	1
□*Fa*	0	0
□*Fb*	0	0
(*x*)□*Fx*	0	

Note that the values for $\Box Fa$ and $\Box Fb$ are false in all worlds. We know that $\sim Fa(k)$ from line 9. This is because each world has access to all in S5, and a does not exist in k, and b does not exist in n, so both $\Box Fa$ and $\Box Fb$ will have to be false in all.

For the value of $(x)\Box Fx(n)$ we eliminate the quantifier for world n for everything that exists in n. Since only a exists in n we get:

$$\Box Fa(n) = 0$$

So: $\quad (x)\Box Fx(n) = 0$

So: $\quad (\Box(x)Fx \supset (x)\Box Fx) \ (n)$
$\quad\quad = (1 \supset 0) = 0$

With the new approach the CBF is now false, given that items from one world do not automatically "carry over" to any other.

This way of dealing with the truth values of negated atomic predicate formulas has introduced quite a new, almost non-classical approach to truth values. On this approach, an open tree could deliver a number of possible counter-examples, depending on what we take to be the logic of each negated atomic predicate formula.

We now turn to the formula $\Diamond \sim (\exists x)(x = a)$ in **S5HRQT=**.

1.	$\Diamond \sim (\exists x)(x = a)$	(n)	*Formula*
2.	nAk		1, $\Diamond$**R**
3.	$\sim (\exists x)(x = a)$	(k)	1, $\Diamond$**R**
4.	$(x) \sim (x = a)$	$(k) \backslash a$	
5.	$\sim (a = a)$	(k)	4, UI a

It still closes and the formula is contradictory. Even with harsh restrictions, it is contradictory.

We have had to make only one restriction in order to rid the logic of the BF. The CBF is quite another issue. We have had to adopt considerable and even contorted restrictions in order to be rid of the CBF. The restrictions all apply to the constants that can be used for the varieties of restricted **UI**.

Compare the restrictions on the **UI** rules, the outcomes with respect to the BF and CBF, and the other main issue that emerges, the truth–value gap issue. We use the particular case of instantiating $(x)Fx$ in world k and the restrictions that apply to constants that we are allowed to use:

$(x)Fx$ (k)	Constants	Formula values with constants
UI	any whatsoever	as usual
RUI	only constants occurring in formulas in (k) or new constants	no value if the constant does not occur in the world
TUI	only constants occurring in formulas in (k) outside the scope of modal operators or new constants	
HRUI	only constants other than those introduced by EI in other worlds	

References and further reading

Barcan (Marcus) R. C. 1947. "Interpreting Quantification". *Inquiry* 5: 252–9.
Fitting, M. & R. L. Mendelsohn 1998. *First-Order Modal Logic*. Dordrecht: Kluwer.
Hintikka, K. J. J. 1961. "Modality and Quantification". *Theoria* 27: 110–28.
Hughes, G. E. & M. J. Cresswell 1996. *A New Introduction to Modal Logic*. London & New York: Routledge.

CHAPTER 8
Quantifiers and existence

8.1 Introduction

We have seen in Chapter 7 that the question of existence is tightly bound up with quantifiers in modal predicate logic.

We simply assumed, for the purpose of setting out some of the intricacies of modal predicate logic, that quantifiers carried existential import. In other words, we assumed that $(\exists x)Fx$ means "*At least one existing entity is F*", and that $(x)Fx$ mean "*Every existing entity is F*".

It turns out that this is not a straightforwardly simple matter. The assumption did not make things as simple as one might have expected. We considered constant and variable domain semantics, and spent some time on the issues that arise in variable domain semantics.

Now we must deal with the issue of existential import itself, and the sorts of matters that have arisen in modal predicate logic as a result.

8.2 Quantifiers and existential import

We begin by considering what is the case when quantifiers do not have existential import. If quantifiers do *not* have existential import then

$(\exists x)Fx$ translates as   *At least one thing is F*

where the "at least one thing" might or might not exist, might be mythical or real, might be fictional or historical. Without existential import the $\exists$ quantifier is not really an *existential* quantifier. It is a *particular* quantifier, as Aristotle termed it. This has an impact on how we interpret the universal quantifier.

Without existential import

(x)Fx   translates as   *Everything is F*

where "everything" includes all the existing and mythical and fictional and historical items.

This is in sharp contrast with the situation where the quantifiers do have existential import.

With existential import we have:

(∃x)Fx   translates as   *At least one **existing** thing is F*

or as   *At least one F exists*
or as   *There exists at least one F*
or as   *There is an F*

Also

~(∃x)Fx   translates as   *Fs do not exist*

or as   *There are no Fs*

If we wish to retain the *duality* of the ∃ and ∀ quantifiers, that is, we want (x)Fx ≡ ~(∃x)~Fx to be a logical equivalence then:

(x)Fx   translates as   *Non-Fs do not exist*

or as   *Every existing item is F*
or as   *All existing things are F*

Two problems arise out of the quantifiers having existential import. The first concerns translating the quantifiers of English. The second concerns the use of names for non-existing entities such as Mr Pickwick, Pegasus or Cair Paravel.

First, if quantifiers have existential import then there is no way that predicate logic can translate:

Some things do not exist

This is a pefectly reasonable thing to say in English. So, let us see what happens if we allow the following dictionary (for the moment anyway), when quantifiers have existential import:

Ex = *x exists*

(∃x)~Ex   translates as   *At least one existing thing does not exist*

This is a certain candidate for logical inconsistency. In a sense this is because if we accept the dictionary above and existential import, then

> $(x)Ex$ (*Every existing thing exists*)

is a logical truth. No wonder $(\exists x)\sim Ex$ turns out to be contradictory in this interpretation.

Many philosophers have objected to the notion that existence is a property. But it is a grammatical predicate. So although the use of *Ex* as an existence predicate may well be challenged on some sort of metaphysical grounds, if the logics we consider are to be neutral about questions of existence so that they might provide an unbiased basis for analysing arguments in this area, then building existential import into the quantifiers is a way of prejudicing the logic with a particular philosophical view. It begs the question. The assumption of existential import will just leave us stranded for a translation of the statement "Some things do not exist".

The second problem concerns the names of fictional, mythical or any non-existing entities. Consider the following:

> $(\exists x)(x = a)$ can be translated as   *At least one existing thing is identical to a*

or as   *a exists*
or as   *There is something called "a"*

So, given existential import, you might think that we could have the following. Let $a = Mr\ Pickwick$:

> $\sim(\exists x)(x = a)$ for *Mr Pickwick does not exist*

There is a problem with this translation because $(\exists x)(x = a)$ is **S5QT**=-Valid. The formula is valid whether we interpret the quantifiers as having existential import or not. So our translation of "Mr Pickwick does not exist" is a contradiction. It is a translation that tries to take advantage of existential import, but that leads into logical inconsistency in a standard predicate logic.

The English sentence "Mr Pickwick does not exist" certainly does not look like a contradiction. So the assumption of existential import places a very powerful restriction on the expressiveness of the standard predicate logic.

8.3 Constants and existential import

Because all formulas of the form $(\exists \lambda)(\lambda = n)$ are **S5QT**=-Valid, we can see that all the constants of predicate logic will have existential import if the quantifiers do, and will lack it if the quantifiers lack it.

We know that $(Fa \supset (\exists x)Fx)$ is **QT**=-Valid. It translates, with existential import, as:

If a is F, then some existing thing is F.

So if we assume the quantifier to have existential import, the constant *a* must name an existing item. Constants have existential import in standard predicate logic if the quantifiers do.

But there is another way of looking at existential import. Instead of seeing the quantifiers as having existential import and everything else deriving existential import from them, we can see the individual constants, the simplest singular terms of predicate logic, as having or lacking existential import in their own right.

There is a predicate logic in which the quantifiers have existential import, but the individual constants do not have existential import. The predicate logic of this kind is *free logic*. We shall look at free logic in a later section of this chapter.

In fact, there are the following possibilities:

	Quantifiers	
Constants	Existential import	No existential import
Existential import	Standard interpretation	NK
No existential import	Free logic interpretation	Open

NK is the "not known" interpretation. "Open" is where there is no existential import of any kind.

If the constants have existential import, then non-existing entities cannot have individual constants as either their logical names or as singular terms referring to them. This interpretation of individual constants is compatible with Parmenides' principle that non-existing entities cannot be referred to nor any statements be made about them. In everyday life, people do no observe Parmenides' counsel at all.

Nonetheless, the assumption of existential import has been fairly dominant in contemporary philosophical logic. We need to consider, also, what follows from the assumption when we look at the Barcan formula and its converse.

On the assumption of existential import

$$\lozenge (\exists x)Fx \supset (\exists x)\lozenge Fx$$

translates as:

*It is possible that F exists **only if** there exists a possible F.*

Whilst the antecedent is fairly straightforward, the consequent is problematic, to say the least. What is a *"possible F"*? And if we know what a *possible F* is, what is meant by saying that at least one of them exists? One way of interpreting this is to interpret ◊ as *in at least one possible world*. This would be compatible with what goes on in modal truth trees and possible world semantics.

$$◊(\exists x)Fx \supset (\exists x)◊Fx$$

translates as:

> In some possible world an F exists **only if** there exists something which, in some possible world, is F.

Consider the consquent in this last translation.

> There exists something which, in some possible world, is F.

This might assert that some existing thing in the actual world has the property *F* in some other world. Or it might assert that, from the perspective of some possible world (remembering that all formulas are true or false *in a world*), some of the things that exist in it have the property *F* in some possible world.

8.4 Predicate logic without existential import

We do not have to go down the complex paths outlined in the last few sections. If we reject existential import, then there is no need to seek complex logics to cope with the possibility that what exists in one world might not be the same as what exists in another. We can have just one domain of quantification, similar to **BE**. But, in this case we would have option **B**; that is, **BE** without existential import.

Instead of saying that there is one domain of *existing* entities, all of which exist in every world and nothing else does, we just say that there is one domain of entities for every world. This is the domain of all possible entities. In each world either some things exist and some do not, or nothing exists or everything exists. We can cope, at the simplest level, by having existence as a syntactic predicate. This is the possibilist approach to interpreting modal predicate logic.

The Barcan formula translates as:

> If everything in all worlds is F, then in all worlds everything is F.

The converse translates as:

If in all worlds everything is F then everything in all worlds is F.

It seems reasonable that both of these are valid provided we take everything to mean just that: everything. Does this more direct route give us the expressive power of **RMQT**=?

Let us assume that we have $Ex = x$ exists. We said that the Barcan formula in **RMQT**= translates to:

If everything that exists in n is, in all worlds to which n has access, F, then in all worlds accessible from n everything that exists is F.

If we generalize this a little, removing all reference to a specific world:

If everything that exists in some world is, in all worlds to which it has access, F, then in all accessible worlds everything that exists is F.

Let us try the formula $((x)\Diamond(Ex \supset \Box Fx) \supset (x)\Box(Ex \supset Fx))$. The test is:

1.	$\sim ((x)\Diamond(Ex \supset \Box Fx) \supset (x)\Box(Ex \supset Fx))$	(n)	NTF
2.	$(x)\Diamond(Ex \supset \Box Fx)$	(n)	1
3.	$\sim(x)\Box(Ex \supset Fx)$	(n)	1
4.	$(\exists x) \sim \Box(Ex \supset Fx)$	(n)	3, **QN**
5.	$\sim\Box(Ea \supset Fa)$	(n)	4, **EI** a
6.	$\Diamond\sim(Ea \supset Fa)$	(n)	5, **MN**
7.	nAk		6, $\Diamond$**R**
8.	$\sim(Ea \supset Fa)$	(k)	6, $\Diamond$**R**
9.	Ea	(k)	8
10.	$\sim Fa$	(k)	8
11.	$\Diamond(Ea \supset \Box Fa)$	(n)	2, **UI** a
12.	nAl		11, $\Diamond$**R**
13.	$(Ea \supset \Box Fa)$	(l)	11, $\Diamond$**R**

14.	$\sim Ea$ (l)		$\Box Fa$ (l)		13
15.	$\uparrow$		Fa (l)		14, $\Box$**T**

The right path on line 15 would not apply for **K**. For **S5**, we could add:

16.		$Fa\ (k)$	14, $\Box$**S5**

But the left path will not close. So, the modal values are as follows:

Every world has access to every world in S5.

	n	k	l
Fa	0	0	1
Ea	0	1	0
$(Ea \supset Fa)$	1	0	1
$(Ea \supset \Box Fa)$	1	0	1
$\Box Fa$	0	0	0
$\Box Ea$	0	0	0
$\Box(Ea \supset Fa)$	0	0	0
$\Diamond(Ea \supset \Box Fa)$	1	1	1

We expand the formula (eliminate quantifiers) for one constant, a:

$$(\Diamond(Ea \supset \Box Fa) \supset \Box(Ea \supset Fa))$$

and assign values in n to get:

$$= (1 \supset 0) \ (n)$$
$$= 0 \text{ in } n$$

So we do have a counter-example and the existentialized BF formula is not valid.

Despite this result, the Barcan formula and its converse are valid in the unrestricted modal predicate logic.

8.5 Identity and existence

Even with all the restrictions, and with contingent identity, the formula $(\exists x)(x = a)$ is still a valid formula. Consider the S5QT= tree:

1.	$\sim(\exists x)(x = a)$	(n)	NTF
2.	$(x)\sim(x = a)$	(n)	1, QN
3.	$\sim(a = a)$	(n)	2, UI a
	$\times$		

The tree began with the supposed assertion that a *does not exist in* n. It closes because it is contradictory to assert that something is not self-identical. But towards the end of §5.7 we agreed that, under certain restrictions, a formula that was a negated atomic predicate formula could be true because one or more of the constants in the formula referred to items that are non-existent in that world. But, if a is non-existent in n, then $(a \neq a)$ is no longer clearly contradictory. If we are really serious about this possibility, then the closure rule for identity should be resticted to:

(RClosure)

$$\vdots$$
$$(\exists \eta)(\eta = \kappa) \qquad (\omega)$$
$$\vdots$$
$$(\kappa \ne \kappa) \qquad (\omega)$$

It is only when we know that κ exists that we can have closure.

But we have already seen that $(\exists \eta)(\eta = \kappa)$ is valid. So it is true in all worlds. So, the rule **(RClosure)** should apply in general anyway. If we want realistic use of **(RClosure)**, then we shall have to go to free logic.

8.6 Free logic

In free logic, the quantifiers have existential import, but constants do not. The formula $(Fa \supset (\exists x)Fx)$ is not valid. It should come as no surprise to discover that the formula $(\exists x)(x = a)$ is not valid in free logic either.

To explain why let's set out the tree rules for a fairly standard free logic, FQT=.

(FEI)
$$(\exists \eta)\alpha \qquad (\omega) \checkmark \kappa$$
$$\vdots$$
$$\beta \qquad (\omega)$$
$$(\exists \eta)(\eta = \kappa) \qquad (\omega)$$
where β is the result of replacing every free occurrence of η in α with an individual constant, say κ, where κ is NEW to this path of tree

(FUI)
$$(\eta)\alpha \qquad (\omega) \backslash \kappa$$
$$(\exists \lambda)(\lambda = \kappa) \qquad (\omega)$$
$$\vdots$$
$$\beta \qquad (\omega)$$
where β is the result of replacing every free occurrence of η in α with κ

These rules make it clear that if some existing item is F, then some arbitrary (new to this path of the tree) item is to be that F, *and it exists*. Also we can only universally instantiate to existing items.

Consider the tree for $(\exists x)(x = a)$.

1. $\sim(\exists x)(x = a)$ (n) NTF
2. $(x)\sim(x = a)$ (n) 1, QN
   ↑

The tree will not close because we do not have $(\exists x)(x = a)$ for universal instantiation.

The situation here is that the domain of quantification, $Q(\delta)$, in any world, δ, will be a sub-set of the domain of items for δ: $D(\delta)$.

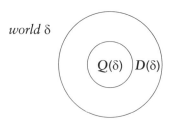

world δ

We assume that:

$$(\eta)\alpha \ (\delta) = 1 \Leftrightarrow \text{for all } \kappa \in Q(\delta), \ \beta \ (\delta) = 1$$

(where β is the result of replacing all free occurrences of η in α with κ)

It follows that if $Q(\delta)$ is empty, then $(\eta)\alpha \ (\delta) = 1$. $Q(\delta)$ will be empty if there is no $(\exists\eta)(\eta = \kappa) \ (\delta)$.

How then do the Barcan formula and its converse fare in **MFQT=** ? First look at the Barcan formula:

1.	$\sim((x)\Box Fx \supset \Box(x)Fx)$	(n)	NTF
2.	$(x)\Box Fx$	(n)	1
3.	$\sim\Box(x)Fx$	(n)	1
4.	$\Diamond\sim(x)Fx$	(n)	3, **MN**
5.	nAk		4, $\Diamond$**R**
6.	$\sim(x)Fx$	(k)	4, $\Diamond$**R**
7.	$(\exists x)\sim Fx$	(k)	6, **QN**
8.	$(\exists x)(x = a)$	(k)	7, **FEI** a
9.	$\sim Fa$	(k)	7, **FEI** a
	↑		

The tree is open because we cannot instantiate the formula at line 2. We can extract a counter-example from the tree:

	n	k
Fa	*	0
$(x)Fx$	1	0
$\Box Fa$	*	0
$(x)\Box Fx$	1	0
$\Box(x)Fx$	0	0

The value of $(x)\alpha \ (n) = 1$, because $Q(n)$ is empty.

So: $(x)\Box Fx \ (n) = 1$
So: $((x)\Box Fx \supset \Box(x)Fx) \ (n)$
$= (1 \supset 0) = 0$

Now for the converse of the Barcan formula:

1.	$\sim(\square(x)Fx \supset (x)\square Fx)$	(n)	NTF
2.	$\square(x)Fx$	(n)	1
3.	$\sim(x)\square Fx$	(n)	1
4.	$(\exists x)\sim\square Fx$	(n)	3, QN
5.	$(\exists x)(x = a)$	(n)	4, FEI a
6.	$\sim\square Fa$	(n)	4, FEI a
7.	$\Diamond\sim Fa$	(n)	6, MN
8.	nAk		7, $\Diamond$R
9.	$\sim Fa$	(k)	7, $\Diamond$R
10.	$(x)Fx$	(k)	2, 8, $\square$R

The tree is open in **K**. For **S5** we add:

11.	$(x)Fx$	(n)	2, $\square$T
12.	Fa	(n)	5, 11, FUI a
	↑		

So, the modal values in **S5** are:

	n	k
Fa	1	*
$(x)Fx$	1	1
$\square Fa$	0	0
$(x)\square Fx$	0	0
$\square(x)Fx$	1	1

This time $Q(k)$ is empty, because there is no $(\exists x)(x = a)$ (k).

So: $(x)\square Fx\,(n) = 0$

So: $(\square(x)Fx \supset (x)\square Fx)\,(n)$
$= (1 \supset 0) = 0$

Free modal predicate logic places the most draconian restrictions on instantiations. But the logic is reasonably intuitive in structure. Each world has its double domain of items.

Free logic has been extended and expanded by adding two additional quantifiers for the whole domain. The quantifiers are Σ for particular quantification, and Π for universal. "Some things do not exist" would translate to:

$(\Sigma x)\sim(\exists y)(x = y)$

Details can be found in Routley (1966) and Girle (1978). We shall not pursue the many extensions here.

Free logic has found application in one of the classic applications of modal predicate logic, epistemic predicate logic. We shall look at that later.

8.6 Exercises

1. Test each of the following formulas for validity in both free logic and S5QT=. If any are invalid, set out a counter-example with a demonstration of invalidity.

a. $((x)Fx \supset (\exists y)Fy)$
b. $(x)(y)(x = y \supset (Fx \supset Fy))$
c. $(((\exists x)(a \neq x) \,\&\, Fa) \supset (\exists y)Fy)$
d. $(x)(\exists y)(x = y)$
e. $(x)\sim (\exists y)(x = y)$

2. Test the following arguments for validity in both free logic and S5QT=. If any are invalid, set out a counter-example with a demonstration of invalidity.

a. $(x)Fx, (x)Gx / \therefore (\exists x)(Fx \,\&\, Gx)$
b. $(x)(Fx \supset Gx), (x)(Hx \supset \sim Gx) / \therefore (\exists x)(Hx \,\&\, \sim Fx)$

References and further reading

Fitting, M. & R. L. Mendelsohn 1998. *First-order Modal Logic*. Dordrecht: Kluwer.

Girle, R. A. 1978. "Logics for Knowledge, Possibility and Existence", *Notre Dame Journal of Formal Logic* 19: 200–214.

Girle, R. A. 2007. "Parmenides Demythologised". *Logique et Analyse* 50(199): 253–68.

Hughes, G. E & M. J. Cresswell 1996. *A New Introduction to Modal Logic*. London & New York: Routledge.

McGinn, C. 2000. *Logical Properties*. Oxford: Clarendon.

Routley, R. 1966. "Some Things do not Exist". *Notre Dame Journal of Formal Logic* 7: 251–76.

PART TWO
Applications

A cornucopia of applications

Modal logic has been used by logicians, philosophers, the "artificial intelligentsia" and computer scientists for many purposes. There is a cornucopia of applications of modal logic to problems and concepts in each of these discipline areas. We shall be looking at a very small number of those applications.

Logicians have used modal logic to try to produce logics that capture the notions of *possibility*, *logical necessity* and *proof*. These applications consider modal logic from an alethic point of view: from the point of view of issues related to *truth*. We turn to these in Chapter 9.

Philosophers, quantum physicists, and artificial intelligence researchers who work in the area of planning all have a deep interest in questions about time. Applications of modal logic to questions of time used to be known as "tense" (from past, present and future tense) applications. But in these days of disdain for grammar, such applications are called **temporal**. In Chapter 10 we introduce temporal applications for modal logic.

Dynamic logic is an application of modal logic that is closely related to temporal logic. Dynamic logic was first generated by computer scientists who applied modal logic to the study of *processes* in machines. It was first seen as a logic for state changes. Philosophers have begun to use dynamic logic in the study of action, and of belief change. In Chapter 11 we consider some elementary dynamic logic.

Philosophers have puzzled over the notions of knowledge (*episteme*) and belief (*doxa*) since the time of Plato. There has been an extensive modern debate about the application of modal logic to the investigation of these notions. The logic of knowledge is **epistemic logic**, and that of belief is **doxastic logic**. We consider some of this in Chapter 12.

In Chapter 13 we introduce the application of modal logic to issues in ethics. Philosophers, lawyers and computer scientists who wish to provide decision support systems are all interested in the logic of *obligation*. **Deontic logic** applies modal logic to decision-making and ethics.

A few of the issues in logic and philosophy that arise from our use of *conditional propositions* are discussed in Chapter 14. The substance of the issues is at the borders of modal logic, but possible world semantics is often used in these discussions. Our discussion centres on the question of the *reliability* of formal evaluations of arguments and propositions.

There are various other applications of modal logic that cannot be covered here, but it is hoped that by considering a variety of applications you will come to see some of the ways in which applications can work, and ways in which they can fail. This should lead to a more realistic approach to the use of logic, especially modal logic.

CHAPTER 9
Alethic modality

9.1 Introduction

We shall consider three main topics in this chapter. They concern the use of modal logic to translate "possibility" and "necessity", the **GL** model for the notion of proof, and the *de dicto–de re* distinction.

We begin with the application of modal logic to the notions of possibility and necessity, especially as they are expressed in ordinary language. It seems intuitively obvious that the formal notion of *possible worlds* should elucidate the notion of possibility and its close relative, necessity. But let the reader beware! Intuitive obviousness is sometimes misleading. Care is needed.

The **S5** modal logic is often suggested as the system for logical possibility and necessity. If we are going to use **S5** to assess the validity of arguments couched in English and containing possibility and necessity terms, then we need to know about the reliability of the **S5** account of logical possibility and logical necessity. We have to consider the question of the relationship between **S5** possibility and necessity, and the concepts of possibility and necessity embedded in ordinary English. So, without further ado we turn to the possibility and necessity terms of English.

9.2 Two kinds of possibility?

It has been suggested that there are two sorts of possibility embedded in ordinary English. First, there is a qualifiable possibility expressed by the phrase "possible for". Second, there is a variable possibility expressed by the phrase "possible that".

• *possible for*

The first can be qualified by words such as "logically", "financially", "legally", "practically" and "physically". Without qualification we might have statements such as:

> *It is possible for Susan to buy a car.*
> *It is possible for John to join the club.*

When qualified we have:

> *It is financially possible for Susan to buy a car.*
> *It is legally possible for John to join the club.*

The term that goes with qualifiable possibility is "necessity". We can replace "possible" with "necessary" in the statements above to get:

> *It is necessary for Susan to buy a car.*
> *It is financially necessary for Susan to buy a car.*

We can also see that the sort of logical equivalences assumed by the possible worlds logics are quite sensible:

> *It is necessary for Susan to buy a car iff*
> > *it is not possible for Susan not to buy a car.*

Even with the qualifications, the equivalences make sense, so long as the qualified modality is treated as a whole:

> *It is financially necessary for Susan to buy a car iff*
> > *it is not financially possible for Susan not to buy a car.*

• *possible that*

The second kind of possibility, "possible that", can be varied by terms such slight, hardly, barely, great, faint, quite and vague. Without such variation we might have statements such as:

> *It is possible that Susan is buying a car.*

When varied we have:

> *It is quite possible that Susan is buying a car.*

The term that goes with variable possibility is "definite". We can replace unvaried "possible" with "definite" in the statements above to get:

It is definite that Susan is buying a car.

The varying term can be inserted to give:

It is quite definite that Susan is buying a car.

The logical equivalences here do not accord with possible worlds logics, which usually link possible and necessary. But the following link "possible" and "definite":

It is definite that Susan is buying a car iff
  it is not possible that Susan is not buying a car.

It has been argued by White (1975) that "certain that", rather than "definite that", pairs with "possible that". But "certain that" brings a psychological dimension that is absent from both "possible" and "definite".

• logical connections

There is a logical connection between variable and qualifiable possibility. It is exemplified by the entailment:

If it is possible that Susan is buying a car
  then it is possible for Susan to be buying a car.

The converse entailment does not hold:

If it is possible for Susan to be buying a car
  then it is possible that Susan is buying a car.   (No!)

If we agree with contraposition and with the logical equivalences between possible, definite and necessary, then we get the following entailments:

If it is not possible for Susan to be buying a car
  then it is not possible that Susan is buying a car.
If it is necessary for Susan not to be buying a car
  then it is definite that Susan is not buying a car.

If the entailments set out above are correct, then there are problems for the possible world accounts of possibility and necessity. The first problem is that the pairing of "possible that" with "necessary that" may well be a mistake.

Diamond and possible for

One response to this problem is simply to say that the box and diamond symbols of modal logic are the translations of "possible for" and "necessary for".

possible for p   translates to $\Diamond p$
necessary for p   translates to $\Box p$

Some logicians would want to argue that the modality is assumed to be qualified to "logically possible" and "logically necessary". This is particularly the case for S5 (and maybe for S4).

This response would be reasonable if "possible for" worked, in English, in much the same way as the diamond works in modal logic.

For example, suppose someone asked me whether Jill was in her office. Suppose that as I was being asked, I looked out the window and saw her getting into her car in the car park. I could reasonably respond, "It is not possible for her to be in her office because I can see her, right now, getting into her car in the car park." My response to the query seems to imply that there are two things that are incompatible. They are that Jill is not in her office and that it is possible for Jill to be in her office. Given the "possible for" translation of the diamond, this pair of incompatible statements translates into instances of the general forms:

$\sim p$ $\Diamond p$

This supposed incompatibility is quite problematic because it seems to arise from a supposed entailment of which the following is an instance:

If Jill is not in her office, then it is not possible for her to be in her office.

But, if the general form:

If not p then not possible for p.

is the form of a general entailment, and if contraposition and double negation are accepted, then we get:

If it is possible for p then p.

But this is clearly false.

We could bypass this unacceptable conclusion by rejecting one or both of double negation and contraposition. At this stage that could be seen as a radical solution. *A* less dramatic way out of the problem might be found by another consideration.

If the contrast between "possible for" and "possible that", so strongly portrayed in White (1975), is not so strictly observed in everyday usage, then the "reasonable" response above should be reconsidered. In everyday English there might not always be a sharp distinction drawn between the two kinds of possibility. So, the response might have been better expressed if it had been, "It is not possible that she is in her office because I can see her, right now, getting into her car in the car park."

The "because" part of the response can be seen as a way of saying, "Jill is *definitely* not in her office". Given the pairing of "possible that" with "definite that", this gives us the incompatabile pair as:

> *It is definite that Jill is not in her office.*

and *It is possible that Jill is in her office.*

These are definitely incompatible, especially since the first is equivalent, on the pairing, to:

> *It is not possible that Jill is in her office.*

Cases like this could be used to support the idea that modal logic will give us a clearer account of possibility and necessity than can be given in English, because people slide over the many distinctions available in English when using it in everyday conversation.

Diamond and possible that

In the cases above we have contended that there is a slide, in casual usage, between "possible for" and "possible that". But if modal logic is to give a clearer account, we would need to use something for "possible that" and "definite that". Perhaps we can use the symbol that has been regularly used for possibility in modal logic. It is the letter **M**. **M** has been used instead of diamond (and it contains the bottom half of the diamond). We could pair it with the letter **D** for "definite that". So,

> **M**α translates as   *It is possible that* α
> **D**α translates as   *It is definite that* α

But any formal system would have to cope with four, not two, modal operators. We would need a *multiply modal* S5. The suggested entailments above would indicate that:

> (**M**$\alpha \supset \Diamond\alpha$)   ($\Box\alpha \supset$ **D**α)

should both be valid in multiply modal S5. For such a logic we would need separate rules for each set of operators, and some inter-connecting rules as well.

The general rules for **M** and **D** would be just like the rules for box and diamond. There would be two modal negation rules, an (MS) rule, a (DS) rule, and a (DT) rule.

The interconnecting rules would be:

$$(\mathbf{M} \Diamond \text{ R}) \qquad \mathbf{M}\alpha \quad (\omega) \qquad\qquad \Box\alpha \quad (\omega)$$
$$\vdots \qquad\qquad\qquad \vdots$$
$$\Diamond\alpha \quad (\omega) \qquad\qquad \mathbf{D}\alpha \quad (\omega)$$

It will be clear that with these interconnecting rules for trees we can show both of the following to be valid:

$$(\mathbf{M}p \supset \Diamond p) \qquad\qquad\qquad (\Box p \supset \mathbf{D}p)$$

The check for this is left to the reader.

In all of this we have not done anything about the qualifications or variations available.

9.3 Qualifying the diamond

Consider the following qualified modalities.

> It is **logically** possible for there to be no hunger.
> It is **theoretically** possible for there to be no hunger.
> It is **physically** possible for there to be no hunger.
> It is **economically** possible for there to be no hunger.
> It is **humanly** possible for there to be no hunger.

These statements seem to be in a sort of hierarchy. The first is entailed by all the others, but it does not entail any of the others.

It would be interesting, in the light of this, to develop a hierarchy of modal logics, and to consider the interrelationships between them. They may well form a partial order of logics.

One interesting question concerns the place of "conceptual possibility" in such a hierarchy. Is it the same as logical possibility, or is it below or above it in the hierarchy? It has been customary to see analytic truths as dividing into the logically necessary and the conceptually necessary.

The top line of the diagram gives us a kind of hierarchy for true, conceptually true, and logically true.

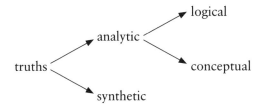

9.4 Varying the M

It is quite possible that a similar sort of hiearchy of modalities can be set up for *possible that*. Consider the following:

It is vaguely possible that Sue will take the job.
It is hardly possible that Sue will take the job.
It is barely possible that Sue will take the job.
It is quite possible that Sue will take the job.
It is certainly possible that Sue will take the job.

These statements show that the situation is not as clear as it was for *possible for*. The reader is invited to try to set up clear logical hierarchies of variable possibilities. It is not easy.

9.5 Proof

"In which modal logic is the box correctly read as 'It is provable that ...'?" is an interesting question. In other words, in which modal logic, if any, is the proof interpretation a satisfactory interpretation? A proof interpretation gives:

$\Box\alpha$ translates to   *It is provable that* α
$\Diamond\alpha$ translates to   *It is not provable that not* α

Given an intuitive understanding that if the negative of α is not provable, then α is consistent, we get:

$\Diamond\alpha$ translates to   *It is consistent that* α

An immediate question will be, "provable in what system?" Much of the work in this area has focussed on provability as it applies in the arithmetical extension of first-order logic known as Peano arithmetic. There are interesting results set out in Boolos and Jeffrey (1989), and in Boolos (1993).

Most of the work begins with a logic built out of **K4** which is called "**GL**" (for the Gödel–Löb logic). **K4** is a non-reflexive normal modal logic. It is, essentially, **S4** without ($\Box A \supset A$). If we add the following axiom schema to **K4**, then we have **GL**:

GL   ($\Box(\Box A \supset A) \supset \Box A$)

If we look at the axioms for **GL** we see that, in the case of first-order logic (propositional and predicate logic), the first two axiom schemas make intuitive sense.

K $\Box(A \supset B) \supset (\Box A \supset \Box B)$
         If ($A \supset B$) *is provable, then if A is provable then B is.*

S4   ($\Box A \supset \Box\Box A$)
         If A is provable then it is provable that it is provable.

The third axiom schema is **GL** above. **GL** is somewhat problematic. It is an expression of what is contained in Löb's theorem. Löb's theorem can be understood as saying that any statement implied by its own provability is provable. Löb's theorem is actually (given that the single quotes are read as corner quotes, and *Prov(x)* is read as "*x* is provable"):

   If ⊢ *Prov*('*S*') → *S, then* ⊢ *S*

Details of why and how Löb arrived at this theorem can be found in Boolos (1993) Boolos says that this theorem is "utterly astonishing". He gives several reasons for its being astonishing.

One concerns the connection between provability and necessity, where necessity is understood as necessary *truth*. He says:

> one might very naturally suppose that provability is a kind of necessity, and therefore, just as $\Box(\Box p \to p)$ always expresses a truth if the box is interpreted as "it is necessary that" – for then $\Box(\Box p \to p)$ says that it is necessarily true that if a statement is necessarily true, it is true – [if we interpret the box as "it is provable that", the formula] would also always be true or at least true in some cases in which *S* is false and not true only in the rather exceptional cases in which *S* is actually provable.   (Boolos 1993: 55)

Löb's theorem has consequences that run quite counter to what one might "naturally suppose".

To get some further idea of what's embodied in the **GL** axiom schema, consider the following for any system of logic. If it is provable that (p & ~p)

in the system, that is, if $\Box(p \mathrel{\&} {\sim}p)$, then the system is internally inconsistent. One of the instances of **GL** (where A is $(p \mathrel{\&} {\sim}p)$) is:

$$(\Box(\Box(p \mathrel{\&} {\sim}p) \supset (p \mathrel{\&} {\sim}p)) \supset \Box(p \mathrel{\&} {\sim}p))$$

If this is true, it follows that either the system **GL** is inconsistent, or some sentence $(\Box A \supset A)$ is not a theorem, or some sentence $\Box(\Box A \supset A)$ is not a theorem.

Since **GL** is not an inconsistent modal logic, it follows that we cannot have the reflexivity axiom schema, because if we do, then both $(\Box A \supset A)$ and $\Box(\Box A \supset A)$ are theorems, the latter as a result of necessitation. So, we have to do without the reflexivity axiom schema.

Truth trees for **GL** require a new rule for the diamond: ($\Diamond$**GL**). Otherwise we have the usual rules for a **K4** like propositional logic: modal negation, the box rule ($\Box$**R**), and Hintikka's transitivity rule ($\Box\Box$**R**). There is, of course, no reflexivity rule ($\Box$**T**).

$$(\Diamond\mathbf{GL}) \qquad \Diamond\alpha \quad (\omega)$$

$$\vdots$$

$$\omega A\upsilon$$

$$\alpha \quad (\upsilon)$$

$$\Box{\sim}\alpha \quad (\upsilon)$$

where υ is NEW *to this*
path of the tree

The reader is invited to test the **GL** axiom.

The **S5** axiom is not in **GL**.

$$({\sim}\Box A \supset \Box {\sim} \Box A)$$

This translates to "If there is no proof of A, then there is a proof that there is no proof of A". It is well known that this is *not* a principle that applies to the proof systems for first-order logic or of systems built upon first-order logic. So, **S5** is *too strong* for provability.

It is possible to generate a provability logic from an **S4** base. Investigation of this is left to the reader. We have only been able to indicate some of the results and themes. To that extent we are leaving out many of the finer points. If your interest in this area has been stirred, then you will need to investigate further to fill in gaps.

The generally important thing to note is that whether we start from **K4** or **S4**, the logic we arrive at is weaker than **S5**. We have already seen that **S5** is the appropriate logic to capture the idea of logical necessity. But **S5** is not appropriate for the notion of provability in first-order logic. Provability is not the same as logical necessity.

A common intuition would be that proof and necessity should be just different perspectives on the same thing. But, this is just not so.

9.6 Modality *de dicto* and modality *de re*

Consider the following statements:

(1)   It is possible that rain is falling in Invercargill.
(2)   Every material object is necessarily in space.

There is a standard way of distinguishing the nature of the modalities in these statements in terms of *de dicto* and *de re*. The first can be taken as a statement about a proposition, the proposition that it is raining in Invercargill, to the effect that it is possibly true. The modality is a *de dicto* modality, since it is about the possible (or necessary) truth of a proposition. The second can be taken as a statement about material objects, namely that they have a certain property necessarily. The modality is a *de re* modality, since it is about things, or reality, and what properties things have necessarily (or possibly) rather than about propositions.

An analogous distinction applies in other areas as well. For example, consider the two statements of belief:

(1′)   Sue believes that John's car is red.
(2′)   Sue believes John's car to be red.

The first can be taken to set out the propositional content of Sue's belief. This is a *de dicto* belief statement. The second can be taken as an assertion about what colour Sue believes a vehicle to have. Sue believes *of* the car, that it is red. This is a *de re* belief statement.

There is some intuitive plausibility about this distinction. It is often applied to the Barcan formula (formula 3 in Chapter 5, §5.5) in the obvious way. The consequent:

$$\Box(x)Fx$$

is seen as having a *de dicto* necessity modality. The antecedent:

$$(x)\Box Fx$$

is seen as having a *de re* necessity modality. From a formal point of view, the difference is clear. The scope of the modal operator in the former (the consequent) contains no free occurrences of individual variables. By contrast, the scope of the modal operator in the latter (the antecedent) does contain a free occurrence of an individual variable. But note that this free occurrence in the scope is, in the complete formula, bound by the universal quantifier outside the scope of the modal operator. This is a case of "quantifing into" the scope of a modal operator.

Hughes and Cresswell give a definition:

> A wff, α, containing a modal operator (*L* or *M*) will be said to express a modality *de re* iff the scope of some modal operator in it contains some free occurrence of an individual variable; otherwise α will be said to express a modality *de dicto*. (1968: 184)

This formal definition is fine for modal predicate logic. Hughes and Cresswell go on to consider whether or not all *de re* modalities can be eliminated in modal predicate logic in favour of modality *de dicto*. This elimination, as it turns out, is very difficult. The formal details can be followed in Hughes and Cresswell (1968: 184–8).

A "rebel" view about the distinction is to be found in White (1975). He claims that the distinction is not the distinction it is claimed to be. He describes the distinction made in modern philosophy as a distinction between how "modals qualify what is said about something" and how modals "qualify the something ... it is said about" (1975: 165).

White claims that the distinction is based on two assumptions.

> The first, and correct, assumption is that modal qualifications can apply either to the whole or to the part of something. The second, and incorrect, assumption is that what is qualified when the whole is qualified is a proposition, that is, something which is said.
> (1975: 165)

An example of the whole/part contrast is "between e.g., 'He possibly (necessarily, certainly) gave a misleading answer' and 'He gave a possibly (necessarily, certainly) misleading answer'". White denies that the latter gives any "evidence for a peculiar composite property being possibly (necessarily, certainly) misleading in addition to the property being misleading" (White 1975: 166ff.).

If White is correct, then much of the debate in this area is vacuous. It is also interesting to note that the *de dicto–de re* distinction is made in Hughes and Cresswell (1968) by reference to the syntax of formulas, but that syntactical distinction does not guarantee any non-syntactic distinction.

The reader is encouraged to investigate further.

References and further reading

Audi, R. (ed.) 1995. *The Cambridge Dictionary of Philosophy*. Cambridge: Cambridge University Press.

Boolos, G. 1993. *The Logic of Provability*. Cambridge: Cambridge University Press.

Boolos, G. & R. Jeffrey 1989. *Computability and Logic*, 3rd edn. Cambridge: Cambridge University Press.

Bradley, R. & N. Swartz 1979. *Possible Worlds*. Oxford: Blackwell.

Hughes, G. E. & M. J. Cresswell 1968. *An Introduction to Modal Logic*. London: Methuen.

Lewis, D. 1983. *Philosophical Papers*, vol. I. Oxford: Oxford University Press.

Loux, M. J. (ed.) 1979. *The Possible and the Actual: Readings in the Metaphysics of Modality*. Ithaca, NY: Cornell University Press.

Smullyan, R. M. 1987. *Forever Undecided: A Puzzle Guide to Gödel*. New York: Knopf.

White, A. 1975. *Modal Thinking*. Oxford: Blackwell.

CHAPTER 10

Temporal logic

10.1 Introduction

Possible worlds can be seen as states of the universe at some point in history. Such states are sometimes called "time-slices". The accessability connections can be seen as time-lines from instant to instant, or temporal relations of "after" or "before". If world n has access to world k, then n is after k. If n can *see* into k, then in n we can "see back" into the past. So begins modal temporal logic.

This instant and state-of-the-universe approach is not the only way to approach temporal logic. An important alternative is the "time interval" approach. A comparison of the two approaches is to be found in van Benthem's *The Logic of Time* (1983).

In this chapter we shall confine ourselves to the instant and state approach. In the last section we shall look very briefly at some philosophical questions about time.

10.2 The worlds of K4

The system **S4** has a close non-reflexive relative called **K4**. The difference between **S4** and **K4** is that while accessibility in **S4** is both transitive and reflexive, **K4** accessibility is transitive only. **K4** is one of the non-reflexive normal modal logics. Look back to the map of systems in §3.6.

Consider a sequence of worlds as in a **K4** system, $\{n, k, l, j\}$.

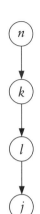

Each of these worlds could be seen as the state of the universe in which we live, at some instant of time. The arrows can be seen as pointing towards the future, with the flow of accessibility being the flow of time. Possible world n (now) might be the state of the universe at the present, k might be the state of the universe at the next instant of time into the future, and so on into the future.

K4 can be interpreted as a temporal logic, or a logic for time.

With this interpretation, the accessibility relation in **K4**, $\omega A \upsilon$, is better as:

$$\omega B \upsilon \quad \text{for} \quad \omega \text{ is } \textbf{\textit{before}} \ \upsilon$$
$$(\text{or } \omega \rightarrow \upsilon).$$

n has access to k means the same as *n is before k*. So we get: *n is before k, k is before l* and *l is before j*. Since accessibilty is transitive in **K4**, it also follows that *n is before l, n is before j*, and *k is before j*.

We can treat **K4** as a temporal logic by interpreting the $\Box$ and the $\Diamond$ as temporal operators. In a sense, they become temporal quantifiers. The $\Box$ is for "at all times in the future", and the $\Diamond$ is for "at some time in the future".

With this temporal interpretation:

$\Diamond p$ translates as   *At some time in the future p*

and $\Box p$ translates as   *At all times in the future p*

Given: L = *There is life on Earth.*

We would translate:

$\Diamond \sim L$ as   *At some time in the future there will be no life on Earth.*

$\Diamond \Box \sim L$ as   *There will be some time in the future such that at all times later there will be no life on Earth.*

     or   *There will be some future time after which there will be no life on Earth.*

$(L \ \& \ \Box L)$ as   *There now is and always will be life on Earth.*

This interpretation of **K4** lacks any way of considering the past, so we do two things. We begin by changing the symbols from $\Box$ to **G** and from $\Diamond$ to **F**. **G** is read as "It is always *going* to be the case that". **F** is read as "At some time in the *future* it will be the case that".

The three formulas about life on Earth become:

F~*L*   **FG**~*L*   (*L* & **G***L*)

We are now in a position to introduce a second logic – a logic for past times.

10.3 Past, present and future

We now consider a **K4** logic for the past. In this case, if *n has access to k*, then *n is after k*. We replace the □ and ◊ with **H** and **P**. **H** is read as "It always *has* been the case that". **P** is read as "At sometime in the *past* it has been the case that". We also define the operator **L** for "always".

Lα = ₍ₓ₎ (**H**α & α & **G**α)

α *is always true* means that α *always has been true, is true, and will always be true.*

This dual logic needs a little more. There need to be some principles that allow the past, present and future to be related to each other in some logical fashion. Two principles have been suggested. They are:

If from some time in the past it is always going to be the case that p, then p is the case now.

and *If at some time in the future it is always had been the case that p, then p is the case now.*

These translate, respectively, to:

(**PG***p* ⊃ *p*)   and   (**FH***p* ⊃ *p*)

The question is, what will tree rules be like for a two-tense logic that validates these interconnecting principles? The rules for the future tense operators alone, **G** and **F**, should be no problem provided we change the accessibility notation from ωAυ to ωBυ (ω *is before* υ). If you look in §3.6, you will see a set of tree rules for **K4** in accordance with the mixed strategy. If we replace the □ and ◊ with the temporal logic symbols, we would get an appropriate set of tree rules.

The set of temporal rules becomes:

(FR)   Fα (ω)   (GR)   Gα (ω)
           ⋮ $\omega B\upsilon$
       $\omega B\upsilon$ ⋮
       α (υ) α (υ)
where υ is NEW *to*
this path of the tree

(Trans) $\omega B\upsilon$
         $\upsilon B\tau$
         ⋮
         $\omega B\tau$

The rule (FR) generates a world, say υ, that is *after* the world ω. So ω is *before* υ, and υ is in the future with respect to ω.

We now adopt a piece of trickery to set up the logic for the past. We use exactly the same accessibility relation, B, but we use the converse in the tree rules. The generation rule creates a world that is *before* the world from which it was generated. It is also useful to add an S5 style rule for Lα. We get:

(PR)   Pα (ω)   (HR)   Hα (ω)
           ⋮ $\upsilon B\omega$
       $\upsilon B\omega$ ⋮
       α (υ) α (υ)
where υ is NEW *to*
this path of the tree

(LR)   Lα (ω)
          ⋮
       α (υ)
for any υ

The accessibility relation as in $\upsilon B\omega$ still reads as υ *is before* ω. The rule (FR) generates a world, υ, that is in the past with respect to ω, so $\upsilon B\omega$ (ω *is after υ*).

The logic with all these rules is known as either K4$_t$ (for K4 two tenses) or as CR (for Cocchiarellia's Relativistic causal time).

Is this all we need to validate the two principles set out above? The following tree shows the situation:

1.	$\sim (\mathbf{PG}p \supset p)$	(n)	NTF
2.	$\mathbf{PG}p$	(n)	
3.	$\sim p$	(n)	
4.	kBn		2, **PR**
5.	$\mathbf{G}p$	(k)	2, **PR**
6.	p	(n)	4, 5 **GR**
	$\times$		

The tree closes, so the formula is valid. Validation of the other principle in $\mathbf{K4}_t$ is left to the reader.

The reason for the "relativistic" reference is because the pattern of time instances (related by accessibility) into the past and the future is compatible with certain features of Einstein's special theory of relativity. Rennie says:

> CR is a "relativistic" system by default only: it is relativistic on account of what it omits rather than what principles it contains. Its most significant omission is any axiom requiring that the [accessibility] relation ... should be connected. In special relativity, the relation "... is causally (or absolutely) before ..." is not weakly connected, since according to the [special theory of relativity], two events can be such that it is physically impossible for them to be causally related, in which case one is neither causally before nor causally after the other.   (Rennie 1970: 19–20)

The set of tree rules for **CR** is **CRTr**:

$$\mathbf{CRTr} = \mathbf{PTr} \cup \mathbf{MN} \cup \{\mathbf{PR}, \mathbf{HR}, \mathbf{FR}, \mathbf{GR}, \mathbf{LR}, \text{Trans}\}$$

10.4 Variations on the flow of time

At this point, there are some features of **CR** that can be noted. First, "before" and "after" are *transitive*. This is usually seen as a desirable feature for time lines described in terms of before and after.

Secondly, the picture of the "flow of time" *allows* for all sorts of systems of instants (worlds). It is clear that **CR** allows the past and the future to have a sort of logical symmetry. So we might expect that maps of systems of instants will *look* symmetrical. But symmetry is not forced on to systems of instants. Such symmetrical maps are allowed, not enforced. The map in Figure 10.1 is one of many allowed by **CR**.

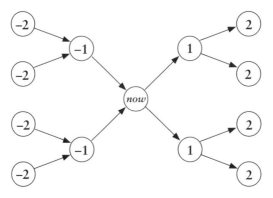

Figure 10.1

In Figure 10.1 the negative numbers are for the past, and positives for the future. The arrow goes from past to future, from instant to instant.

The **CR** logic allows for many things. Another intuitive picture of past, present and future, allowed by **CR**, is in Figure 10.2. For example, some people see the past as a fixed, single line, or sequence, of instances up to the present. The future is an amorphous blob.

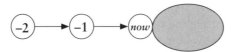

Figure 10.2

In Figure 10.3 the future is not a blob but a set of branching possibilities. This is also allowed by **CR**.

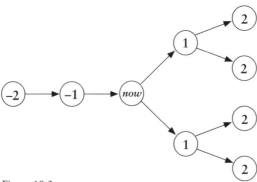

Figure 10.3

There is yet another picture allowed by **CR**. The past and the future are a single line as in Figure 10.4. This picture is compatible with the **CR**.

Figure 10.4

But there will be some things allowed in **CR** that might be considered quite undesirable. For example, a system of four instants could have the arrangement in Figure 10.5 and still be compatible with **CR**.

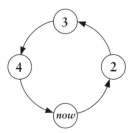

Figure 10.5

Figure 10.5 is a picture of *circular* time: *now* is before 2, 2 is before 3, 3 is before 4, and 4 is before *now*. This circular time is non-ending and non-beginning. Circular time is not what we would have expected for non-ending and non-beginning time. There is an interesting variation on circular time (Figure 10.6).

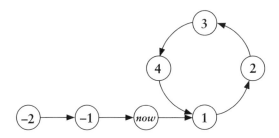

Figure 10.6

This is the picture of time that is (contingently) linear up to the present and then it goes circular (and non-ending). A system with a circular past might be easy to draw, but what it means is quite another thing.

The extreme case of circular time (Figure 10.7) was pointed out by Smiley (cited in Prior 1967: 49). Accessibility is turned into *identity*. Arthur Prior (1967) called the systems of this kind, systems of "instantaneous time". This is not only instantaneous time, it is *static* time.

Figure 10.7

Burnet says that Parmenides, the Greek philosopher, claimed that: "What *is* (το eon) is, therefore a finite, spherical, motionless continuous plenum, and there is nothing beyond it" (1968: 54). Parmenides would have certainly liked static time to go with the plenum.

All this and much more is allowable in **CR**. The question is, "Do we want to allow such a diversity?" If the answer is "yes", then we have it. If the answer is "no", then we have to add conditions to prevent the systems of instants we do not want. We have to find a different logic.

10.5 Linear time

Consider the two cases we have been looking at. They are the cases of branching time and circular time. In this section we consider what is needed if we want our temporal logic to disallow branching time. In the next section we consider ways of stopping circular time.

Suppose we want the whole of time to be *linear*, as in Figure 10.4. The standard way is to add another property to the accessibility relation. The property is *connectedness* [$(x)(y)(z)((yBx$ & $zBx) \supset (yBz \lor zBy)$); that is, if y and z are both before x, then either y *is before* z or z *is before* y]. This "pulls" the instants into line.

The rules to ensure that accessibility is a connected relation for both the future and the past are:

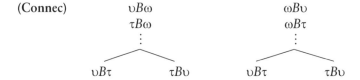

To see what the addition of **Connec** to **CR** means, consider the following argument form and the truth-tree test of its validity in **CR** plus **Connec**:

$$\frac{\textbf{F}(\textbf{G}q \ \& \ {\sim}p)}{\therefore \quad \textbf{G}(p \supset (\textbf{G}p \supset q))}$$

Consider the first thirteen steps of the tree:

1.	$\mathbf{F}(\mathbf{G}q \,\&\, {\sim}p)$	(n)	Premise
2.	${\sim}\mathbf{G}(p \supset (\mathbf{G}p \supset q))$	(n)	NC
3.	$\mathbf{F}{\sim}(p \supset (\mathbf{G}p \supset q))$	(n)	2, MN
4.	nBk		1, FR
5.	$(\mathbf{G}q \,\&\, {\sim}p)$	(k)	1, FR
6.	nBm		3, FR
7.	${\sim}(p \supset (\mathbf{G}p \supset q))$	(m)	3, FR
8.	p	(m)	7
9.	${\sim}(\mathbf{G}p \supset q)$	(m)	7
10.	$\mathbf{G}p$	(m)	9
11.	${\sim}q$	(m)	9
12.	$\mathbf{G}q$	(k)	5
13.	${\sim}p$	(k)	5

The tree, so far, is not going to close. But that is not the whole story.

The tree shows that there are three instants, n, k and m. The accessibility relation between them gives the picture in Figure 10.8. The arrows indicate that n *is before* both k and m.

Figure 10.8

If the accessibility relation is a connected relation, then either k *is before* m, or m *is before* k.

So, the tree should make those alternatives clear with a branching. In one branch we should have kBm, in the other mBk. These are the options for pulling the instants into a line, either $n \to m \to k$ or $n \to k \to m$.

Such a branching will extend the tree above, extend the logic by adding **Connec**, and close the tree:

12.	$\mathbf{G}q$	(k)	5
13.	${\sim}p$	(k)	5

14.	mBk	kBm	4, 6, **Connec**
15.	p (k)	q (m)	10, 14 and 12, 14, **GR**
	$\times$	$\times$	

The tree has closed and the argument is valid. The argument is a key argument for deciding whether a logic has linear accessibility or not.

If we add (**Connec**) to **CRTr** then we get the rules for the system **CL**. Rennie says that this is for Cocchiarella's Linear time. The rules for **CLTr** are (where **PMNTr** = **PTr** ∪ **MN**):

CLTr = PMNTr ∪ {**PR, HR, FR, GR, LR**, Trans, Connec}

This system is linear, but that does not stop its being circular, strange as this may seem.

Note also, circular time in Figures 10.5–10.7 is non-ending. In Figures 10.5 and 10.7 it is also never-beginning. Things are never simple when it comes to time.

10.6 Non-circular time

We now consider what is needed if we want our temporal logic to disallow circular time. If you look at any of the circular time pictures you will see that the accessibility relation allows *nBn* to result from transitivity. In Figure 10.5 we have:

> *now B 2*   *2 B 3*   *3 B 4*   *4 B now*

Since *B* is transitive, it follows that *now B now*, or *now is before now*. Similarly, in Figure 10.6 a consequence of transitivity is *1 B 1*. In Figure 10.7 the consequence is *now B now*. These are all the consequences of accessibility being transitive, even if they are somewhat unexpected, or even paradoxical.

One way of stopping this is to make accessibility *irreflexive* [$(x)\sim xBx$; nothing is before itself] or *asymmetric* [$(x)(y)(xBy \supset \sim yBx)$; that is, if *x is before y* then *y is not before x*]. If a relation is asymmetric then it follows that it is irreflexive. Irreflexivity is included in asymmetry. We can disallow circular time in our logic by making accessibility into an irreflexive relation. Either irreflexivity or asymmetry would add an extra closure rule to our tree rules. The two rules are:

(**Irrfl**) $\omega B \omega$ (**Asym**) $\upsilon B \omega$
      ×   ⋮
                                 $\omega B \upsilon$
                                 ×

The addition of asymmetry and connectedness gives us a logic that has no looping back or forward.

If we add (**Asym**) to **CLTr** then we get the rules for the system **CLA** (for **CL** with Asymmetry). The rules for **CLATr** are:

CLATr = PMNTr ∪ {PR, HR, FR, GR, LR, Trans, Connec, Asym}

But the interesting feature of such systems is that, although we can set out a clear semantic description of such a logic, there are no crucial formulas that we can use to set out an axiomatic logic.

There is no formula that "captures" irreflexivity in the way in which $(\Box A \supset A)$, for example, captures reflexivity. In technical terms, the systems with asymmetric accessibility are *incomplete*. Some logicians think incompleteness is a fatal flaw. The discussion of that topic is beyond the ambit of this text; we shall simply fly in the face of the flaw.

The addition of asymmetry and connectedness does not allow the mixed linear and branching time shown in Figure 10.3. This would require us to have two sorts of accessibility: a linear accessibility for the past, and a branching (non-circular?) accessibility for the future. The complications are quite formidable, but not beyond reach. The development of such a logic is left in abeyance for the moment (but the reader is in no way prevented from experimenting).

10.7 Never-beginning and never-ending time

Consider the formulas $(\mathbf{G}p \supset \mathbf{F}p)$ and $(\mathbf{H}p \supset \mathbf{P}p)$. These are the temporal analogues of $(\Box p \supset \Diamond p)$, the consistency principle. If the consistency principle is tested in **CR**, it is invalid. If we add the appropriate tree rules to validate the consistency principle we get **D4**. The temporal analogue of **D4** is **D4**$_t$.

The additional tree rules are:

(GD)	$\mathbf{G}\alpha$	(ω)		(HD)	$\mathbf{H}\alpha$	(ω)
	$\vdots$				$\vdots$	
	$\mathbf{F}\alpha$	(ω)			$\mathbf{P}\alpha$	(ω)

The set of tree rules for **D4**$_t$ is **D4**$_t$**Tr**:

D4$_t$**Tr** = PTr ∪ MN ∪ {PR, HR, HD, FR, GR, HD, GD, LR, Trans}

The consistency conditions constrain accessibility to conform to both:

$(\forall w)(\exists y)wBy$
$(\forall w)(\exists y)yBw$

This means that every instant has an instant to its future and an instant to its past.

Nevertheless, with **D4**$_t$ we can still have branching and/or circular time. All the diagrams in §10.4 are allowed by **D4**$_t$. Things are never simple when it comes to logics for time.

We can, of course, add connectivity and asymmetry to the rules for **D4**$_t$ to get linear non-branching, non-circular, never-ending, never-beginning time. If we add (**Connec**) to **D4**$_t$**Tr** then we get the rules for the system **CS** (for Scott's system of never-ending and non-beginning time). The rules for **CSTr** are:

CSTr = PMNTr ∪ {**PR, HR, HD, FR, GR, HD, GD, LR**, Trans, Connec}

CS is linear, but that does not stop its being circular, strange as this may seem. Note also, circular time in Figures 10.5–10.7 is non-ending. In Figure 10.5 and 10.7 it is also never-beginning.

When we add asymmetry we get the system **CSA**, which gives linear, non-branching, non-ending, non-beginning time:

CSATr = PMNTr ∪
            {**PR, HR, HD, FR, GR, HD, GD, LR**, Trans, Connec, Asym}

This system is also incomplete.

10.8 Beginning and ending time

There is a well-known view that time began some finite number of years ago with the Big Bang and may well end with a "Big Crunch". This view might lead someone to suggest that we need a temporal logic that does not allow infinite extension into the past and the future. In other words, there is a first instant of time and a last instant of time. If we consider just the past, there is an instant that *is before* all instants other than itself:

$$(\exists x)(\forall y)(x \neq y \supset xBy)$$

This, of course, is a condition that can be imposed on the accessibility relation. But this accessibility condition, with asymmetry, is incompatible with the never-beginning principle. So, we cannot simply add this condition to the **CSA** tree rules. We have to go back to the **K** systems. Since **CLA** lacks the consistency principles, we can qualify accessibility in this system to get beginning time.

A formula closely related to the condition above is (**P**p ⊃ **P**~ **P**p). This states that if p was true at sometime past, then at sometime past there is no further past time at which p is true. Since this applies to all p, this indicates that, eventually, everything has no past in which to be true, or that everything is false in all the past of sometime in the past.

We can contemplate several systems. In the first there is beginning and ending time. For ending time we need the principle:

$$(\mathbf{F}p \supset \mathbf{F}\sim\mathbf{F}p)$$

and the accessibility condition:

$$(\exists x)(\forall y)(x \neq y \supset yBx)$$

Another system would have beginning but non-ending time. A third would have never-beginning but ending time. We already have non-ending non-beginning time.

Consider a tree to test the first of these formulas:

1.	$\sim(\mathbf{P}p \supset \mathbf{P}\sim \mathbf{P}p)$	(n)	NTF
2.	$\mathbf{P}p$	(n)	1
3.	$\sim\mathbf{P}\sim \mathbf{P}p$	(n)	1
4.	$\mathbf{H}\mathbf{P}p$	(n)	3
5.	kBn		2
6.	p	(k)	2
7.	$\mathbf{H}\mathbf{P}p$	(k)	4, 5
8.	$\vdots$		

This tree can continue on forever, generating endless past instants, but that is contrary to the condition imposed on accessibility. So, the tree is generating an inconsistent system of worlds. To that extent, the tree is inconsistent, and should be "closed".

10.9 Axiom systems

We turn to the axiomatic systems for some of the logics above. The axiomatic accounts of the systems assist us in comparisons. The axiom schemas for the systems are drawn from those below. There is some redundancy in the sets we give. The first three schemas and *modus ponens* give standard propositional logic.

1. $(A \supset (B \supset A))$
2. $((A \supset (B \supset C)) \supset ((A \supset B) \supset (A \supset C)))$
3. $((\sim A \supset \sim B) \supset (B \supset A))$

4p. $(H(A \supset B) \supset (HA \supset HB))$
4f. $(G(A \supset B) \supset (GA \supset GB))$
5p. $(PGA \supset A)$
5f. $(FHA \supset A)$
6p. $(HA \supset HHA)$
6f. $(GA \supset GGA)$
7p. $(HA \supset PA)$
7f. $(GA \supset FA)$
8p. $(H(A \supset (HA \supset B)) \vee H(HB \supset A))$
8f. $(G(A \supset (GA \supset B)) \vee G(GB \supset A))$

The axiom schema sets are:

$$CR = K4_t = \{1, 2, 3, 4p, 4f, 5p, 5f, 6p, 6f\}$$
$$CL = CR \cup \{8p, 8f\}$$
$$D4_t = \{1, 2, 3, 4p, 4f, 5p, 5f, 6p, 6f, 7p, 7f\}$$
$$CS = D4_t \cup \{8p, 8f\}$$

The rules of inference are all the following for all systems:

(*Modus ponens*)	$\vdash A, \vdash(A \supset B) \Rightarrow \vdash B$
(Necessitation)	$\vdash A \Rightarrow \vdash HA$
(Necessitation)	$\vdash A \Rightarrow \vdash GA$
(Necessitation)	$\vdash A \Rightarrow \vdash LA$

There are no axiomatic systems for **CLA** and **CSA**.
A map of all the systems is:

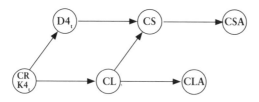

Figure 10.9

10.10 Philosophical problems

Philosophical debate about time began, in an important sense, with St. Augustine, Bishop of Hippo. His discussions are to be found in his *Confessions* (e.g. Lovill 1993). Augustine remarks at one point that, when we have to address the problem of just what time is: "If no one asks me, I know; but if any Person should require me to tell him, I cannot."

We look at three philosophical topics. The first arises from the notion of branching time, as in Figure 10.1. The second is a major twentieth-century issue to do with the unreality of time. The third arises from the science fiction stories of time travel.

Time and necessity

The branching picture of time in Figure 10.1 is supposed to allow for all the possibilities of the past and the future. The picture in Figure 10.3 depicts the idea of the past as fixed and the future as full of possibility. Diodorus of Megara is often said to have maintained that necessity and possibility are definable in terms of time. There is much argument about what Diodorus was actually supposed to have said, and we have no space to enter into exergetical arguments. Instead we shall look at the following two theses as of interest in their own right:

1.   All true past tensed propositions are necessarily true.
2.   Propositions which are or will be true are possibly true propositions.

The first thesis picks up on the intuition that the past *cannot* be altered. Prior gives the interpretation, "Whatever has been the case cannot now not have been the case" (1967: 32). This gives us:

1'. $(Pp \supset \Box Pp)$

or

1''. $(Pp \supset \sim \Diamond \sim Pp)$

The second thesis "cashes in" the idea that if something is not now true and never will be, then it is not possible for it to be true.

2'. $((\sim p \;\&\; \sim Fp) \supset \sim \Diamond p)$

or

2''. $(\Diamond p \supset (p \lor Fp))$

The last of these is highly compatible with possible world semantics where the truth of $\Diamond p$ in a world entails that p is true in some world, either the same one or one to which there is access.

There are many problems with this tight link between time and possibility and necessity. We look at three problems. The first concerns the role of the diagrams in clarifying the semantics of logics such as **CR**. The second concerns how we describe the differences between what is in fact the case right now, what might have been the case right now, and what must be the case right now. The third concerns the combination of alethic and temporal logic.

First we need to understand what a diagram like Figure 10.1 is supposed to tell us about the relationship between time and possibility. It is tempting to see the branches as "possibility" branches instead of seeing them as branches allowed by just one reading of "before and after". The diagram just tells us about a system of states that CR allows to be related by the before/after relation. The fact that CR allows such a system might be a good reason for declaring that the logic is not a suitable logic for time. We might argue that in the world in which we live only one sequences of states correctly describes the past, and only one will describe the future. So, we should accept only a logic with a linear accessibilty (before/after) relation for time. Questions about what might have been the case should be left to alethic logic. We should beware of diagrams leading us to confuse notions of temporality and necessity.

The second question can be approached as follows. Temporal logic treats propositions as "now" tensed. If R is for *It is raining*, then **F**R asserts that at some time in the future *It is raining*. Similarly, **P**R asserts that at some time in the past *It is raining*. We must distinguish between **P**R and **P**$\Box R$ and $\Box$**P**R. The second asserts that at some time in the past *It is necessary that it is raining*, or that at some time in the past *It is necessary for it to be raining*. The third asserts that, necessarily, at some time in the past *It is raining*.

It is not clear that these readings of **P**R, **P**$\Box R$ and $\Box$**P**R give one the entailments set out in 1 and 2 above. Of course, one might assert 1 and 2 as fatalistic doctrines, but that is another matter.

So, we come to the third matter. The intuition that the past is unalterable is not quite the same as the idea that the past is the way it is *of necessity*. It may well be true that we cannot "go back" and change the past (we discuss time travel later). Consider the situation where, right now, there is an object falling to the planetary surface on Mars. If we were there we could catch it. But, given the limits imposed on us by present technology, not to mention the speed of light, we cannot get there and catch the object, and so prevent it hitting the surface. It does not follow that the object will *of necessity* strike the surface. Our inability to change what's going on now on Mars does not make what is going on go on necessarily. Similarly with the past.

It is also true that we cannot go forward and change the future. It does not follow that truths about the future are necessarily true. Even if we accept that "There is a sea battle in progress" is true at noon tomorrow, it doesn't follow in any obvious way that it is necessarily true either now or at noon tomorrow.

McTaggart and time

Second, we consider the problem raised by J. M. E. McTaggart in 1908 as part of his general point that time (as well as many other things) is unreal.

Schlesinger says: "I may assert confidently that no other thesis advanced in the twentieth century in the philosophy of time has attracted as much attention as McTaggart's thesis that time is unreal. Most discussions of it endeavour to refute the thesis" (1980: 41).

McTaggart asserted that there were two ways of looking at time. These can be pictured in terms of two series of events, the A-series and the B-series. The A-series puts events into past, present and future. The B-series puts events into a series based on the relationships of "before" and "after". McTaggart claimed that the A-series was contradictory, and that the B-series did not cope satisfactorily with the essential features of time.

There is a common view that now, the present, is crucial in our understanding of time. An event begins, as it were, in the future, becomes a present event, and then becomes a past event. Some would want to assert that the event does not exist when it is future and does not exist when it is past, but exists only now. This approach is sometimes allied with the view that events "approach" us from a non-existent future to become momentarily real, and then recede into the non-existence of the past.

This future-to-present-to-past picture is what underlies McTaggart's A-series, the series that is absolutely fundamental. Events have A-series characteristics, the characteristics of being in the future, being in the present, and being in the past. The birth of Oliver Cromwell is in the past. The heat death of the universe is in the future. Your reading of these words is in the present. Of course, before you read these words, the reading of them was in the future, and after you have finished, the reading of the words will be in the past. At no point was the reading of the words in the past and in the future and in the present. The reading of the words changed from being in the future to being in the present, and then to being in the past. In this way events change their A-series characteristics, and, if they don't, then there is no change. Since change is essential to time, if there's no change, then there is no time.

At one point McTaggart says "If one of the determinations past, present, future can ever be applied to [an event] N, then one of them has always been and always will be applicable, though of course not the same one" (1908: 459n). Van Benthem claims that this means that "being tensed once means being tensed always" (1983: 154), and leads to the six principles:

past:	(1) $(\mathbf{P}p \supset \mathbf{H}(\mathbf{F}p \vee p \vee \mathbf{P}p))$	(2) $(\mathbf{P}p \supset \mathbf{GP}p)$
present:	(3) $(p \supset \mathbf{HF}p)$	(4) $(p \supset \mathbf{GP}p)$
future:	(5) $(\mathbf{F}p \supset \mathbf{HF}p)$	(6) $(\mathbf{F}p \supset \mathbf{G}(\mathbf{F}p \vee p \vee \mathbf{P}p))$

McTaggart saw all this as problematic. He:

> tried to show that a vicious infinite regress is involved in affirming the existence of a series ordered by A-series characteristics. Each member of such a series must have all the A-series characteristics, he said, but those characteristics are incompatibile. If we try to remove the contradiction by saying that each member possesses all the characteristics at different times, we are presupposing the existence of different moments of time at which the A-series characteristics are possessed. But each of these moments, to be temporal, must itself possess all the A-series characteristics, which, again, is impossible; the attempt to relieve this contradiction by appeal to yet another set of moments only gives rise to another set of contradictions, and so on.   (Edwards 1968: vol. 5, 230)

By contrast, B-series characteristics do not change. Your reading of these words is after the birth of Oliver Cromwell and before the heat death of the universe (student failings aside). These before/after relations never change. The problem with this concerns the status of *now*. In fact, it has no status, because the relation of *now* to the birth of Oliver Cromwell is that "at one time" it was before the birth, and at another it was after, and at another it was right then. The now changes its before/after relation with events. But events, or whatever, that change their before/after relations are not in the B-series. This seems to be a real blow to the status of the present, the now. The B-series is just incomplete, on this account. To make it complete we need the A-series, but that road leads to contradiction, and the A-series is unreal.

One other way of arguing that the B-series is incomplete is to argue that all the B-series characteristics can be understood in A-series terms, but not conversely. This is supposed to show that the B-series characteristics are derivative, or can be derived from the A-series.

There are many arguments against McTaggart's approach and conclusion. McTaggart's approach can be attacked at many points, and has been. Philosophers have questioned his claim that there are the two series. They have questioned his account of one or both of the series, his account of the relationship between the series, his claim that the B-series is incomplete, his claim that the A-series is superior, and his account of the contradictoriness of the A-series. The debate is extensive and many faceted.

It can be noted that the temporal logics we have been looking at are all logics that make use of both the before/after relation (accessibility) and the past/present/future division of time. The maps of temporal instants (possible worlds) combine, in some sense, both an A-series and a B-series. This it does, in the tradition of Prior, by distinguishing between the explicit operators for past and future and the ordering of instants along the one or many time lines. The ordering by means of "before/after" accessibility is to be found in the semantical meta-language (see van Benthem 1983: 10). If there is a real combination of these in consistent formal systems, then it could be argued that they are compatible with each other and are not an inconsistent whole.

We leave the debate at this quite inconclusive point. The reader is encouraged to investigate further.

The paradoxes of time travel

Enthusiastic readers of Wells' *The Time Machine* (Geduld 1987) and viewers of *Dr Who* (BBC) cannot but consider the strangeness of time travel. In both cases we have people going back in time (is this A-series or B-series?) and doing things. They become part of the events of the past. We consider two sorts of problems.

The first is of the following sort. Let us consider this in two steps: first step, a simple point of logic; second step, a case.

The point of logic is just that if a conclusion is validly derived from a set of premises, and the conclusion is a contradiction, then the set of premises is inconsistent.

Now we consider the case. Say that someone, quite ruthless in a "good" sort of way, gets hold of a time machine. This person despises Adolf Hitler so they go back to Austria in 1920 and assassinate him. Unbeknown to the assassin, their parents met only because of the injuries the father suffered in the air raids in London in 1940. So the parents now never meet and the assassin is never born. Since the assassin is never born, nobody goes back to 1920 to assassinate Hitler. So the air raids happen, and the assassin is born, and the assassin does go back, and Hitler is assassinated, and the assassin is never born, and so on, and so on. Given the time machine, is Hitler assassinated in 1920?

There seems to be a paradox. If Hitler is assassinated, then he is not assassinated; and if he is not assassinated, then he is. This formalizes in simple propositional logic (where $H = $ *Hitler was assassinated in 1920*) as:

$$((H \supset \sim H) \mathbin{\&} (\sim H \supset H))$$

which is equivalent to:

$$(H \equiv \sim H)$$

The latter is certainly a contradiction.

Now our first point above comes into play. Since this contradiction is derived on the assumption that there is a time machine in a world very much like ours, it follows that this is an inconsistent notion. So, we cannot have our world, or worlds like it and consistently suppose that there are time machines in any of them.

The second sort of problem is of less drastic kind, but still puzzling. In Paul Nahin's *Time Machines* (1993) he pulls together a set of cases under the heading of "causal loop" problems. They include the case where someone goes back in time and does something that enables them to invent a time machine, later in time, to go back in time. Other similar cases, cited in Nahin, include the case where someone cannot decide who to marry. So they go forward in time to see who they do marry, then come back and marry that person.

Nahin is very interested in the cases where the causal connection is simply the transfer of information. David Lewis's paper, "The Paradoxes of Time Travel", is cited with approval in Nahin. Lewis considers the case of the time traveller who goes back in time to tell his younger self how to build a time machine.

Nahin claims that it would be a mistake to interpret such a story in a repetitive cycle way. Some have told stories like this, but have proposed that the person who goes back is the *first* voyager to go back to meet the younger self. The younger person then lives, invents, and goes back as a *second* voyager, to meet his younger self. The younger self *of the second voyager* then lives, invents, and goes back as a *third* voyager, to meet his younger self, and so on.

Nahin claims that there is no need to think of the cycle as repetitive. It is just a "standing loop" in the time sequence.

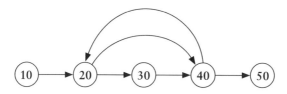

It should be noted that any temporal logic which rules out loops or cycles will not allow for standing loops. **CSA** and **CLA** will both certainly be anti-time-travel. Any logic containing both transitivity and asymmetry will also rule out loops.

Some have claimed further, as Nahin points out, that the information that gets passed back via the voyager in time has no real origin. Lewis says of this:

> But where did the information come from in the first place? Why did the whole affair happen? There is simply no answer. The parts of the loop are explicable, the whole of it is not. Strange! But not impossible, and not too different from inexplicabilities we are already inured to. Almost everyone agrees that God, or the Big Bang, or the entire infinite past of the Universe, or the decay of the tritium

atom, is uncaused and inexplicable. If these are possible, why not the inexplicable causal loops that arise in time travel?

(Lewis 1986: "The Paradoxes of Time Travel")

There are other problems to do with the notion of time travel. Some philosophers have opined that time travel is logically impossible because of these problems. It is not clear that the arguments are as conclusive as the mathematical proof that it is not possible, in general, to trisect the angle. If the arguments are not as conclusive, then, to pun a little, only time will tell. The reader is encouraged to investigate further.

References and further reading

Several of these volumes have massive bibliographies.

Audi, R. (ed.) 1995. *The Cambridge Dictionary of Philosophy*. Cambridge: Cambridge University Press.

Burnet, J. 1968. *Greek Philosophy: Thales to Plato*. New York: Macmillan.

Davies, P. 1995. *About Time*. Harmondsworth: Penguin.

Edwards, P. (ed.) 1968. *The Encyclopedia of Philosophy*. New York: Macmillan. (Refer to this encylopedia for articles on time and McTaggart.)

Geduld, H. M. (ed.) 1987. *The Definitive Time Machine*. Bloomington, IN: Indiana University Press.

Goldblatt, R. 1987. *Logics of Time and Computation*. Stanford, MT: CSLI.

Hinckfuss, I. 1975. *The Existence of Space and Time*. Oxford: Oxford University Press.

Lewis, D. 1986. *Philosophical Papers*. Oxford: Oxford University Press.

Lovill, J. 1993. *St Augustine Bishop of Hippo Confessions, based on a translation by J. G. Pilkington*. London: Folio Society. (Or see any other translation of the *Confessions* of St Augustine.)

McTaggart, J. M. E. 1908. "The Unreality of Time". *Mind* 68 (October): 457–74.

Nahin, P. J. 1993. *Time Machines*. New York: AIP.

Ohrstrom, P. & P. F. V. Hasle 1995. *Temporal Logic: From Ancient Ideas to Artificial Intelligence*. Dordrecht: Kluwer.

Prior, A. N. 1957. *Time and Modality*. Oxford: Oxford University Press.

Prior, A. N. 1967. *Past, Present and Future*. Oxford: Oxford University Press.

Prior, A. N. 1968. *Papers on Time and Tense*. Oxford: Oxford University Press.

Rennie, M. K. *c*.1970. *Tense Logic Notes*, Philosophy Department, University of Queensland.

Schlesinger, G. N. 1980. *Aspects of Time*. Indianapolis, IN: Hackett.

van Benthem, J. F. A. K. 1983. *The Logic of Time*. Dordrecht: Reidel.

CHAPTER 11
Dynamic logic

11.1 Introduction

If we interpret the □ as "After any change", then we have a dynamic inter-pretation of modal logic. The ◊ is then interpreted as "After some change".

Most change is by means of some specific process. We can use an index within the modal operator to indicate the specific process of change. If the process were a, then we would have either $[a]$ or $\langle a \rangle$. We translate:

$[a]p$ as "Always on completion of a it is the case that p"

and $\langle a \rangle p$ as "Sometimes on completion of a it is the case that p"

In dynamic logic the possible worlds are seen as states of some system. The states are just like instants in the history of a system for temporal logic. The states change from one to the next by means of processes. So the processes are just like accessibility relations. In dynamic logic, a process π is taken to be an accessibility relation between states.

11.2 States and processes

Consider a sequence of states (worlds) as in a fairly typical **T** or **DT** system, $\{n, k, l\}$. Each of these worlds could be seen as a state of some system. The arrows are the process of change that moves the system from state to state. This is not unlike the basis for temporal logic. Indeed, there are some strong parallels.

Remember, the difference between **T** and **DT** is that accessibility in **T** is reflexive, while in **DT** accessibility is not. **DT** is one of the non-reflexive normal modal logics which contains the consistency rule or axiom. We shall focus on **DT** for the time being.

Consider the following tree rules in which the process, π, is the accessibility relation. We begin with modal negation style rules:

$(\langle\;\rangle N)$ $\sim\langle\pi\rangle\alpha$ (ω)
$\vdots$
$[\pi]\sim\alpha$ (ω)

$([\;]N)$ $\sim[\pi]\alpha$ (ω)
$\vdots$
$\langle\pi\rangle\sim\alpha$ (ω)

$(\langle\;\rangle R)$ $\langle\pi\rangle\alpha$ (ω)
$\vdots$
$\omega\pi\upsilon$
α (υ)
where υ is NEW to this path of the tree

$([\;]R)$ $[\pi]\alpha$ (ω)
$\omega\pi\upsilon$
$\vdots$
α (υ)

$([\;]D)$ $[\pi]\alpha$ (ω)
$\vdots$
$\langle\pi\rangle\alpha$ (ω)

There would not be anything of much interest in dynamic logic if it were just to be the sort of adaptation for a single process that we see above. But we can add a whole set of simple processes: a, b, c, ... Such processes are known as **atomic processes**. What these do is expand the logic to a multiply modal logic for as many processes as we need to refer to.

The really interesting thing in dynamic logic is the move to *complex* processes. The atomic processes can be combined in the following ways. Take the two processes: a and b. A state might change by means of a and then b. So we can have the complex process $(a;b)$. We can also have either a or b (non-deterministically). This is the complex process $(a\cup b)$. We can also have a process that occurs some number of times, say n times, where $n>0$. This is the complex process a^n. There is also the null process θ. This is the process of "doing nothing".

So we have:

$(a;b)$ the process of a and then b
$(a \cup b)$ the process of either a or b
    θ the process of doing nothing
    a^n the process of a n times

The last is best defined as doing a and then a, ... until a is done n times. There are tree rules for each of these:

$(\langle ; \rangle R)$ $\langle (\pi ; \tau) \rangle \alpha$ (ω)
           $\vdots$
          $\omega \pi \upsilon$
          $\upsilon \tau \mu$
          α (μ)
where υ and μ are NEW *to this path of the tree*

$([;]R)$ $[(\pi ; \tau)] \alpha$ (ω)
          $\omega \pi \upsilon$
          $\upsilon \tau \mu$
           $\vdots$
          α (μ)

$(\langle \cup \rangle R)$ $\langle (\pi \cup \tau) \rangle \alpha$ (ω)
          $\vdots$

    $\omega \pi \upsilon$ $\upsilon \tau \mu$
   α (υ) α (μ)
where υ and μ are NEW *to these paths of the tree*

$([\cup]R)$ $[(\pi \cup \tau)] \alpha$ (ω)
      $\omega \pi \upsilon$ (or $\omega \tau \upsilon$)
          $\vdots$
        α (υ)

It is also usual to have a "test" process. This is the process of testing a proposition for truth. For the purposes of such tests it is usual to distinguish between formulas which contain process terms and those which do not. The latter are known as process free formulas. So we get (where P is process free):

    P?   the process of testing P for truth.

In the truth-tree formulation of a logic to include the test process it is by far the easiest thing to treat the test in terms of the rather fortunate equivalence:

$$[P?]\, Q \equiv (P \supset Q)$$

So the tree rules are:

$([?]R)$ $[\beta?]\alpha$ (ω)
          $\vdots$

   $\sim\!\beta$ (ω) α (ω)

$(\langle ? \rangle R)$ $\langle \beta? \rangle \alpha$ (ω)
          $\vdots$
        β (ω)
        α (ω)

The practical effect of the left tree rule for the test process is that if β is true then α is true in world ω. This is the same as translating:

[β?]α (ω) as   "If β is true in ω then α is true in ω".

It is also usual to introduce the * operator on processes:

π*   the process of doing π n times where $n \geq 0$

The condition given means that π is repeated a finite number of times. So, the asterisk is the *repeat* operator.

It is not possible to provide a complete set of truth-tree rules for *repeat*. But there are two things that can be done that will go part of the way:

1. Processes of the form π* can often just be handled with the rules we already have.
2. When we get ωπ*υ, we can subsequently treat π* as a transitive and reflexive accessibility relation.

This will give us the following tree rules:

(Trans)	ωπ*υ	(Trans)	ωπυ	(Refl)	ωπ*υ
	υπτ		υπ*τ		⋮
	⋮		⋮		ωπ*ω
	ωπ*τ		ωπ*τ		

For example, say we wish to test:

([a*]p ⊃ [a][a*]p)

for validity in dynamic logic. The tree is:

1.	~([a*]p ⊃ [a][a*]p)	(n)	NTF
2.	[a*]p	(n)	1
3.	~[a][a*]p	(n)	1
4.	⟨a⟩~ [a*]p	(n)	3
5.	nak		
6.	~[a*]p	(k)	4
7.	⟨a*⟩~p	(k)	6
8.	ka*m		
9.	~p	(m)	7
10.	na*m		5, 8, **Trans**
11.	p	(m)	2, 10
	×		

The reader might try trees for the following:

$([a*](p \supset [a]p) \supset (p \supset [a*]p))$
$([a*]p \supset (p \ \& \ [a][a*]p))$

In Goldblatt's *Logics of Time and Computation* (1987) the following are introduced:

If P then π, otherwise τ	for	$(P?;\pi) \cup (\sim P?;\tau)$
While P do π	for	$((P?;\pi)*;\sim P?)$
Repeat π until P	for	$(\pi;(\sim P?;\pi)*)$
Skip	for	$(p \supset p)?$
Abort	for	$(\sim p \ \& \ p)?$
π^0	for	*Skip*
π^{n+1}	for	$(\pi^n;\pi)$

These abbreviations make it clear that one of the important applications of dynamic logic is in the logic of computer programming.

The first of the abbreviations make it very clear that the "If ... then ..." of computing languages is not a conditional in any straightforward way. This should be obvious from the fact that such "If ... then ..."s have an instruction or command, not a proposition, in their consequents.

The tree rules we have given will provide an incomplete tree system for the logic known as **PDL**, for propositional dynamic logic.

11.3 Actions and processes

Dynamic logic is of considerable philosophical interest. For example, consider the proposition:

1.   *John enters the room by walking through the door.*

It has often been suggested that such propositions are really conditionals with their antecedent confirmed:

> *If John walks through the door, then he enters the room; and he walked through the door.*

This translates to:

$((W \supset E) \ \& \ W)$

Given the standard problems with conditionals, this approach to doing things "by means of" something turns out to be very risky.

If we look at 1 from the point of view of dynamic logic we would be most likely to get:

After walking through the door John enters the room.

This translates either to $\langle w \rangle E$ or to $[w]E$.

We have to decide whether we see 1. as expressing a general statement about how John's walking through the door *always* gets him into the room, or about how his walking through the door *sometimes* gets him into the room.

If the emphasis is on the processes of walking and entering, then we might even get:

John's walking through the door is just his entering the room.

This translates to:

$$w = e$$

The use of dynamic logic allows us specifically to treat actions as processes. The act of walking through the door is treated as the process w.

Some arguments that would be very difficult to analyse in first-order logic become relatively simple in dynamic logic. For example:

Bill's kicking the television starts it.
Therefore, Bill's repeatedly kicking the television starts it.

The translation of this argument into predicate logic is quite problematic. But it translates easily into dynamic logic to give:

$$[k]S$$
$$\therefore \quad [k*]S$$

The argument is valid. The reader is invited to try a test with a truth tree. It should close. The reason why the argument turns out valid, contrary to first expectations, is because the premise has no restriction, such as "sometimes". As translated, the premise is taken to say that, always after Bill kicks the television, it starts.

The reader is encouraged to investigate dynamic logic further.

References and suggested reading

Goldblatt, R. 1987. *Logics of Time and Computation*. Stanford, CA: CSLI.
Harel, D. 1979. *First-Order Dynamic Logic*. Berlin: Springer Verlag.

CHAPTER 12
Epistemic logic

12.1 Introduction

If we interpret the □ as "It is known that", then we have an **epistemic** interpretation of modal logic. If we interpret the □ as "It is believed that", then
we have a **doxastic** interpretation of modal logic. Epistemic logic gives us a
logic for knowledge, and doxastic logic gives us a logic for belief.

Since knowledge and belief both involve some knower or believer, many
epistemic and doxastic logics use a subscript with the modal operator to indicate the agent. If the agent were a, then we would have $\square_a$. If several agents
were to be considered, then we would have a logic for each agent.

It is usual to distinguish epistemic from doxastic logic by replacing the □
with K for knowledge, and with B for belief. So we translate:

$K_a p$ as   *a knows that p*

and $B_a p$ as   *a believes that p*

Epistemic and doxastic logics were proposed by a variety of people. One
classic early paper was Lemmon's "Is there only one correct system of modal
logic?" (1959). The classic summary and complete proposal for epistemic and
doxastic logic is to be found in Hintikka's *Knowledge and Belief* (1962).

We shall focus mainly on the propositional part of Hintikka's epistemic
and doxastic logics. We then discuss some of the issues generated by these
logics. There will be a brief discussion of epistemic free logic.

12.2 S4 Knowledge

Hintikka's epistemic logic is straightforwardly an epistemic interpretation of S4. If we assume that epistemic logic is to cope with more than one epistemic agent, then the logic will be a multiply modal S4 (see Rennie 1970). Given agents: $a, b, c, d, \ldots$, there will be a knowledge operator for each agent:

$$K_a, K_b, K_c, K_d, \ldots$$

We also define the operators:

$$P_a, P_b, P_c, P_d, \ldots$$

such that, for any agent x:

$$P_x =_{df} {\sim}K_x{\sim}$$

The truth-tree rules for this multiply modal S4 will be similar to those for single modality S4. The main difference will be that there will be a distinct accessibility relation for each epistemic agent. The accessibility relation in epistemic logic is often called "epistemic accessibility". So we use E for the accessibility relation:

$$E_a, E_b, E_c, E_d, \ldots$$

The tree rules for standard propositional logic, **PTr**, are the same as for any S4 modal logic. The remaining rules are:

(KPN)
$$
\begin{array}{ll}
{\sim}K_x\alpha & (\omega) \\
\vdots & \\
P_x{\sim}\alpha & (\omega)
\end{array}
\qquad
\begin{array}{ll}
{\sim}P_x\alpha & (\omega) \\
\vdots & \\
K_x{\sim}\alpha & (\omega)
\end{array}
$$

(PR)
$$
\begin{array}{ll}
P_x\alpha & (\omega) \\
\vdots & \\
\omega E_x\upsilon & \\
\alpha & (\upsilon)
\end{array}
$$
where υ is NEW *to this path of the tree*

(KR)
$$
\begin{array}{ll}
K_x\alpha & (\omega) \\
\omega E_x\upsilon & \\
\vdots & \\
\alpha & (\upsilon)
\end{array}
$$

(KT)
$$
\begin{array}{ll}
K_x\alpha & (\omega) \\
\vdots & \\
\alpha & (\omega)
\end{array}
$$

(KKR)
$$
\begin{array}{ll}
K_x\alpha & (\omega) \\
\omega E_x\upsilon & \\
\vdots & \\
K_x\alpha & (\upsilon)
\end{array}
$$

As well as these obviously **S4** style rules, there is need for the rule which Hintikka calls the "Transmissibility of knowledge rule". It puts into effect the principle that *If* a *knows that* b *knows that* p, *then* a *knows that* p. We get:

(TrKR)　　$K_x K_y \alpha$　　(ω)
　　　　　　　⋮
　　　　　　$K_x \alpha$　　(ω)

This last rule is the rule that links the many **S4** epistemic operators together into one logic. The possible worlds that are generated by the **PR** rules are often referred to as "epistemically possible worlds" or "epistemically alternate worlds."

Hintikka also translates:

　　$P_a p$　as　"It is possible, for all that *a* knows, that *p*"

We shall not use this translation. There are problems about whether the "possible for" is qualified by "logically" or "epistemically". For the moment we shall avoid those issues by sticking to the more literal translation:

　　$P_a p$　as　"*a* does not know that *p* is not the case"

If we set out the axiomatic version of this logic we have the usual axioms of propositional logic, *modus ponens*, and the following axiom schema:

K1　$(K_x(X \supset Y) \supset (K_x X \supset K_x Y))$
K2　$(K_x X \supset X)$
K3　$(K_x X \supset K_x K_x X)$
K4　$(K_x K_y X \supset K_x X)$

and the inference rule of Epistemic Necessitation:

EN　$\vdash X \Rightarrow \vdash K_x X$

The axiom schema are known by the following names:

K1　Distribution
K2　Veridicality
K3　**KK**-thesis or positive introspection thesis
K4　Transmissability of knowledge

We shall discuss the many interesting and controversial features of the logic in later sections of this chapter. There is one uncontroversial principle, embodied in K2: the reflexivity axiom schema.

The general idea is that someone knows something only if it is true. So, if an agent claims to know something, and what they claim to know is not true, then their claim to know is mistaken. It is false that they know it.

By contrast, someone can believe all sorts of falsehoods, and it is still belief. If someone claims to believe something, and what they say they believe is not true, then the content of their belief is incorrect, but it will still be true that they believe it (unless they are insincere, or have changed their mind). This contrast between knowing and believing is sometimes said to be a contrast between the objectivity of knowledge and the subjectivity of belief. We go at once to Hintikka's doxastic logic.

12.3 D4 belief

Hintikka's belief logic is a doxastic interpretation of a multiply-modal **D4**. This logic is simply non-reflexive **S4**. Given agents: $a, b, c, d, \ldots$, there will be a belief operator for each agent:

$$B_a, B_b, B_c, B_d, \ldots$$

We also define the operators:

$$C_a, C_b, C_c, C_d, \ldots$$

such that, for any agent x:

$$C_x =_{df} {\sim}B_x{\sim}$$

Hintikka translates:

$C_a p$ as "It is possible, for all that a believes, that p"

We shall not use this translation. We shall use the more literal:

$C_a p$ as "a does not believe that p is not the case"

We set out the tree rules for multiply modal **D4** and use D for doxastic accessibility. The rules are analogous to the epistemic logic rules above, but **(KTR)** has no analogue but is replaced by **(BCR)**:

(BCN) $\quad {\sim}B_x\alpha \quad (\omega)$ $\qquad\qquad\qquad\qquad {\sim}C_x\alpha \quad (\omega)$
$\qquad\qquad\qquad \vdots \qquad\qquad\qquad\qquad\qquad\qquad\qquad \vdots$
$\qquad\qquad\quad C_x{\sim}\alpha \quad (\omega) \qquad\qquad\qquad\qquad B_x{\sim}\alpha \quad (\omega)$

(CR) $\quad C_x\alpha \quad (\omega) \qquad$ (BR) $\quad B_x\alpha \quad (\omega)$
$\qquad\qquad \vdots \qquad\qquad\qquad\qquad\qquad\qquad \omega D_x\upsilon$
$\qquad\quad \omega D_x\upsilon \qquad\qquad\qquad\qquad\qquad\qquad \vdots$
$\qquad\qquad \alpha \quad (\upsilon) \qquad\qquad\qquad\qquad\qquad \alpha \quad (\upsilon)$
$\quad$ *where υ is* NEW *to*
$\quad$ *this path of the tree*

(BBR) $B_x\alpha$ (ω) (BCR) $B_x\alpha$ (ω)
           $\omega D_x\upsilon$ $\vdots$
           $\vdots$ $C_x\alpha$ (ω)
           $B_x\alpha$ (υ)

There is no interconnecting rule for doxastic logic, so each believer's beliefs entail nothing for any other believer's beliefs on the scale of the principle of the transmissability of knowledge.

If we set out the axiomatic version of this logic we have the usual axioms of propositional logic and *modus ponens*, together with:

B1 $(B_x(X \supset Y) \supset (B_xX \supset B_xY))$
B2 $(B_xX \supset \sim B_x\sim X)$
B3 $(B_xX \supset B_xB_xX)$

and the inference rule of doxastic (belief) necessitation:

DN $\vdash X \Rightarrow \vdash B_xX$

The reflexive axiom is replaced with a consistency axiom. If someone believes that X, then they do not believe the negation of X. The transmissability axiom schema is missing.

The major controversial features of epistemic logic are paralleled in doxastic logic. We turn to the interesting and often controversial features of epistemic logic.

12.4 Looking at epistemic logic: two ways and four topics

We set out two ways of looking at epistemic logic. These can help us to understand the model of the knowledge agent that a particular epistemic logic gives. These ways of looking at epistemic logic will be applied to the interpreting of a sequence of epistemic logics, one of which is Hintikka's S4-style epistemic logic. What is involved in adopting any particular logic in the sequence will then become clearer. Many of the points to be made here can be analogously made for doxastic logic (see Girle 1989a). Finally, desirable and undesirable characteristics of any model will be set out for future reference.

One general way of looking at epistemic logic is set out by Lemmon (1959). He made the suggestion that, to interpret the epistemic logician's "X knows that": "We may make a start, however, by treating X as a kind of logical fiction, the rational man ... (A rational man knows (at least implicitly) the logical consequences of what he knows.)" (Lemmon 1959: 39).

Lemmon is suggesting that the epistemic agent be seen as *ideal* in some respect that is appropriate to the debate. He is aware of some of the "queer consequences" of this ideal. As he writes: "There are some queer consequences: X knows that T, let us say, where T is some very long tautology containing 396 propositional variables. But this is not to worry us..." (1959: 40).

Clearly, the "rational man" of Lemmon is logically very knowledgeable (at least implicitly). This follows from the fact that the logical system which Lemmon is interpreting as an epistemic logic has as one of its rules the rule of weak necessitation:

If T is a tautology then □T is a theorem

This rule is interpreted in epistemic logic as:

If T is a tautology then X knows that T

Lemmon gives us a snapshot picture of his preferred rational man by looking directly at the axiomatization of the logic, and drawing a *prima facie* picture of the ideal epistemic agent from the axioms and rules of inference. It is no surprise that Lemmon does this. He is one of the great systematic axiomatizers of modal logics. This way of developing a *prima facie* picture of the model to which the ideal knower and believer conforms is the *axiomatic way* of seeing an ideal epistemic agent modelled by a logic. This will be our first way of looking at epistemic logics.

The second way, which is somewhat less direct, is to look at the semantics for epistemic logics, and to give some account of the function of the concept of knowledge in terms of the semantic model. This tends to be Hintikka's way of arguing for his model for the epistemic agent. This is the *semantic way* of seeing an ideal epistemic agent modelled by a logic.

When we look at a logic in either of the two ways we need to know the focus of our attention. We set out four topics that we shall consider when looking at the logics. These topics have been the subject of extended debate, and attitudes to them have a direct bearing on the model of knowledge that is accepted.

The first two topics concern the extent to which the concept of knowledge involves innate or automatic knowledge. Should we assume that every knower automatically knows the "laws of logic", or even the "laws of epistemic logic"? Should we assume that every knower automatically knows all the consequences of their knowledge? In the original debates these topics were debated under the general heading of **epistemic omniscience**. It will help if we begin with some definitions of *omniscience*, particularly with respect to epistemic and doxastic logic. We define three kinds of omniscience: **logical, deductive,** and **factual**. We divide logical omniscience into two kinds: strong and weak. We begin with logical omniscience.

Logical omniscience

Where the knowledge agent depicted by some epistemic logic automatically knows all the logical truths defined by that logic, the agent is *strongly logically omniscient*. Logics that attribute strong logical omniscience to agents are said to assert a *strong logical omniscience thesis (SLOT)*.

We now turn to *weak logical omniscience*. Where the knowledge agent depicted by some epistemic logic automatically knows all the logical truths of first-order logic, the agent is *weakly logically omniscient*. Weak logical omniscience is included in strong logical omniscience. Logics that attribute weak logical omniscience to agents are said to assert the *weak logical omniscience thesis (WLOT)*. This was viewed with some warmth by Rene Descartes. He says that there are some eternal truths that dwell in our minds: "To this class belong: *It is impossible that a given thing should at once be and not be*; ... and countless others. It would not be easy to enumerate them all; but one is not either likely to be ignorant of them when occasion arises to think of them and when we are not blinded by prejudice" (1964: 191). Agents depicted as being at least weakly logically omniscient can be described as **Cartesian agents**.

Deductive omniscience

The second kind of omniscience is deductive omniscience. Where the knowledge agent depicted by some epistemic logic automatically knows all the logical consequences of known propositions, the agent is *deductively omniscient*.

Logics that attribute deductive omniscience to agents are said to assert a *deductive omniscience thesis (DOT)*.

Factual omniscience

The third kind of omniscience is factual omniscience. Where the knowledge agent depicted by some epistemic logic automatically knows, for any proposition A, whether A is true or not, the agent is *factually omniscient*.

Factual omniscience includes the other two. There are no logics that attribute such epistemic divinity to their epistemic agents.

We shall consider the extent to which epistemic logics attribute logical and deductive omniscience to epistemic agents under the two topic headings of *SLOT* and *DOT*. There has been limited debate about these two groups of theses, and usually under the heading of **deductive closure**. Hintikka does refers at some length to the topics in one of his papers (1975), but in general, it was as if the problem was of such enormity that hardly anyone was prepared to concede that it existed, let alone tackle it.

The third topic concerns the extent to which knowers know what they know. In the original debates the discussion centered on the *KK-thesis*:

If a knows that X, then a knows that a knows that X

In any epistemic logic with both the *KK-thesis* and the *SLOT*, it has to follow that everyone knows that the *KK-thesis* is necessarily so. Why then all the argument? (And there was extended argument.) Perhaps the opponents of the *KK-thesis* are people who know the *KK-thesis* to be true but don't know that they know this? If so, then they are the proof of its incorrectness. The only other alternative seems to be that they are not ideal epistemic agents.

The fourth topic concerns the suggestion to be found in some recent computing literature that (machine) knowers should also be taken to know when they are ignorant. That is, if an agent does not know something, then they know that they do not know it. Even further, knowers should also know when they *cannot* know. That is, if something is false, an agent should know that they do not know it (see Halpern 1986).

12.5 The ideal agent and the axiomatic way

We begin with the axiomatic way of seeing the epistemic agents modelled by several logics. How does logical and deductive omniscience vary from system to system? What is the status of the *KK-thesis* from system to system? To what extent does the system reflect knowledge of ignorance? To find out, we begin by looking at three normal modal logics – **T**, **S4**, and **S5** – and three non-normal logics – Lemmon's preferred **S0.5**, **E2**, and the logic of pure necessity, **N**. From a logical point of view the five systems are related as in the following map:

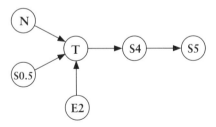

So **S5** includes all the theses of all the others. We shall start with **S5** and work down through the systems, seeing what is lost at each point, and maybe lost to advantage.

The S5 agent

Consider an axiomatization for epistemically interpreted multiply-modal S5. We simply extend the axiomatization above for epistemic S4. The rules of inference are unchanged. We need only a single axiom schema to be added. The additional axiom is K5:

K5 $(P_x X \supset K_x P_x X)$

It is important to note that the following are theorem schema of this S5 logic:

T1 $(\sim X \supset K_x \sim K_x X)$
T2 $(\sim K_x X \supset K_x \sim K_x X)$

For cross-reference we add the rule of weak necessitation:

WN $\vdash_{PL} T \Rightarrow \vdash K_x T$

We call T1 the **Platonic principle**. T2 is the **negative introspection thesis**. This last inference rule, WN, is the weak necessitation referred to above. "$\vdash_{PL} T$" is read as either "T is a theorem of **PL**" or "T is a tautology".

We have already noted that the veridicality axiom, K2, is unchallenged in philosophical debate. So we leave well enough alone, and move on to consider other matters.

We begin with the agent depicted by epistemic S5. Consider first the necessitation rule. This rule means that the ideal S5 agent is strongly logically omniscient. We saw above that Lemmon's knower knew all the tautologies, but the S5 knower knows all the theses of epistemic logic as well. We have full, not weak, necessitation. Under epistemic interpretation we have:

If T is a thesis of this epistemic logic then a knows that T.

This is strong logical omniscience.

It is important to be clear about just what epistemic necessitation means. Let us start with *weak necessitation*. The rule is:

$\vdash T \Rightarrow \vdash K_x T$ (where T is a tautology).

It is not:

$\vdash T \Rightarrow \vdash K_a (T \text{ is a tautology})$

The rule does not mean that if T is a tautology then an agent, a, knows that T is a tautology. This is not about knowing logic. The agent would simply know that T. For example, *If it is raining, then it is raining* is a tautology. Weak necessitation asserts that any agent, a, would know automatically that *If it is raining, then it is raining*. That's all. We might note that any ideal agent for whom weak necessitation holds will be an ideal Cartesian agent.

These observations say something about the Cartesian model for knowledge. But in S5 there is more. There is full epistemic necessitation. The rule is:

$$\vdash X \Rightarrow \vdash K_a X$$

In this case X is any thesis of epistemic logic. For example, it is a thesis of Hintikka's epistemic logic, and included in the S5 ideal, that "If a knows that X, then a knows that a knows that X". It follows from epistemic necessitation that every agent knows automatically that "If they know that X, then they know that they know that X".

This surely shows that real-life epistemic agents are neither S4 nor S5 agents. If they were, then there would be no controversy about the thesis that "If a knows that X, then a knows that a knows that X". Weak necessitation is not too difficult to accept, but the strong is too strong for mere mortals.

Secondly, consider the axiom that expands knowledge. It is the distribution axiom, K1. The axiom reads as:

If a knows that if X then Y, then if a knows that X then a knows that Y

This axiom ensures that the agent does draw all the obvious conclusions that follow from what is known. But it does more. This axiom, when put together with epistemic necessitation, gives full strength to the *DOT*. For example, say it follows logically from X that Y. That is: *If X then Y* is a logical truth. It follows that every agent will know that *If X then Y*. So, *if a knows that* X, it must follow that *a knows that Y*. This can be displayed formally by:

$$\vdash (X \supset Y), K_x X \Rightarrow K_x Y$$

Every ideal S5 agent will know everything that follows logically from whatever they know. Every ideal S5 agent is deductively omniscient. It should be noted that all ideal agents depicted by normal modal logics will be deductively omniscient.

Thirdly we turn to the Platonic principle:

If not X then a knows that a does not know that X

The truly Socratic person is here exemplified, the person who knows just how ignorant they are. The full force of this axiom is often avoided by considering only the apparently weaker T2 theorem. This theorem, the negative introspection principle is, in a sense, more reasonable:

If a does not know that X then a knows that a does not know that X

But we cannot have the weak without the strong in S5.

Finally we consider the S4 axiom, the *KK-thesis*:

If a knows that X, then a knows that a knows that X

This has been the subject of much controversy. We begin by noting the standard counter-example to the *KK-thesis*. The standard counter-example is one in which there is an element of self-deception. "I knew all along that my partner was being unfaithful, but I refused to believe it" (so I refused to know that I knew).

There are two fairly standard responses. One response has centred on the question of the "primary" meaning of the concept of knowledge. In particular, there has been debate about whether the "primary" meaning of the concept is of an active and aware sense of knowing or whether the "primary" sense of the concept is a minimal sense where an agent might know something but without being aware of knowing it (see Hintikka 1962; Girle 1973). It would be difficult not to assume that any epistemic logic should be based on a univocal sense for the concept of knowledge. In a univocal account, the interpretation of X *knows that* should not change from place to place in the reading of sentences. This is particularly important in the reading of sentences in which there is an iterated occurrence of knows that (see Girle 1989b).

Hintikka has, for all practical purposes, asserted that his account of knowledge is of an active and aware sense of knowing (1962: 103–23). It follows that since the **S4** axiom has unrestricted application in the **S5** model, the agent modelled there has to be a fully aware knower. This is not to rule out the possibility of a multiply modal system to cope with both fully aware knowing and minimal knowing, but as long as we are looking at the possibility of the simpler, single system model, then the **S5** model has to be of the fully aware knower. Such an agent cannot truthfully assert that they knew all along that their partner was being unfaithful, but were not aware that they knew it. Hintikka copes with such assertions in everyday life by arguing that the sense of knowledge under self-deception is non-standard or residual (1962: 114).

The second response is, in a sense, parasitic on the fully aware sense. It is based on the logical equivalence in S5 and in S4 of $\Box \ldots \Box X$ and $\Box X$. For the S5 knower there is no logical difference between *knowing that X* and *knowing that one knows that … one knows that X*. If the notion is quite univocal, then the counter-example fails. On this basis the apparent introspection boils away into logical equivalence. The *KK-thesis* is not a thesis about introspection. It is about logical equivalence.

Summary for S5

The ideal **S5** agent is therefore a fully aware knower who has immediate access to all the consequences of his or her knowledge, to all the theorems that constitute the logical structure of knowledge, and knows what he or she does not know. Knowledge will, for the S5 knower, constitute a maximal consistent theory, totally accessible. It is arguable that there is one and only one possible S5 knower: an omniscient God. Total accessibility is the key. No mere mortal could aspire to such heights.

The S4 agent

The ideal S4 agent is the knower who conforms to Hintikka's epistemic logic. The S4 agent is almost the same as the S5 agent. The model contains both the S4 axiom (the *KK-thesis*), the distribution axiom, and the necessitation rule. The difference is to be found in the absence of the S5 axiom, K5. The S4 model also lacks both T1 and T2. It follows from this that the following sets, while inconsistent in S5, are quite consistent for the S4 agent:

{not X, a does not know that a does not know that X}

and

{a does not know X, a does not know that a does not know X}

So it is possible for the S4 agent not to know that he or she does not know something when, in fact, they do not know it. The S4 agent can be blissfully ignorant. For example, if *a* were an S4 agent then *a* could believe that he or she knew that X, but X could be false, and so *a*'s belief would be a false belief. So, the S4 agent is permitted to have false beliefs about what he or she knows. This is in contrast to the S5 agent, who cannot have false beliefs about what he or she knows.

Nevertheless, the similarity between the S4 and S5 agents is great. The S4 agent is a fully aware knower who knows all the consequences of what he or she knows, and who knows the logical structure of knowledge. The S4 agent can have mistaken beliefs about what he or she knows. The S4 agent is beginning to look a little lower than the angels, but not low enough for mere mortals.

The T agent

The modal system T lacks both the S5 and S4 axioms. But it contains epistemic necessitation and the distribution axiom. This means that the T agent knows all the logical consequences of what he or she knows. The lack of the S5 axiom means that the T agent can be mistaken about what he or she knows, that is, can falsely believe that he or she knows something.

The lack of the S4 axiom means that it is possible for the T agent to know something, but not to know that he or she knows it. In other words, the following is not inconsistent in a T based epistemic logic:

{a knows that X, a does not know that a knows that X}

So it is possible to distinguish between fully aware knowledge and knowledge without active awareness for the **T** agent without two epistemic operators.

But, the epistemic necessitation rule has one strange effect in **T**. It follows from epistemic necessitation that all the theses of epistemic logic are known, and furthermore, it is known that they are known. So although there is no overall *KK-thesis* in **T**, there remains a restricted *KK-thesis* in **T**. It can be set out as:

If T is a thesis of epistemic logic then a knows that a knows that T

The intriguing result of this is that the **T** agent is fully aware of the structure of knowledge without necessarily being fully aware of everything he or she knows.

The **T** agent, unlike the **S4** and **S5** agents, is not necessarily a fully aware knower. The **T** agent does know all the logical consequences of what he or she knows, but knowledge of contingencies may be unknown knowledge, implicit knowledge. The **T** agent knows the structure of knowledge, and is fully aware of that knowledge.

The S0.5 agent (Lemmon's ideal)

The **S0.5** model contains the distribution axiom, but it lacks the **S5** and **S4** axioms, and it lacks the full-blooded epistemic necessitation rule. It contains the weak necessitation rule:

*If T is a theorem of **PL** then a knows that T*

In a quantified **S0.5**, this would become:

If T is a theorem of first-order logic then a knows that T

The **S0.5** agent, like the **T** agent is not necessarily a fully aware knower. Indeed, there are no theorems in epistemic **S0.5** of the form $K_x K_x \alpha$. So, if being self-aware, or fully aware, is to be represented by formulas of the form $K_x K_x \alpha$, then self-awareness for the **S0.5** agent is a purely contingent matter. So it is appropriate to consider here the question of what it means for an agent to know something and not to know that it knows it. The most obvious answer to this question is that self-aware knowledge must be explicitly represented in the store of knowledge that the agent has.

Now, unlike the **T** agent, the **S0.5** agent does not, of necessity, know the structure of knowledge, not even implicitly. The **S0.5** agent does know all the consequences of what he or she knows, but may not be fully aware of them. The **S0.5** agent knows all the theorems of first-order logic, but may not know that he or she knows them.

While there is a limit on the extent of the automatic logical knowledge of the **S0.5** agent, the knowledge of all the theorems of non-epistemic first-order logic will constitute exactly the same barrier to a mortal's being an **S0.5** agent as to a mortal's being a **T**, **S4** or **S5** agent. The **S0.5** agent is an ideal Cartesian agent.

The E2 agent

The **E2** system contains the distribution axiom, but it has no theorems of either the form $K_x\alpha$ or (of necessity) of the form $K_xK_x\alpha$. So there is no automatic knowledge of anything at all. The agent is not Cartesian.

The N agent

Remember that the **N** system is, as far as modality is concerned, a system based on argument analysis. It is concerned with deductive consequence. There are no theorems beyond standard propositional logic, and their single or repeated necessitation.

N contains the weak necessitation rule:

*If T is a theorem of **PL** then a knows that T*

So, $(p \supset p)$ is a theorem, and so is $\Box(p \supset p)$ and all of $\Box \ldots \Box(p \supset p)$.

The **N** model does not contain the distribution axiom. So, for example, although $((p \vee p) \supset p)$ is a theorem, $(\Box(p \vee p) \supset \Box p)$ is not a theorem.

This means that the **N** agent is logically omniscient but not deductively omniscient. The agent is Cartesian.

N does not contain the reflexivity principle. The assumption is that if a proposition is a premise of an argument, then it is known.

Summary

First, five of these epistemic logics, **S5**, **S4**, **T**, **S0.5** and **N**, seen as theoretical models for ideal epistemic agents, have one thing in common: all of the ideal agents modelled by these systems are Cartesian in the sense outlined above. Second, **E2** is not Cartesian. The **E2** system has no theorems of the form $K_a\alpha$. It lacks the *SLOT* (see Girle & McRobbie 1988). Third, the ideal agent in each of the first four systems, **S5**, **S4**, **T** and **S0.5**, is deductively omniscient. But the ideal agent in **N** is not deductively omniscient.

It would be good if we could combine the best features of **N** and **E2**. The reader is urged to investigate further.

At this point we turn to the second, *semantic*, way of looking at epistemic logics and the models they present of epistemic agents. Hintikka's semantic picture of knowledge, and of the epistemic agent, is our main concern.

12.6 Indefensibility and the semantic way

In all of the models considered the ideal agent knows, necessarily, the theses of first-order logic. In the case of S5, S4 and T, that knowledge is actively aware knowledge. But Hintikka is more careful, and deliberately so. The theses of these models, or theories if you will, are said by Hintikka to be "self-sustaining". A sentence is "self-sustaining" if and only if its negation is "indefensible". The semantic notions of *defensibility* and *indefensibility* are basic ones for Hintikka.

Hintikka's notion of *defensibility* is the notion of, in his words, *immunity to certain kinds of criticism*. He writes:

> suppose that a man says to you, "I know that *p* but I don't know whether *q*" and suppose that *p* can be shown to entail logically *q* by means of some argument which he would be willing to accept ... If he is reasonable, you can thus persuade him to retract one of his statements without imparting to him any fresh information beyond certain logical relationships. If he really does know that *p*, he could by means of these logical relationships come to know *q* all by himself if he had followed far enough the consequences of what he already knew. (1962: 31)

What Hintikka says here can be put in a more technical way, in terms of his definitions, by saying that

$$\{\vdash (p \supset q), a \text{ knows that } p, a \text{ does not know that } q\}$$

is an indefensible set of statements, that is, it is not immune to logical criticism.

It follows that when *p* entails *q*

If a knows that p then a knows that q

is a self-sustaining sentence, that is, that its negation is not immune to criticism.

When we apply these principles to the theses that collectively state that any epistemic agent knows all the theorems of first-order logic, the following account would seem appropriate.

If *T* is a thesis of first-order logic, and someone says that they do not know that *T* (and that they do not know that not *T* for that matter), then they can be persuaded to retract one of the statements without anyone imparting to them any information beyond certain logical truths.

Now, of logical truths Hintikka says: "Logical truths are not truths which logic forces on us; they are not necessary truths in the sense of being unavoidable. They are not truths we must know, but truths which we can know without making use of any factual information" (*ibid.*: 37).

Of course, Hintikka is not just telling us about his epistemic logic when he makes these remarks. He is telling us something about his view of what knowledge is. Knowledge is not merely being aware of the facts. What an agent knows must form a coherent defensible whole, immune from criticism. But that is not all. There is something else of crucial import. If anyone claims *not to know* something, that claim should also be immune from criticism. In the case of the theses of first-order logic, the claim not to know them is not immune from the sort of "persuasive criticism" which Hintikka outlines.

But this means that, for Hintikka, *X knows that P* is far more than what is normally taken to be knowledge. It might be put in the following way:

$K_a X$ is to be read as   *a knows that, or can work out whether, X*

So, if *a can work out that* X, setting aside all questions of the temporal or intellectual limitations of human agents, then *a knows that X*. Indeed, a somewhat stronger reading will show how much Hintikka is prepared to integrate into knowledge:

a knows that, or it is provable, given what a knows, that X

The rational person is assumed to be accepting of all proof, so his or her limitations are totally discounted. This reading also discounts the usual contrast that people commonly make between what is known and what has been proved. "I know he has been sneaking in but I cannot *prove* it."

In Chapter 7 we noted that the contrast between logical necessity and provability can be understood in terms of the contrast between S5 and S4 style logics. If we are to maintain a contrast between knowledge and provability, then we need a logic that is weaker than S4. The strongest modal logic for such a contrast would be T.

Furthermore, it does not follow from a proposition's immunity to criticism in an epistemic context that the agent has to know all the things, the whole theory, by virtue of which the proposition is immune to criticism. Knowledge is far more contingent than this.

Hintikka's model of the epistemic agent is not the model of a knower. It is the model, if anything, of the *commitments* of a knower. The picture given by S4 is the picture of what an epistemic agent could be said to be logically committed to by claims to know.

It is also sometimes claimed that sense can be made of the semantics only if we make certain assumptions about the possible world nature of the semantics. Emphasis is placed on the usual modal valuation function, which states that $K_a X$ is true in world ω iff X is true in all worlds that are *epistemically accessible* to ω. So, it is argued, since all the theorems of first-order logic are true in all worlds, epistemic agents will know them all. It does not seem to have occurred to many of those who argue this way that this argument could be taken as a *reductio ad absurdum* against this way of looking at the semantics.

A better way of looking at the semantics would be to take Hintikka's *model-set/model-system* semantics more seriously. Our modal truth trees are a direct implementation of the Hintikka semantics. In the truth trees, the only way in which epistemically alternate worlds are generated is by statements of the form $P_x\alpha$. These are equivalent to statements of the form *x does not know that not* α. Since the agent is ignorant about *not* α, α might be true or might be false. In the generated epistemic alternative for all our logics we find that α is true; only true. But, would it not be better if there were two possible alternatives? In one α would be true, in the other α would be false. The epistemic alternatives are best seen as worlds in which ignorance, rather than knowledge, is set out.

This would give us truth-tree rules like (where **PIR** is for **P** ignorance rule):

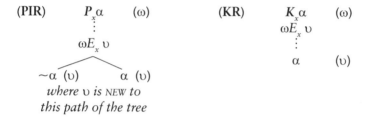

Worlds generated by **PIR** account for two situations rather than just one. A logic with the **PIR** rule would be non-normal and very weak (see Girle 1973). As Sylvan says of such weaker modal systems, "Philosophical virtue lies in weakness" (1986: 3).

12.7 Belief logics

There are a series of problems with doxastic logic that run in parallel with problems in epistemic logic. We have seen that the normal Cartesian modal logics (**T**, **S4**, and **S5**) are too strong, and that plausible models for knowledge are more likely to be found in the weaker non-normal non-Cartesian modal logics such as **N**, and the hinted at **E** systems. Similarly, the doxastically interpreted strong modal systems (**DT** and **D4**) are implausible, while the weaker non-normal non-Cartesian doxastic logics, such as **N** and other weak systems, are more likely to provide plausible models for belief.

If we were to combine epistemic and doxastic logic, then we would need to consider the rule that embodies the principle that *If a knows X, then a believes X.*

(KBR) $K_x \alpha$ (ω)
          $\vdots$
          $B_x \alpha$ (ω)

This principle is not altogether uncontroversial. But it is generally accepted.

Inconsistency and para-consistency

One major problem with belief logics based on classical logic is that they cannot cope with inconsistent belief. Most doxastic logics are interpretations of *classical* modal logics. Classical modal logics are built on classical propositional and predicate logic. Classical logic is utterly intolerant of inconsistency, and is reduced to uncontrollable inferential idiocy in the presence of contradiction. It is vital, therefore, that inconsistency tolerant logics be investigated as a base on which doxastic logic can be built. Such non-classical logics are to be found in the family of **para-consistent logics**. These logics have been thoroughly investigated. Now is the time for us to acknowledge their application as a base for doxastic logic. We have no real space for a full account of para-consistent logic; we can only point out the area of investigation.

The problem that classical logic has with inconsistency can be exemplified by the classical theorems of the form:

EFQ $((P \, \& \sim P) \supset Q)$

known as *ex falso quodlibet* (whatever you wish follows from contradiction). So when a contradiction is deduced from a set of beliefs, it also follows by *ex falso* that any proposition, including every possible contradiction, follows validly from that set of beliefs. There is no restriction of the consequences of inconsistency to related or relevant beliefs. So if we apply a classical inference engine to drawing conclusions from an inconsistent set of beliefs, a malignant inconsistency spreads across absolutely everything.

But this does not happen in real-life belief systems. Reasonable people isolate inconsistency, suspend judgement, or follow other inconsistency handling procedures. Classical inference systems cannot deal so easily with the inconsistency of real-world belief systems. So when doxastic logics are built on a classical base they are equally unable to cope sensibly with inconsistency. One standard classical response has been to develop restricted doxastic logics by interpreting doxastic logics as logics for rational belief. But this interpretation begs a wide range of questions concerning rational and reasonable belief in favour of classical logical consistency. Not only is there no conceptual impossibility about declaring that someone has inconsistent beliefs, but it is by no means clear that everyone with logically inconsistent belief systems is irrational. There are at least three important concerns.

First, it is not clear that a necessary condition for a rational belief system is classical logical consistency. Second, it is not even clear that the attributions of rationality should depend on the logical structure of a system of beliefs. It can be argued that rationality should depend on the way in which an agent deals with contradictions when they are detected in a system of beliefs.

Third, there is a need to develop some taxonomy for inconsistency in belief systems. We might consider a taxonomy related to the *depth* of its occurrence. Some inconsistencies occur on the *surface* of belief systems. The most obvious are the *prima facie* contradictions of the form (p & $\sim p$).

Because of the classical threat of global inconsistency there is a fairly standard, but not uncontroversial, expectation that a rational agent will resolve such contradictions. But in some contexts it might be better to leave such inconsistencies unresolved for the time being. In this case we need a logic that will at least quarantine the inconsistency. Para-consistent logics will do just this, since they lack EFQ and its related theorems. Such logics will help us to deal with contradiction in a more rational fashion than indicated by classical logic. On the other hand, not all inconsistency is on the surface. Some inconsistencies are very deeply buried in belief systems. They often become apparent only after the malignancy has been widely spread, even to totally unrelated areas. If a logic lacks *ex falso quodlibet* it will give us an inference system that is inoculated against the spread of more deeply buried contradiction.

Much more work remains to be done on logical systems for belief.

12.8 Epistemic predicate logic

We turn briefly to epistemic and doxastic predicate logic. There are two topics of interest. They are existential import and quantification into epistemic and doxastic contexts.

We have already seen that some of the problems of existential import can be avoided with free logic. It should be no surprise to discover that Hintikka's epistemic and doxastic predicate logics are free logics. In particular, consider the statement:

a believes that Holmes exists.

This translates easily to:

$B_a(\exists x)(h = x)$

Similarly:

Although Holmes does not exist, a believes that Holmes does exist.

This translates easily to:

$$\sim (\exists x)(b = x) \;\&\; B_a(\exists x)(b = x)$$

If we used standard predicate logic then the last translation would be contradictory simply becase the left conjunct is a contradiction, as we saw in Chapter 8. If we used standard predicate logic then the second last translation would attribute a trivial belief to *a* because the content of *a*'s belief would be a logical truth. Standard predicate logic is clearly quite out of court in both cases. We have, in a sense, covered these issues in Chapter 8.

We turn to the problem of quantifying into epistemic contexts. This problem is closely related to the *de dicto/de re* problem that we looked at in Chapter 9. The problem appears in its most acute form when we contrast the following two formulas:

1. $K_a(\exists x)(b = x)$
2. $(\exists x)K_a(b = x)$

Formula 1 is fairly easy to interpret. It is the "*de dicto*" formula. It simply says that:

1'. *a knows that b exists.*

But, what does 2 mean? Hintikka translates it as:

2'. *a knows who b is.*

This translation is derived from the more literal:

2''. *There is something which a knows to be b.*

In the light of 2'' we get a slightly more detailed idea of what 2' is supposed to mean. It really means that *a* knows on whom to pin the name "*b*". So, knowing who *b* is is knowing who bears the name *b*.

This is a very weak sense of knowing who. Usually, when we say that we know who someone is, we mean that we know some distinguishing property (or relationship) that picks them out in an appropriate context. If somone says that they know who *b* is, and we challenge this with "Who?", then we would expect something like "*b* is the Mayor of Waitakere" or "*b* is the lady who lives five doors down the street".

On the other hand, if we were with Hintikka and saw someone across the room, we might ask Hintikka, "Who is that?" The response might be, "Peter Gärdenfors". We now know who that person is, but we might not know who Peter Gärdenfors is. We could still ask, "But who is Peter Gärdenfors?"

It is true that for us, for *a*, that there is someone we know to be Peter Gärdenfors, *b*, but we don't know who he is. So, 2 and 2'' are true, but 2' is not true.

Furthermore, there is no acknowledgement in 2' or in 2'' that the existential quantifier carries a strong existential import. Such is acknowledged in 1'.

We might have expected something like the following for 2″:

2‴   *Some existing thing is known by a to be b.*

or even:

2″″   *Some existing thing is known by a as b.*

This does not entail that *a* believes that *b* exists. Nor does it entail that *a* believes that *b* does not exist. That is left open. Consider what happens in the trees for 1 and 2:

1. $K_a(\exists x)(b = x)$ 2. $(\exists x)K_a(b = x)$
        $(\exists x)(b = x)$ $(\exists x)(c = x)$
                                         $K_a(b = c)$

It follows from 1 that *b* exists. That seems quite straightforwardly correct. It follows from 2 that something exists, namely *c*, and that *a* knows that *b* is *c*. This means that *a* knows of some existing thing that it bears the name "*b*". *a* does not, of necessity, know that *b* exists. This is 2‴. This allows *a* to know that Cicero, an existent person (in the past), also is called "Tully", but to believe that Cicero is a figure of Roman mythology.

Knowing who seems to be something other than what is asserted in 2.

12.9 Characteristics for a knowledge agent

It must be clear by now that we can say what is undesirable in a model of the ideal knower. The ideal knower, as far as knowledge is concerned, should not be logically omniscient. The *SLOT* should not be a feature of any epistemic logic.

It is also desirable that the ideal knower not be fully deductively omniscient. In fact, there is a stronger and a weaker deductive power in epistemic logics. In the stronger case, we have the full *DOT*. In four of these logics the epistemic agent knows all the logical consequences of all that they know. In the N system, since there is no distribution axiom there will be no *DOT*.

The *KK-thesis* is less of a problem than might at first be thought from the volume of philosophical debate that it generated. If we are to have an always "fully aware" epistemic agent, then we shall want the *KK-thesis*; otherwise not. Since human epistemic agents are not fully aware, a model closer to human agents will not have the *KK-thesis*.

At this stage it looks as though **N** is the best of the systems we have considered. But we need to look at weaker non-normal systems, systems even weaker than **N**. The reader is encouraged to look further, starting with Lemmon's **E** systems.

References and further reading

Descartes, R. 1964. "Principles of Philosophy". In his *Philosophical Writings*, E. Anscombe & P. T. Geach (trans.). Melbourne: Nelson.

Girle, R. A. 1970. *Explanatory Models for Knowledge and Belief*. Unpublished MA thesis, University of Queensland.

Girle, R. A. 1973. "Epistemic Logic, Language, and Concepts". *Logique et Analyse* **63–4**: 359–73.

Girle, R. A. 1989a. "Contradictory Belief and Logic". In *Proceedings of the Second Florida Artificial Intelligence Research Symposium*, Orlando, Florida, 3–6 April: 133–7.

Girle, R. A. 1989b. "Indubitibility and Deductive Omniscience". Paper presented to the Research Seminar in the Department of Logic and Metaphysics, St Andrews University.

Girle, R. A. & M. A. McRobbie 1988. "Exploring the Epistemic Labyrinth". In *Proceedings of the Australian Joint Artificial Intelligence Conference*, Adelaide, SA, 15–18 November: 104–24.

Halpern, J. Y. (ed.) 1986. *Theoretical Aspects of Reasoning about Knowledge: Proceedings of the 1986 Conference*. Los Altos, CA: Morgan Kaufmann.

Hintikka, J. J. 1962. *Knowledge and Belief: An Introduction to the Logic of the Two Notions*. Ithaca, NY: Cornell University Press.

Hintikka, J. J. 1975. "Impossible Possible Worlds Vindicated". *Journal of Philosophical Logic* **4**: 475–84.

Hocutt, M. O. 1972. "Is Epistemic Logic Possible?". *Notre Dame Journal of Formal Logic* **13**(4): 433–53.

Kripke, S. A. 1965. "Semantical Analysis of Modal Logic II: Non-normal Modal Propositional Calculi". In *The Theory of Models*, J. W. Addison, L. Henkin & A. Tarski (eds), 206–20. Amsterdam: North-Holland.

Lemmon, E. J. 1959. "Is there Only One Correct System of Modal Logic?". *Aristotelian Society Supplementary Volume* **33**: 23–40.

Lemmon, E. J. 1966. "Algebraic Semantics for Modal Logics I, II". *Journal of Symbolic Logic* **31**: 46–65, 191–218.

Lenzen, W. 1978. "Recent Work in Epistemic Logic". *Acta Philosophica Fennica* **30**(1). Amsterdam: North-Holland.

Michie, D. & R. Johnston 1985. *The Creative Computer*. Harmondsworth: Penguin Books.

Rennie, M. K. 1970. "Models for Multiply-modal Systems". *Zeitschrift für mathematische Logik and Grundlagen der Mathematik* **16**.

Rescher, N. 1968. "Epistemic Modality: The Problem of a Logical Theory of Belief Statements". In *Topics in Philosophical Logic*. Dordrecht: Reidel.

Schotch, P. K. & R. E. Jennings 1981. "Epistemic Logic, Skepticism, and Non-normal Modal Logic". *Philosophical Studies* **40**: 47–67.

Sylvan, R. 1986. "Relational Semantics for all Lewis, Lemmon and Feys' Modal Logics, most Notably for Systems between S0.3° and S1". Paper presented to the 1986 *Australasian Association for Logic Conference*, Auckland, Aotearoa.

CHAPTER 13
Deontic logic

13.1 Introduction

If we interpret the $\square$ as "It is obligatory to bring it about that", then we have a **deontic** interpretation of modal logic. The $\lozenge$ is then interpreted as "It is permissable to bring it about that".

Some deontic logicians have insisted that the deontic modal operators operate not on propositions but on acts. In that case the translation of the $\square$ is "It is obligatory to do", and the $\lozenge$ is translated as "It is permissable to do". This means that the p and q of standard logic become the names of *acts*, not the descriptions of states of affairs. We shall try to present the deontic interpretation in such a way as to be neutral about the act versus proposition approaches. In what follows we shall assume that the alternative to "is true" of "is done" can be used instead of "is true", and so on. In the next paragraph only we shall insert the alternatives. After that we use the states of affairs locutions.

Just as $\lozenge p$ generates a world in which p is true (or is done), a permission to bring it about that p generates a world in which p is true (or is done), and all the truths (or actions) that it is obligatory to bring about (or do) are true (or are done). In deontic logic, the accessible worlds, the worlds we *see into*, are the worlds in which at least one permitted state of affairs (or action) occurs, and all obligations are fulfilled.

Deontic logics are drawn from the non-reflexive logics, because we cannot assume that just because something is obligatory it will be true. So we cannot have $(\square p \supset p)$.

13.2 A basic deontic logic

In a classic paper, "Deontic logic", von Wright (1951) presented a foundational system of deontic logic. The main features are as follows.

Two operators are introduced to replace $\Box$ and $\Diamond$. They are O and P. They are inter-defined by the obvious equivalence:

(C1) $(Op \equiv {\sim}P{\sim}p)$

Four other principles are proposed. They can be translated into:

(C2) $(Pp \vee P{\sim}p)$
(C3) $(P(p \vee q) \equiv (Pp \vee Pq))$
(C4) "$(O(p \vee {\sim}p))$" and "${\sim}P(p \,\&\, {\sim}p)$" are not valid.
(C5) If p and q are logically equivalent, then Pp and Pq are logically equivalent.

The second principle is "the principle of permission". It can also be expressed as:

Not both p and not p are forbidden.

The third principle is the "principle of deontic distribution". Follesdal and Hilpinen say, of these two principles:

> Both (C2) and (C3) have alethic analogues: Either p or ${\sim}p$ is possible (i.e. both p and ${\sim}p$ cannot be impossible), and a disjunctive proposition $p \vee q$ is possible if and only if p is possible or q is possible. The analogy between deontic and alethic modalities breaks down in the case of the *ab esse ad posse* principle for alethic modalities: if p is true, it is possible, but a state of affairs (or an act) is not necessarily permitted, if it is the case (or the act performed).
> (Follesdal & Hilpinen 1981: 9)

The fourth principle is the principle of deontic contingency. In axiomatic formulations of von Wright's system, the fourth principle holds anyway, because neither $O(p \vee {\sim}p)$ nor ${\sim}P(p \,\&\, {\sim}p)$ are deducible as theorems.

The fifth principle is known as the **rule of extensionality**. It is essentially the principle of the substitutivity of material equivalents.

There are some interesting features of the formulas of this deontic logic. Since the operators of this logic are prefixed to names of acts, then the *iteration* of operators is not permissable. So, neither $(OOp \equiv Op)$ nor $(OPp \equiv Pp)$ is a well formed formula of this system. For similar reasons, the system does not allow for the truth functional combination of deontic and non-deontic propositional logic elements. So, neither $(p \supset Pq)$ nor $(p \vee Oq)$ are well formed formulas.

These limitations simply mean that the set of modal formulas interpreted as deontic formulas is a sub-set of the total set of modal logic formulas. The reader might try to constuct a proper recursive definition of the set of formulas of von Wright's deontic logic.

Without setting out the actual logical mechanism for deciding on validity (see Follesdal and Hilpinen), we note that the following are valid in the system:

1. $(O(p \ \& \ q) \equiv (Op \ \& \ Oq))$
2. $((Op \lor Oq) \supset O(p \lor q))$
3. $(P(p \ \& \ q) \supset (Pp \ \& \ Pq))$

The converses of 2 and 3 are not valid.

The following are discussed by von Wright:

4. $((Op \ \& \ O(p \supset q)) \supset Oq)$
5. $((Pp \ \& \ O(p \supset q)) \supset Pq)$
6. $((\sim Pq \ \& \ O(p \supset q)) \supset \sim Pp)$
7. $((O(p \supset (q \lor r)) \ \& \ \sim Pq \ \& \ \sim Pr) \supset \sim Pp)$
8. $\sim (O(p \lor q) \ \& \ \sim Pp \ \& \ \sim Pq)$
9. $((Op \ \& \ O((p \ \& \ q) \supset r)) \supset O(q \supset r))$
10. $(O(\sim p \supset p) \supset Op)$

Formula 4 is equivalent to the familiar K formula:

11. $(O(p \supset q) \supset (Op \supset Oq))$

Formulas 4–10 are called "the laws of commitment". They spell out what holds when the performance of p commits one to perform q.

A commitment of this kind is translated as: $O(p \supset q)$.

Follesdal and Hilpinen comment on 7 and 8 in terms of a distinction drawn by Thomas Aquinas.

> Aquinas draws a distinction between a man's being *perplexus simpliciter* and a man's being *perplexus secundum quid*. The former is the case if a man, without having done anything forbidden, is, as such, obliged to choose between forbidden alternatives. Aquinas denies that a man can be *perplexus simpliciter*, and this is also denied by [8]. A man is *perplexus secundum quid* if he is obliged to choose between forbidden alternatives as a result of a previous forbidden act. According to Aquinas, this case is possible. Aquinas's view is in accord with [7]. [7] says that an obligation to choose between forbidden alternatives implies that the person in question has committed a forbidden act.   (Follesdal & Hilpinen 1981: 12)

13.3 Standard deontic logic

The basic system in the previous section is included in the standard deontic logic, but usually with one exception. The departure from von Wright's system is usually the rejection of (C4) and the acceptance of:

(C4') $\sim P(p \ \& \ \sim p)$

This is equivalent to accepting:

(ON) $O\sim(p \ \& \ \sim p)$

This looks like at least weak necessitation for obligation at work. If something is a tautology then it is obligatory. This sounds strange. But, given that tautologies are true, no matter what, the obligation to "bring them about" is an *empty* obligation. It is the one obligation that we all fulfil all the time with no effort at all. In fact, the standard system turns out to be **DT**. In some cases this is strengthened to **D4**.

Apart from the obvious modal negation rules we have:

(PR)	$P\alpha$	(ω)		(OD)	$O\alpha$	(ω)
	$\vdots$				$\vdots$	
	$\omega A\upsilon$				$P\alpha$	(ω)
	α	(υ)				
	where υ is NEW *to*					
	this path of the tree					

(OOR)	$O\alpha$	(ω)		(OR)	$O\alpha$	(ω)
	$\omega A\upsilon$				$\omega A\upsilon$	
	$\vdots$				$\vdots$	
	$O\alpha$	(υ)			α	(υ)

The last rule, (OOR), adds transitivity to the accessibility relation to give **D4**. If this is left out we have the system **DT**.

13.4 Paradoxes

Deontic logic is an interpretation of modal logic rife with disagreements about what should be the case. At the very start, the formula:

12. $(Op \supset O(p \lor q))$

is clearly valid in **DT**, but it runs counter to our intuitions about what we are committed to when we are obliged to bring about p. Formula 12 can translate to:

If I ought to hand in my essay, then I ought to either hand it in or burn it.

This paradox is known as Ross's paradox, because Alf Ross brought it to attention in "Imperatives and Logic" (Ross 1941). There is a permission analogue which seems quite bizarre:

13. $(Pp \supset P(p \vee q))$

This can translate to:

> *If I am allowed to write an essay, then I am allowed to either write an essay or plagiarize an essay.*

There are quite explicit university rules about this sort of thing, and they cast quite a lot of doubt on 13.

One way around these paradoxes is to assume that worlds generated from ours, for example, are "deontically perfect" worlds. As was said above, permission generates them, and then in them all obligations are fulfilled. So, they are deontically perfect with respect to the world from which they are generated.

Given this account of the perfect worlds, it becomes easy to see that if the obligation to bring about p is fulfilled in a world, then of course, all the logical consequences of p will be true in that world. So, if p is true, then so is $(p \vee q)$. So 12 and 13 are not quite as problematic as it might have seemed.

There are a group of paradoxes that have been generated by the paradoxes of the material conditional. We know that while some arguments are invalid when couched in English, their standard translation into propositional logic is valid. The problems often centre around the material conditional. In many cases the material conditional is not suitable, and not reliable in argument analysis, as a translation of conditionals. We shall look at an interesting example in Chapter 14.

The same sort of thing happens in deontic logic. We saw earlier that formulas of the form $O(p \supset q)$ display a commitment. From p flows the consequent obligation to do q. This idea is reinforced by the fact that, by 11, $(Op \supset Oq)$ follows from $O(p \supset q)$. Now consider the case of the valid formula of standard deontic logic:

14. $(O{\sim}p \supset O(p \supset q))$

This says, if we are unwary, that if one is forbidden to do p, then one is committed, on doing p, to doing anything and everything (since q can be anything whatsoever).

Most of the ways of explaining away 14 rely on the fact that the material conditional is equivalent to an inclusive disjunction. But, this is much the same as the warning that the material conditional does not translate reliably into the English "If ... then ...".

13.5 The content

In all the above discussion it is assumed that the appropiate content of deontic operators is propositions of a particular kind. The kind of proposition is usually some description of an action. For example:

If I ought to give to the poor, then I ought to either give to the poor or burn my money.

The antecedent could be translated to *OG*, where the *G* translates as *I give to the poor* or *I will give to the poor*. In the case of the latter, *OG* is something like *I ought to bring it about that I give to the poor at some future time*.

Ray Bradley has suggested (in informal discussion) that the deontic operators could be treated as qualified necessity and possibility operators, the qualification being a moral or practical qualification. The operators might be taken to mean "morally necessary", and either "morally possible" or "permissable." The content of these operators would then be something more like a statement of obligation. For example, *OG* would translate as

It is morally necessary that I should give to the poor.

In accordance with Bradley's suggestion, the standard content of deontic operators would be "should" statements.

Under this interpretation, a straightforward S5 logic makes good sense. Consider the S5 modal axioms with *G* for *I should give to the poor* and *S* for *I should sell all my goods*:

$(\Box(G \supset S) \supset (\Box G \supset \Box S))$

If it is morally necessary that if I should give to the poor then I should sell all my goods, then if it is morally necessary that I should give to the poor, then it is morally necessary that I should sell all my goods.

$(\Box G \supset G)$

If it is morally necessary that I should give to the poor, then I should give to the poor.

$(\Diamond S \supset \Box \Diamond S)$

If it is permissable that I should give to the poor, then it is morally necessary that it is permissable that I should give to the poor.

This interpretation falls in well with the notions of qualified necessity and possibility that were discussed in Chapter 9. But, the problem with the rule of necessitation still remains. Vacuous assertions of moral necessity seem quite counter-intuitive.

There are many such problems with deontic logic, but we leave them to the reader to investigate. There are also many ways, other than by means of modal logic, of approaching the notions of obligation and permission. The investigation of these is also left to the reader.

References and further reading

Follesdal, D. & R. Hilpinen 1981. "Deontic Logic: An Introduction". In *Deontic Logic: Introductory and Systematic Readings*, R. Hilpinen, 1–35. Dordrecht: Reidel.
Hilpinen, R. 1981. *Deontic Logic: Introductory and Systematic Readings*. Dordrecht: Reidel.
Prior, A. N. 1954. "The Paradoxes of Derived Obligation". *Mind* 63: 64–5.
Prior, A. N. 1962. *Formal Logic* (2nd edn). Oxford: Oxford University Press.
Ross, A. 1941. "Imperatives and Logic". *Theoria* 7: 53–71.
von Wright, G. H. 1951. "Deontic Logic". *Mind* 60: 1–15.

CHAPTER 14
Conditionals and reliability

14.1 Introduction

Conditionals invite us to use our imagination and to consider possibilities. The antecedent "If *A*" turns us towards hypothetical circumstances and prepares us to consider what follows from them. The consequent "then *C*" expresses the claim that *C* follows from *A* or is implied by *A*. When we know that *A* is false, contrary to fact or *counterfactual*, then the speculations invite contention. There is a "what if" dimension to conditionals. Public figures are often asked conditional questions such as: what would you do if *A*? They will often decline to answer such questions. The element of speculation raises all sorts of difficulties in giving answers. These difficulties are not just for public figures. Logicians and philosophers face the same questions about speculation and possibility when discussing conditionals and what makes for their being true or false.

If we set aside conditional or hypothetical questions for the moment, then the key question about conditional statements is what makes a conditional true. One quite standard answer has been that a conditional is true when either the antecedent is false or the consequent is true. This is the *material conditional* interpretation. This is problematic for several reasons, not least because it makes all counterfactual conditionals true, and all conditionals with true consequents true.

Almost since the first propositional logic more than two thousand years ago, there has been dissatisfaction and controversy about the use of the material conditional as the interpretation and translation for "If … then …" and "… only if …". We do not intend to discuss the history of this controversy, but it is worth noting just how long conditionals, and especially the material conditional, have been the focus of interest and controversy. In what follows we focus on the relevance of modern modal logic to some of the problems and issues. We have seen some of the formal systems developed as conditional logics in Chapter 6. We saw there that the resort to possibility and necessity has not been the only approach to the problem of conditionals.

The formal logics in Chapter 6 are only one kind of attempt to resolve the issues. There are many proposals. We shall discuss three. We begin with the issue of the *reliability* of formal systems and a proposal to ensure reliability. We discuss the formal systems that were set out in Chapter 6. This is done in consort with the topic of reliability. Then we turn to some general issues about conditionals. We turn first to reliability.

14.2 Reliability in evaluating formulas and arguments

At heart, the problem with conditionals is part of the problem of the *reliabilty* of formal systems for evaluating ordinary language arguments as valid or invalid and of propositions as theorems or logical truths. In what follows we shall assume that formal logics are artificial languages with defined semantics and proof systems. They are unlike ordinary language in many ways, particularly because of their stipulated semantics and proof systems. The semantics or the proof system are used to evaluate arguments and propositons couched in the artificial language. The evaluated arguments and propositions are often *translations* from ordinary language. Those evaluations are then transferred to the arguments and propositions expressed originally in ordinary language.

It is absolutely vital to this discussion that propositions expressed in ordinary language be carefully distinguished from those expressed in a formal system, unless there is some explicit defined sameness such as at the atomic level. Similarly, the logical form of propositions expressed in ordinary language should be distinguished from that of propositions in formal systems. Similarly, there should be no confusing of arguments and argument forms in ordinary language with those in the artifacts.

Translation is not the same as abbreviating or symbolizing or regimenting. Translation involves the shift from one language to another. The deceptive part of translation from ordinary language to an artifact is the sharing of basic or atomic propositions. Translation is moving from the logical words and phrases of ordinary language to the logical operators of the formal language. In practice, translation mostly relies on standard rules of thumb. These are to be found in all introductory logic texts and are taken to be so obvious that they are rarely questioned, except in the case of conditionals. And even in the case of conditionals there is little demurring and a great deal of apologetic.

Many formal systems are *pure* logics in the sense set out by Church. They deal only with *argument forms*. But many formal systems are able to deal with actual arguments. Their traffic is translated arguments. We distinguish between abbreviated and translated arguments and propositions. Translated arguments rely on propositional meaning given to the atomic sentences by an abbreviation dictionary, which will contain entries such as:

H = *The figure on the board is a hexagon.*
S = *The figure on the board has six sides.*

In what follows we abbreviate in ordinary language, not translate,

The figure on the board is not a hexagon   as   *not H*;

and   *If the figure on the board is a hexagon then the figure on the board has six sides*   as   *If H then S.*

H and S are then treated as having exactly the same meaning in both ordinary language and the artificial language into which the propositions are translated. This sameness of atomic or basic propositions is wont to mislead about what is going on in translation. An artificial language that allows such abbreviations and sameness is, in something like Church's sense, an *applied* language. Compound formulas in the artificial language have a meaning determined by the stipulated meaning of the abbreviation letters and the *stipulated semantics* of the logical operators.

The formal language meaning is not necessarily the same as the meaning of the translated ordinary language sentences which contained the (abbreviated) sentences in combination with logical words and phrases. At the same time, the meanings of translated and translation might be so close as to be virtually the same. For example, *not H* and its standard translation as $\sim H$ would usually be considered to be the same or virtually the same in meaning. The question of the closeness or difference in meaning is at the heart of the question of the reliability of formal systems.

Despite the applied nature of the formal systems used to evaluate ordinary arguments, the formal translations are mostly treated as if they were argument *forms* rather than arguments. In this text we have no lengthy discussion of what constitutes an argument form. We rely on the intuition that there are repeated patterns of argument in ordinary language and that these patterns are argument forms. There are recurring patterns or argument forms such as *modus ponens* and *modus tollens* and *affirming the consequent*. It is often said that an argument *has* a certain form. These forms will be valid or invalid. If an argument has a valid form then it is valid, but if it has an invalid form, then it does not follow that it is invalid, but we might be rather suspicious of it. In case this asymmetry seems wrong, then consider the following argument:

A.   If the figure on the board either has four sides or does not have four sides,
     then the figure on the board is a hexagon.
     The figure on the board is a hexagon.
     So, the figure on the board either has four sides or does not have four
     sides.

We add to the dictionary above:

F = *The figure on the board has four sides.*

A abbreviates in ordinary language to:

A.   *If either F or not F then H*
               H
        So, either F or not F

The argument has at least three forms:

If either r or not r then q	*If p then q*	*t*
q	*q*	*u*
So, either r or not r	*So, p*	*So v*

The form on the left is sometimes said to be the *explicit form* of argument A.
The form on the right is the form common to all arguments of two premises.
The middle form is the form of *the fallacy of affirming the consequent*.

On one standard analysis, the first form is valid, the second and third are
invalid. Having one valid form is sufficient for validity, but having invalid
forms is not sufficient for invalidity. Showing an argument to be invalid is
not the same as showing that it has an invalid form. Form and argument are
not the same thing.

The evaluation of patterns of argumentation is a key concern of logic.
Ordinary language arguments are instances of ordinary language argument
forms. If an argument form has an instance with true premises and a false
conclusion then the form is invalid and the instance is a *counter-example*. For
example, we set out an argument, B, and the explicit form, B′, of which B is
an instance. They are set out in abbreviated English:

F = *The figure on the board has four sides.*
H = *The figure on the board is hexagon.*
R = *The figure on the board is a rectangle.*
S = *The figure on the board has six sides.*

B. *If R then F*
    If H then S

    Therefore at least one of the
    following:

    (a) if R then S, and
    (b) if H then F

B'. *If p then q*
    If t then u

    Therefore at least one of the
    following:

    (a) if p then u, and
    (b) if t then q

We can appeal to geometrical definitions for our evaluation of the truth of the premises and conclusion of B. Clearly the premises are true and the conclusion false in B. B' has an instance with true premises and a false conclusion. So the form, B', is invalid, and B is a counter-example to B'. An additional counter-example is found in *INCL* (Priest 2008: 13, example 2).

If the form B' is translated from ordinary language to some formal language and then tested for validity, we would expect the formal evaluation to be that the argument form is not valid. If the evaluation in the formal system is valid, then the formal system is *unreliable*. The evaluations of translations in that formal system cannot be reliably transferred to all the arguments translated.

The general process of evaluation can be shown in the diagram:

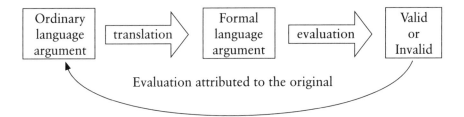

The evaluation is not directly of the original but of its translation. The value is then attributed to the original. The issue is whether the evaluation of the formal argument gives a reliable evaluation of the argument of which the formal language argument is a translation. Let's see what happens with our argument form B' above.

The standard translation of the argument form B' into classical propositional logic is:

B_{PL}.
$$(p \supset q)$$
$$(t \supset u)$$
$$\therefore \quad ((p \supset u) \vee (t \supset q))$$

The evaluation in classical propositonal logic is *valid*. The reader can confirm this with a truth-tree or a truth table.

This is one of the many cases by means of which it can be shown beyond reasonable doubt that classical propositonal logic is *unreliable* given the standard rules for translation, especially in the cases of arguments containing conditionals.

There are various other responses to the case of B′ and B$_{\text{PL}}$, and we shall consider some of them later. At this point it is worth discussing one of the obvious responses.

The most obvious response would be that we should not have used the standard translation for *If p then q* when translating B′. This point is of little use to us if it is made *after* the translation gives us the wrong evaluation. If the argument form in ordinary language is so clearly invalid then there is no need to use a formal system for its evaluation unless we want to show just how useful a formal system might be. In that case our demonstration is definitely not good for classical propositional logic. But the important point is that if we accept the standard translation of *If p then q* to $(p \supset q)$, then the classical logic evaluation of B′ is worse than unreliable, it is wrong.

At this point some would object that logics, especially classical propositional logic, are not artificial languages. They are abstractions from ordinary language and reveal the *real* underlying logical structure of ordinary language. We consider this further in the section below about defending the material conditional.

What can be said? Is there any way around this problem with conditionals, or should we simply abandon the use of classical logic for the evaluation of arguments containing conditionals? The problem might not require such a radical course of action. We propose a less radical approach.

14.3 Systematic determination of reliability

There is a general view of what is needed for a formal system to be reliable. It was first proposed by Phillip Staines. This view enables us to decide in a systematic way whether any evaluation will be reliable before one is made. Otherwise we would be driven to *ad hoc post hoc* decisions about correct translation.

The general idea is that when sentences are translated from one language to another, including ordinary to formal, there are logical relationships between the propositions expressed by the sentences (formulas) of the languages. The original proposition can entail or be entailed by the translation proposition, or there can be no entailment either way. For logical purposes the ideal translation of the original entails and is entailed by its translation. This will be so if the meaning is the same. Entailment equivalence is the ideal.

But it is not necessary to have entailment equivalence for reliability. If one language is to be used for the reliable evaluation of arguments in another, then certain minimum conditions should be met. There should be at least the following for the reliable attribution of validity, invalidity, etc.:

P1. For the reliable attribution of validity to an argument or argument form the premises should entail their translation, and the translated conclusion should entail the original conclusion.

P2. For the reliable attribution of invalidity to an argument form the premises should be entailed by their translation, and the translated conclusion should be entailed by the original conclusion.

P3. For the reliable attribution of theoremhood or logical truth to a proposition or propositional form the formal translation should entail the proposition expressed in ordinary language.

P4. For the reliable denial to a sentence form of theoremhood or being a logical truth the formal translation should be entailed by the ordinary language sentence.

We set out P3 and P4 especially because much of the debate about conditionals stems from debate about the single sentence paradoxes of material implication.

The reader is invited to work out what should hold for contradictions, and for relations between pairs of propositons such as contrary, contradictory, sub-contrary, and for contradictory sets of propositions.

This systematic approach is more rigorous than the "Can Do principle" set out in Gabbay and Woods. But it very much in the same spirit. They write that the:

> Can Do Principle bids an investigator of a question Q in a domain D to invest his resources in answering questions $Q_1^*, \dots, Q_n^*$ from domain D^* when the following conditions appear to have been met. First, the investigator is adept at answering the Q_i^*; and second, he is prepared to attest that answering the Q_i^* facilitates the answering of the initial question Q.   (Gabbay & Woods 2003: 49)

The shift from domain D to D^* is the shift from ordinary language to formal language, and the questions, Q and Q^* are questions about validity and logical truth and such. The system we shall use relies on the assumption of the transitivity and contrapositivity of entailment, and that if an argument is valid then the premises jointly entail the conclusion. P1 can be represented in the following diagram for reliable evaluation when the formal language gives a valid evaluation of the translated argument. We use "**OL**" for ordinary language argument and "**FL**" for a formal language translation and "$\Rightarrow$" for entailment:

P1.   OL   FL

P_1 $\Rightarrow$ p_1
$\vdots$ $\vdots$
P_n $\Rightarrow$ p_n
$\therefore$ C $\Leftarrow$ c

The inter-language entailment can be assessed before the formal language evaluation is made. So, we know *ahead* of the formal evaluation whether the formal test will be reliable. If we go ahead in unreliable cases then *caveat emptor*.

There is wide agreement that "If ... then ..." conditionals entail their material conditional translations. Jackson calls this the *uncontested principle*. The uncontested principle supports the view that the standard translation conforms to:

E1.   *If p then q* $\Rightarrow$ $(p \Rrightarrow q)$
E1$_\supset$.   *If p then q* $\Rightarrow$ $(p \supset q)$

where E1$_\supset$ is E1 for the material conditional.

The converse entailment is at least highly controversial. It is denied or contested by many, and agreed to be problematic by most. Before we return to argument B above, let's see what happens when we check *modus ponens*:

MP   *If p then q* $\Rightarrow$ $(p \supset q)$
p $\Leftrightarrow$ p
_____
So, q $\Leftrightarrow$ $\therefore$ q

The test of *modus ponens* for validity in classical propositional logic will be reliable because it satisfies P1. The reader can easily check that the same holds for *modus tollens* and *the uncontested principle*.

When we turn to case B above we have:

B'.   B$_{PL}$.

If p then q $\Rightarrow$ $(p \supset q)$
If t then u $\Rightarrow$ $(t \supset u)$ $\Downarrow$
_____
Therefore at least one of the ? $\therefore$ $((p \supset u) \vee (t \supset q))$
following:
(a) if p then u, and
(b) if t then q

The lack of entailment from right to left for the conclusion will mean that despite B$_{PL}$'s being valid, the evaluation does not reliably transfer to B' and, we might well add, "nor should it".

While we are at it, it might be as well to show the entailment relation between three of the other ordinary language forms and their standard translations. Jackson offers the *truth-functionality principle*, which says, "the standard, familiar, two-valued truth-table accounts of 'not', 'or', and 'and', in their typical uses are correct" (1987: 4). That principle is, in our terms, saying that the following apply:

E2. *Not p*   ⟺ $\sim p$
E3. *Both p and q*   ⟺ $(p \mathbin{\&} q)$
E4. *Either p or q*   ⟺ $(p \vee q)$

From E1 and the contrapositivity of entailment we also have:

E5. *Not if p then q*   ⟸ $\sim (p \Rightarrow q)$

Our immediate interest, as with E1, is in:

E5$_\supset$. *Not if p then q*   ⟸ $\sim (p \supset q)$

We set aside for the moment the disagreement that will come from intuitionist logicians about negation, and from the exclusive disjunction and intentional disjunction advocates when it comes to disjunction. These can be the subject of debate elsewhere. It will ease our debate about conditionals to accept the *truth functionality principle* for the time being.

It is clear from the account of reliability above that if ordinary conditionals are entailment equivalent to the material conditional, then the *truth functionally principle* can be expanded to include the material conditional. But if that were the case, then there would be very deep problems with argument B and its evaluation.

Finally, it is very important not to misinterpret the result of unreliability. It does not follow from a system's unreliabilty in assessing an argument as valid that the argument is invalid, nor does it follow from a system's unreliability in assessing an argument as invalid that it is valid. There is considerable asymmetry in the conclusions we may draw.

14.4 Whence entailment?

The reliability methodology forwarded above appears to cut through a huge Gordian knot of debate. But is it realistic? We cannot just produce the methodology and expect acquiescence. There are two issues.

First, in the abstract, the methodology appears sound but only if we accept the three properties of the entailment we are using.

Secondly, what is the basis for the specific claims above about entailment between propositional languages? Even if the methodology in the abstract is seen as good, and we accept the three properties of entailment, the application of it depends on the acceptance of E1 to E5 for every operator. At this stage we accept E2 to E4 simply to ease the discussion. Debate on them is postponed to another place. E5 is the contrapositive of E1, and we shall take it that it stands or falls with E1. The real issue is twofold. There is the contrast between E1 and:

E6.　*If p then q* $\Leftrightarrow$　　$(p \Rightarrow q)$

for the conditional operators in all the logics.

There is the question of how we justify either of them. This is a key question if we are to accept the reliability methodology above.

In considering the formulas and arguments above we have been taking the approach that assumes that the best logic is one that either refutes or does not support certain formulas and certain argument forms. Many of these are controversial. But there is good reason to expect the best logic to confirm the validity of some tautologies and some argument forms.

In his predicate logic Aristotle argued that "Barbara" (*Every M is P, Every S is M, So every S is P*) is a perfect syllogism. One might suppose that any predicate logic which invalidated a standard translation of "Barbara" had failed a crucial test. Is there any such test for conditional logics?

The first three formulas and argument forms listed in Chapter 6 might well be seen as providing a benchmark. They are the *uncontested principle* (UP), *modus ponens* (MP) and *modus tollens* (MT). Whatever the final analysis of conditionals is to be, in ordinary language it seems clear that MP and MT should be valid. Ordinary conditionals obey not just one uncontested principle, but the other two as well. It seems quite contrary to the central meaning of any conditional that we should deny that when a conditional is true and its antecedent is true that its consequent is true. The same applies to the case when a conditional is true and its consequent is false. The antecedent is false. This is in conformity with the *uncontested principle*. Even for those who want to include the cases where propositions are both true and false, and where they have no value at all, would deny MP and MT at the risk of misunderstanding the basic nature of any ordinary conditional.

If a logic does not sustain UP, MP and MT then we can argue that it will be inveterately unreliable. There will be no entailments between ordinary language conditionals and the "conditionals" of the logic. They will be *logically indifferent* to each other.

The system C does not evaluate UP, MP and MT as valid. The system C⁺ does value UP, MP and MT as valid. So, without further ado we can rule C as unreliable in the sense that its alleged conditionals are entailment indifferent to ordinary conditionals. C might be correct some of the time, but we cannot rely on it. Our interest in **C** is simply because it is formally interesting as the logic on which **C⁺** and others are built.

Some will argue that *contraposition* and *hypothetical syllogism* should be included in the benchmark set of formulas and arguments. If they are, then our whole system above of pre-evaluation determination of reliability will collapse, especially because of our inter-language entailments set out in E1 to E5.

At this point we can note two interesting cases of the pre-evaluation determination of reliability. *Modus tollens* can be seen as a variation on *contraposition*. Compare them:

$$\frac{\text{If } p \text{ then } q}{\therefore \quad \text{If not } q \text{ then not } p} \qquad\qquad \frac{\begin{array}{c}\text{not } q \\ \text{If } p \text{ then } q\end{array}}{\therefore \quad \text{not } p}$$

The form on the right can be seen as a modification of the form on the left. The modification is that the antecedent of the conclusion on the left is removed and added as a premise, and the consequent of the conclusion on the left becomes the conclusion of the argument on the right.

The same modification will give us the following pair where the left is **HS**.

$$\frac{\begin{array}{c}\text{If } p \text{ then } q \\ \text{If } q \text{ then } r\end{array}}{\therefore \quad \text{If } p \text{ then } r} \qquad\qquad \frac{\begin{array}{c}p \\ \text{If } p \text{ then } q \\ \text{If } q \text{ then } r\end{array}}{\therefore \quad r}$$

Let us call the form on the right "categorical **HS**" or "**CHS**" for short. In a sense, **MT** is categorical **Contra**. Both **MT** and **CHS** conform to the standards for reliable assessment of validity in logics where E1 to E5 are accepted. But **Contra** and **HS** do not. The difference centres on whether the argument forms have conditional conclusions. This reflects a common scepticism about reasoning to hypothetical conclusions, a scepticism that is often used when people refuse to answer questions on the basis that it is a "hypothetical question". The common scepticism also reflects negatively on *Weakening*.

If E6 applies, then there is no problem. But if E6 applies there are worse problems.

For the aficionados of meta-logic, this contrast has interesting implications for logics with a deduction theorem. Such logics are definitely distinct from ordinary language.

14.5 The cases – the material conditional and its rivals

We now take up the cases which are often counted as telling for conditional logic. The cases are indicated in the eight formulas and six argument forms we dealt with in Chapter 6. We look first at the material conditional interpretations. The first case is the simplest. We have the pair:

6.1. $\qquad (\sim (p \Rightarrow q) \Rightarrow (p \ \& \ \sim q))$
6.1'. $\qquad \dfrac{\sim (p \Rightarrow q)}{\therefore \quad (p \ \& \ \sim q)}$

The material conditional interpretation gives:

6.1$_\supset$. $\qquad (\sim (p \supset q) \supset (p \ \& \sim q))$
6.1'$_\supset$. $\qquad \dfrac{\sim (p \supset q)}{\therefore \quad (p \ \& \sim q)}$

Consider the following argument:

C. *It is not true that if Bill has applied [A] for a job, then he will get [G] one. So, Bill has applied for a job and he will not get one.*

With the obvious dictionary indicated the abbreviation and form of which it is an instance are:

C. $\quad \dfrac{\textit{Not if A then G}}{\textit{So, A and not G}} \qquad\qquad \dfrac{\textit{Not if p then q}}{\textit{So, p and not q}}$

C gives us the problem of negated conditionals in argument form. In terms of reliability we have:

$$\dfrac{\textit{Not if p then q}}{\textit{So, p and not q}} \quad \Leftarrow \quad \dfrac{\sim(p \supset q)}{\therefore \quad (p \ \& \ \sim q)}$$
$$\Leftrightarrow$$

Although the argument on the right is valid, the valuation cannot be reliably attributed to the argument on the left. The entailments are in breach of P1.

None of **S1**, **C**$^+$ and **RM** allow 6.1 as a theorem in their respective interpretations:

6.1$_\prec$. $(\sim(p \prec q) \prec (p \ \& \ \sim q))$
6.1$_>$. $(\sim(p > q) > (p \ \& \ \sim q))$
6.1$_\rightarrow$. $(\sim(p \rightarrow q) \rightarrow (p \ \& \ \sim q))$

Also, all four of the systems value the related argument forms as invalid.

If we accept that for all the systems we are dealing with we have at least the entailment E5 for all three connectives, then the invalidity result can be reliably attributed to the translated arguments. So, the ordinary argument C cannot be reliably valued as valid by classical logic but will be reliably valued as invalid by **S1**, **C⁺** and **RM**. In summary, 6.1′ is invalid.

The second case is the formula and argument form known as *Weakening*. In its material conditional interpretation:

6.2$_\supset$. $((p \supset q) \supset ((p \, \& \, r) \supset q))$

and

6.2′$_\supset$. $$\frac{(p \supset q)}{\therefore \quad ((p \, \& \, r) \supset q)}$$

The following example from Priest (2008: 74) makes 6.2′ look very questionable:

D.   *If it does not rain tomorrow we will go to the cricket.*
     So, if it does not rain tomorrow and I am killed in a car accident tonight
     then we will go to the cricket.

Apart from morbid jokes, most would want to say that if the premise is true it does not follow that the conclusion is true. One could think of situations where the premise is true, and in such situations the conclusion would be definitely false. So, the form of which D is an instance, namely 6.2′, is invalid. But the classical and **S1** interpretations of 6.2′ are valid. The reliability situation, with an obvious abbreviation dictionary, is:

D. $$\frac{\textit{If not R then C.}}{\textit{So, if not R and K, then C.}} \qquad \begin{array}{c} \Rightarrow \\ \Rightarrow \end{array} \qquad \frac{(\sim R \supset C)}{\therefore \quad ((\sim R \, \& \, K) \supset C)}$$

Classical logic cannot give a reliable assessment of D as valid because it fails P1.

Another way of looking at *weakening* is to see it as a principle applying to arguments as a whole. Consider the following two argument schema, **L** and **R**:

L   **R**

$$\frac{p}{\therefore \quad q}$$ $$\frac{\begin{array}{c} r \\ p \end{array}}{\therefore \quad q}$$

Weakening states that: *If* **L** *is valid then* **R** *is valid.*

If you have a valid argument, then no matter what premises you add to it, the resulting argument will be valid. You can even add the negation of one of the premises. If *weakening* applies, then validity is impervious to additional information, even to additional information that contradicts one of the premises. *Weakening* is quite counter-intuitive, although that is not conclusive. We also note that the **S1** translation of D is also valid. The C, C^+ and **RM** translations await the reader's attention.

If either of C^+ and **RM** evalaute 6.3' as invalid, then that valuation will be unreliable for D if all we have is E1 and E5 for all three connectives.

The third and fourth cases, *contraposition* and *hypothetical syllogism*, are straightforwardly clear as concerns the reliability of the material implication interpretation. The standard translation of both is valid in classical logic. In both cases the translated arguments are unreliable for attributing validity to the original, simply because their conclusions are material conditionals.

What is the fate of the argument forms in the other systems? Again, validity assessment will be unreliable, and so will invalidity assessment.

We turn to the fifth case, or set of cases. The fifth case concerns the *paradoxes of material implication*. These are a group of tautologies of classical logic that seem to give clear expression to *prima facie* undesirable features of the material conditional. There are many that fall into this category.

Consider now the paradoxes of material implication. Let us take just one of those given in Chapter 6 in its classical form:

$6.5_\supset$. $(p \supset (q \supset p))$

This often forwarded as the translation of:

E'. *If p then if q then p.*

which is the form of:

E. *If William of Normandy won the Battle of Hastings, then if the world is flat then William of Normandy won the Battle of Hastings.*

With an appropriate dictionary we get the abbreviation:

E. *If W then if F then W.*

Whether the instance of *q* is relevant to the instance of *p* or not does not matter. $6.6\supset$ is a tautology of classical logic. But, on the basis of the entailment relations we have:

$$\text{If } p \text{ then if } q \text{ then } p \qquad \Rightarrow \qquad (p \supset (q \supset p))$$

So, given E1$_\supset$, any evaluation of 6.5$_\supset$ as a tautology will give us an unreliable evaluation of E′. E′ cannot be reliably evaluated as a tautology by evaluating its standard translations in classical logic. The entailment relation does not meet the minimum requirement in P3 for tautology evaluation. The case is similar for 8.6$\supset$. The next two are somewhat more difficult to test. It would appear that if we either conjoin or disjoin two formulas which are each entailed by the propositions of ordinary langue so translated, then the conjunction and the disjunction are also entailed. So for the following:

6.7$_\supset$. $((p \supset q) \vee (q \supset p))$
6.8$_\supset$. $((p \supset q) \vee (q \supset r))$

we have:

Either if p then q or if q then p	$\Rightarrow$	$((p \supset q) \vee (q \supset p))$
Either if p then q or if q then r	$\Rightarrow$	$((p \supset q) \vee (q \supset r))$

In either case the classical evaluation will not be reliable. So, across all the paradox formulas, when they are translations their tautological status does not reliably transfer to the translated propositional forms.

We now turn to the related argument forms for the first two paradoxes.

6.5$_\supset$. $(p \supset (q \supset p))$

and

6.5′$_\supset$. $$\frac{p}{\therefore \quad (q \supset p)}$$

6.6$_\supset$. $(\sim p \supset (p \supset q))$

and

6.6′$_\supset$. $$\frac{\sim p}{\therefore \quad (p \supset q)}$$

Classical evaluations of 6.5′$_\supset$ and 6.6′$_\supset$ give no reliable evaluation of translated ordinary language arguments.

This is borne out by the following considerations. Given:

R = *It will rain.*
C = *The match will be cancelled.*

then consider the following arguments and their standard translations:

F.
$$\frac{not\ R}{\therefore\quad If\ R\ then\ C} \qquad\qquad \frac{\sim R}{\therefore\quad (R \supset C)}$$

and

G.
$$\frac{not\ R}{\therefore\quad If\ R\ then\ not\ C} \qquad\qquad \frac{\sim R}{\therefore\quad (R \supset \sim C)}$$

The translated arguments on the right are both valid in classical logic.

Of the abbreviated ordinary language arguments on the left Jackson writes that both are surely invalid, certainly at first sight. Of the first he writes:

> From the mere fact that it will not rain, I cannot infer that if it rains, the match will be cancelled. ... I could equally infer from the fact that it will not rain, that if it rains, the match will *not* be cancelled, and surely it is absurd to maintain *together* both "If it rains, the match will be cancelled" and "If it rains, the match will not be cancelled", even if I hold that it will in fact not rain.   (1987: 5)

And we might add that this can be made even more pointed with:

H.
$$\frac{not\ R}{\therefore\quad If\ R\ then\ both\ C\ and\ not\ C} \qquad\qquad \frac{\sim R}{\therefore\quad (R \supset (C\ \&\ \sim C))}$$

To extend Jackson's comments we might add that from the mere fact that it will not rain, I surely cannot infer that if it rains the match will be both cancelled and not cancelled. The ordinary language argument on the left is invalid. But the standard translation on the right is valid.

The third paradox says that for any two propositions whatsoever, either the first implies the second or the second implies the first. The fourth says that any proposition, say q, will be either the consequent of a true conditional or the antecedent of a true conditional.

All of this adds up to a very serious problem for using logics. Jackson forwards a case for saying that the problem is illusory for these paradoxes of material implication.

When we turn to those logical systems that do not attribute theoremhood to the paradoxes, suitably transformed, we still face the unreliability issues for attribution of theoremhood. But not all the systems attribute theoremhood. The table below shows the situation. "T" is for "is a theorem or tautology" and "NT" for "is not a theorem or tautology."

		CL	S1	C$^+$	RM
6.5	$(p \Rightarrow (q \Rightarrow p))$	T	NT	NT	NT
6.6	$(\sim p \Rightarrow (p \Rightarrow q))$	T	NT	NT	NT
6.7	$((p \Rightarrow q) \vee (q \Rightarrow p))$	T	NT	NT	T
6.8	$((p \Rightarrow q) \vee (q \Rightarrow r))$	T	NT	NT	T

In accordance with P3 and P4, and given entailments as set out above, the attributions of theoremhood are all unreliable, but the attributions of non-theoremhood are reliable. So we might well say of the paradoxes that the systems (other than C) tell us the pre-translation paradoxes are not theorems. There are similar outcomes for the related argument forms for the first two paradoxes. Jackson's initial intuitions about those argument forms are very well based and supported by several logical analyses.

14.6 Defending the material conditional

Many philosophers have defended the material conditional as the correct and reliable translation of *If … then …* conditionals. One line has been mentioned already. It is the abstraction line of defence in which it is claimed that logics, especially classical propositional logic, are not artificial languages. They are abstractions from ordinary language and reveal the *real* underlying logical structure of ordinary language.

In response it needs to be pointed out that while the process of creating logics might rely on abstraction from ordinary language, the resultant logic takes on a life of its own with recursively defined formulas, semantics and deduction systems. None of this is to be found in ordinary language. Furthermore, one might ask what has been shed in the abstraction, and how one checks that the abstraction has not left pared away a vital element of the original. Our claim would be that if it is a correct abstraction then there should be no failures of reliability. So, if it is an abstraction, classical propositional logic is a faulty and misleading one that has pared away vital elements, especially when it comes to conditionals.

One counter to our response would be that when we consider arguments such as B, the figures on the board argument, we are simply wrong about its being invalid. There is an *illusion* of invalidity that can be accounted for in terms of either context, assertibility or some other communication dimension.

These responses and all their casuistry depend crucially on the idea that there is an *illusion* of invalidity. In other words, the argument is really valid. This line of reasoning can be maintained only if we assume that people do not really know what they mean when they make statements such as "If the figure on the board is a rectangle then it has six sides". In particular, we are asked to accept that people are not able correctly to assign the truth-value *false* to this statement. The same apples to the example in *INCL*: "If John is in Paris then he is in Italy." But we all know that both of these are false.

So, we claim the opposite. It is against the highly reliable assignment of truth to the statements above that the material conditional should be measured, not the other way around. The material conditional analysis and subsequent use in translation do not add up.

The same applies to the case of the negated conditional. It is simply not true that when a person denies a conditional that they are catagorically asserting the truth of its antecedent. The whole point of an ordinary conditional is its hypothetical dimension. Denying its truth is also a non-categorical matter. To argue that it is categorical is akin to the modal fallacy of assuming that the modal operator in *If Socrates is human then he **must** be mortal* has only the consequent as its scope rather than the whole conditional. The one thing that really rings true about the creation of modal logic to deal with negated conditionals is the idea that the negation of a conditional, *It is not true that if p then q* is equivalent to or very much like *It is possible that p and not q*.

The defence of the material conditional often relies on the distinction between indicative conditionals and subjunctive conditionals. On many occasions the subjunctive is used to emphasize the counter-factual nature of the conditional under consideration, especially when it is being denied. A counter-factual conditional is one where it is clear that the antecedent is false. An example is: *If Queen Anne had given birth to a male heir, then there would have been no pressure to bring the Pretender to the throne.* We know that the antecedent is false. Someone might deny the conditional in a speculative and hypothetical sense. They might point to the general antipathy in Britain to having a German King, and to the subsequent events that led to the 1745 rebellion by some of the Scots. But there is no way that such a denial involves the assertion that Queen Anne did give birth to a male heir. The material conditional will just not do for the translation of the conditional, so something else is required.

But, it is not clear that a distinction can be drawn between the indicative and counter-factual conditional. One might draw an analogy between the use of "and" and the use of "but" in the assertion of conjunctions. *John was very drunk but quite steady on his feet.* The use of "but" indicates that the second conjunct is unexpected given the first. Nonetheless, both conjuncts are true. The unexpectedness does not lead us to say that there are indicative and subjunctive conjunctions and the former have a logic different to the latter.

Priest points out that when we compare conditionals in order to claim that there is a definite indicative–subjunctive divide, the examples have other differences that actually make the distinction. The difference is not in the conditionality. His example is (with his numbering):

(1) *If Oswald didn't shoot Kennedy someone else did.* (True)
(2) *If Oswald hadn't shot Kennedy someone else would have.* (False)

The differences that result in differing truth evaluations are actually dependent on *time* rather than conditionality.

Thus we evaluate (1) as true from the present, where Kennedy has, in fact, been shot. The difference of tense and mood of (2) asks us to to evaluate the conditional "If Oswald doesn't shoot Kennedy, someone else will" from the perspective of a time just before Kennedy was shot. It is, in a certain sense, the past tense of the conditional. Notice that no difference of kind between (1) and (2) arises in the case of present-tense conditionals. There is no major difference between "If I shoot you, you will die" and "If I were to shoot you, you would die" (Priest 2008: 12).

14.7 Conclusion

There is no real conclusion. and there is certainly no closure. We have not looked at the spherical semantics accounts of conditionals given by Lewis and Stalnaker. The reader is invited to look further. The search for a reliable account of conditionals continues.

References and further reading

Anderson, A. R. & N. D. Belnap 1975. *Entailment: The Logic of Relevance and Necessity*. Princeton, NJ: Princeton University Press.

Gabbay, D. M. & J. Woods 2003. *Agenda Relevance: A Study in Formal Pragmatics*. North Holland: Amsterdam.

Girle, R. A. 2007. *Introduction to Logic*, 2nd edn. Auckland: Pearson Educational [esp. Ch. 6].

Jackson, F. 1987. *Conditionals*. Oxford: Basil Blackwell.

Jackson, F. (ed.) 1991. *Conditionals*. Oxford: Oxford University Press.

Priest, G. 2008. *An Introduction to Non-Classical Logic*, 2nd edn. Cambridge: Cambridge University Press [esp. Ch. 5].

Routley, R., with R. K. Meyer, V. Plumwood & R. T. Brady 1982. *Relevant Logics and Their Rivals 1*. Atascadero, CA: Ridgeview.

Staines, P. J. 1981. "Some Formal Aspects of the Argument-Symbolization Relation". *Australian Logic Teachers' Journal* 5(3) (August): 1–17.

Staines, P. & R. A. Girle 1992. "The Reliability of Formal Systems". *Proceedings of the Fifth Australian Joint Artificial Intelligence Conference*, 16–18 November, A. Adams & L. Sterling (eds), 272–7. Hobart: World Scientific.

CHAPTER 15
Synthesis and worlds

15.1 Introduction

In this final chapter we shall look at some of the gains that come from combining modal logics. We shall also look at the question of the status of possible worlds.

15.2 Multiple modality

There is great interest, particularly in the artificial intelligence community, in combining some of the logics we have considered. There are advantages when we just look at single propositions. For example:

1. *Anne has forgotten that the capital of Australia is Canberra.*

can be taken as asserting that, at some time in the past, Anne knew that Canberra is the capital of Australia (*Ac*), but that now she does not know it. A combined temporal and epistemic translation would be:

1′. $PK_aAc \ \& \sim K_aAc$

Other examples are:

2. *Chris believes that he can trisect the angle, but I know that it is impossible for him to do it.*
2′. $B_c \Diamond T \ \& \ K_i \sim \Diamond T$
3. *Every time we have marked the examination scripts for this group of students there has been evidence of cheating.*

3'. $H[m]C$
4. *The Head of Department believes that there is always going to be evidence of cheating.*
4'. $B_b G C$
5. *There was a time when Bob was obliged to give money to the committee.*
5'. $PO_b G$
6. *Everybody knows that it is not possible for anyone to jump seven metres.*

This proposition requires quantification over the agents of knowledge. Our epistemic logic has not extended to this, but let's just try it anyway.

6'. $(\forall x)(Px \supset K_x \sim\Diamond (\exists y)(Py \ \& \ Jy))$

It is fairly obvious that it would be a good idea to extend epistemic logic in this way. The same will certainly apply to deontic logic.

7. *Everybody knows that no one should ever steal anything.*
7'. $(\forall x)(Px \supset K_x L (\forall y)(Py \supset O_y \sim(\exists z)ySz))$
8. *If I ought to give to the poor, then I ought to either give to the poor or burn my money.* (from Chapter 13)
8'. $(O_i LG \supset (O_i LG \vee O_i LB))$ or
8''. $L (O_i G \supset (O_i G \vee O_i B))$
9. *Some people believe some contradictions.*
9'. $(\exists x)(Px \ \& \ B_x (p \ \& \sim p))$

This is not really satisfactory. This says that some person believes $(p \ \& \sim p)$. But the formula is not really any particular contradiction. It is the form of many contradictions. We need to be able to say that there are some propositions that are contradictions, and some people believe them. Let's try [$Sx = x$ *is a proposition; $Cx = x$ is a contradiction*]:

9''. $(\exists x)(Px \ \& \ (\exists y)(Sy \ \& \ Cy \ \& \ B_x y))$

But, we have made a variable of quantification, y, the content of belief. It might be better if we simply quantified over propositions:

9'''. $(\exists x)(Px \ \& \ (\exists p)B_x(p \ \& \sim p))$

This looks fine, but there is a problem. When we start quantifying over propositions then we have moved to what is known as "higher order logic." There are problems with higher order logic that are beyond our scope here. We have touched on this kind of logic. It looks interesting. But we should back off at this point.

The reader is encouraged to investigate further.

15.3 Possible worlds

This text cannot finish without some remarks about the status of possible worlds. There are at least three views on their status. The first and very controversial view is that possible worlds are real, just as real as the world we live in. The distinction is that the world we live in is *actual*, and all other possible worlds are *not actual*. The proponents of this view are said to be *modal realists* and their view is *modal realism*. David Lewis was the major twentieth-century proponent of this doctrine.

Some see modal realism as the doctrine that there are *parallel* worlds, worlds existing parallel to the actual world, worlds in which there are real objects, spaces and times. Some of these worlds are very like the actual world, some are radically different. Lewis would agree in a way, but held that there is no physical or spatiotemporal traffic between possible worlds, parallel or not, like or unlike. They run parallel in logical space not in some sort of meta-spatiotemporal space. Lewis would not have much sympathy with the principles assumed to underlie a television series such as *Sliders*, where people can shift from reality to reality. It is the shifting/sliding that Lewis would object to. But he would be happy with the idea of like worlds in parallel with ours.

The second view is that possible worlds are real, but real in the sense that *abstract objects* are real. They have much the same status as mathematical objects such as numbers, sets, algebraic entities and other such abstract objects.

The third view is that possible worlds are simply the objects of imagination or belief. This view could be labelled the *epistemic* view. Interestingly enough, one of the major direct uses of possible world semantics is to be found in epistemic and doxastic logic where Hintikka uses sets of sentences or propositions, the objects belief and knowledge and imagination, as the interpretation of possible worlds.

The epistemic view is given support in several areas of the application of modal logic and in the related logics of belief revision.

This text is not intended to provide even a partial discussion of these views. The reader who is interested should pursue the topic in the vast and readily available literature.

15.4 Concluding remarks

There are many questions that have been left for the reader to investigate further. The task of applying modal logic is ongoing. New systems are being generated to try to meet new needs. You are invited to participate.

References and further reading

Baader, F. and Schultz, K. (eds) 1996. *Proceedings of FroCoS'96*, Applied Logic Series, Kluwer.

Bradley, R. & N. Swartz 1979. *Possible Worlds*. Oxford: Blackwell.

Girle, R. 2003. *Possible Worlds*. Chesham: Acumen.

Girle, R. A. 1978. "Logics for Knowledge, Possiblity and Existence". *Notre Dame Journal of Formal Logic* 19: 200–214.

Answers

In what follows I provide solutions to some exercises and answers to some. In particular, I provide solutions to at least the first of any particular sort of question.

Chapter 2

2.3 Exercises

1. All trees close. We set out five sample solutions.

(a) 1. $\sim(\Box p \supset p)$ (n)   NTF
     2. $\Box p$ (n)   1, PC
     3. $\sim p$ (n)   1, PC
     4. p (n)   2, $\Box$T
                ×

(b) 1. $\sim(\Diamond p \supset \Box \Diamond p)$ (n)   NTF
     2. $\Diamond p$ (n)   1, PC
     3. $\sim\Box\Diamond p$ (n)   1, PC
     4. $\Diamond\sim\Diamond p$ (n)   3, MN
     5. $\sim\Diamond p$ (k)   4, $\Diamond$S5
     6. $\Box\sim p$ (k)   5, MN
     7. p (l)   2, $\Diamond$S5
     8. $\sim p$ (l)   6, $\Box$S5
                ×

(d) 1. $\sim(\Box(p \supset q) \supset \Box(\Box p \supset \Box q))$ (n)   NTF
     2. $\Box(p \supset q)$ (n)   1, PC
     3. $\sim\Box(\Box p \supset \Box q)$ (n)   1, PC

4.	$\Diamond \sim (\Box p \supset \Box q)$	(n)	3, **MN**
5.	$\sim (\Box p \supset \Box q)$	(k)	4, $\Diamond$**S5**
6.	$\Box p$	(k)	5, **PC**
7.	$\sim \Box q$	(k)	5, **PC**
8.	$\Diamond \sim q$	(k)	7, **MN**
9.	$\sim q$	(l)	8, $\Diamond$**S5**
10.	p	(l)	6, $\Box$**S5**
11.	$(p \supset q)$	(l)	2, $\Box$**S5**

12. $\sim p$ (l) ——— q (l)
      ×   ×

(g) 1. $\sim (\Box (p \,\&\, q) \equiv (\Box p \,\&\, \Box q))$ (n)   NTF

2. $\Box (p \,\&\, q)$ (n) —— $\sim \Box (p \,\&\, q)$ (n)
3. $\sim (\Box p \,\&\, \Box q)$ (n) $(\Box p \,\&\, \Box q)$ (n)
                                          $\Box p$ (n)
4. $\sim \Box p$ (n) —— $\sim \Box q$ (n) $\Box q$ (n)
5. $\Diamond \sim p$ (n) $\Diamond \sim q$ (n) $\Diamond \sim (p \,\&\, q)$ (n)
6. $\sim p$ (k) $\sim q$ (l) $\sim (p \,\&\, q)$ (m)
7. $(p \,\&\, q)$ (k) $(p \,\&\, q)$ (l) p (m)
8. p (k) p (l) q (m)
9. q (k) q (l)
10. ×   × $\sim p$ (m) —— $\sim q$ (m)
                                    ×   ×

(h) 1. $\sim (\Box (\sim p \supset p) \equiv \Box p)$ (n)   NTF

2. $\Box (\sim p \supset p)$ (n) —— $\sim \Box (\sim p \supset p)$ (n)   1, **PC**
3. $\sim \Box p$ (n) $\Box p$ (n)   1, **PC**
4. $\Diamond \sim p$ (n) $\Diamond \sim (\sim p \supset p)$ (n)   3, 2, **MN**
5. $\sim p$ (k) $\sim (\sim p \supset p)$ (l)
6. $(\sim p \supset p)$ (k) p (l)
7. $\sim p$ (l)
8. $\sim\sim p$ (k) —— p (k) $\sim p$ (l)
9. p (k)   ×   ×
     ×

2. All the arguments are valid. We set out translations.

(a) $\sim \Diamond (A \,\&\, T), A / \therefore \sim T$

(b) $\Box (R \supset M), (M \supset G), \sim G / \therefore \sim R$

(c) $\Box (M \supset A), \sim A / \therefore \sim M$ (the "must" modifies the "since")

(d) $\sim \Diamond (A \,\&\, U) / \therefore \Box (U \supset \sim A)$

(e) $(\Diamond S \supset S), \sim \Diamond (S \,\&\, \sim H), \Diamond S / \therefore H$

2.4 Exercises

1.

(a) S5-Valid

1.	$\sim(p \supset \Box\Diamond p)$	(n)	NTF
2.	p	(n)	1, **PC**
3.	$\sim\Box\Diamond p$	(n)	1, **PC**
4.	$\Diamond\sim\Diamond p$	(n)	3, **MN**
5.	$\sim\Diamond p$	(k)	4, $\Diamond$**S5**
6.	$\Box\sim p$	(k)	5, **MN**
7.	$\sim p$	(n)	6, $\Box$**S5**
	$\times$		

(b) S5-Invalid. A counter-example is:

$p\,(n) = 0$; $p\,(k) = 1$; $p\,(l) = 0$

$\Diamond p\,(n) = 1$ [since $p\,(k) = 1$ i.e. 1 in at least one world]

$\Diamond p\,(k) = 1$ [since $p\,(k) = 1$]

$\Diamond p\,(l) = 1$ [since $p\,(k) = 1$]

So $\Box\Diamond p\,(n) = 1$ [since $\Diamond p = 1$ in every world]

$\Box p\,(n) = 0$ [since $p\,(n) = 0$ i.e. 0 in at least one world]

$\Box p\,(k) = 0$ [since $p\,(n) = 0$]

$\Box p\,(l) = 0$ [since $p\,(n) = 0$]

So $\Diamond\Box p\,(n) = 0$ [since $\Box p$ is not true in any world]

So $(\Box\Diamond p \supset \Diamond\Box p)\,(n) = (1 \supset 0)\,(n) = 0\,(n)$

(c)   S5-Valid

(d)   S5-Invalid. A counter-example is: $p\,(n) = 1$; $q\,(n) = 1$

(e)   S5-Invalid. A counter-example is: $p\,(n) = 1$; $p\,(k) = 1$

                                                  $q\,(n) = 1$; $q\,(k) = 0$

(f)   S5-Valid

(g)   S5-Valid

(h)   S5-Valid

(i)   S5-Valid

(j)   S5-Invalid A counter-example is: $p\,(n) = 1$

Chapter 3

3.3 Exercises

In both 1 and 2, all parts should have an appropriate closed tree. All the trees for 1 should be **K** trees. Trees for 1a and 2a, 2c and 2j are set out below.

2.   (a) S5   (b) S5   (c) S5   (d) S4   (e) S5

         (f) S5   (g) T   (h) S5   (i) S5   (j) S4

We now set out for the four trees.

1.

(a)

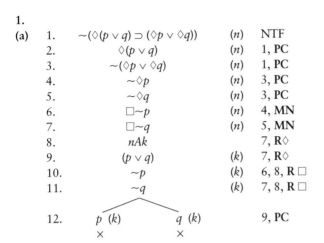

1.	~(◇(p ∨ q) ⊃ (◇p ∨ ◇q))	(n)	NTF
2.	◇(p ∨ q)	(n)	1, PC
3.	~(◇p ∨ ◇q)	(n)	1, PC
4.	~◇p	(n)	3, PC
5.	~◇q	(n)	3, PC
6.	□~p	(n)	4, MN
7.	□~q	(n)	5, MN
8.	nAk		7, R◇
9.	(p ∨ q)	(k)	7, R◇
10.	~p	(k)	6, 8, R□
11.	~q	(k)	7, 8, R□
12.	p (k) q (k)		9, PC
	× ×		

All the tree rules used were **K** rules.

2.

(a)

1.	~(□(□(p ⊃ □p) ⊃ □p) ⊃ (◇□p ⊃ □p))	(n)	NTF
2.	□(□(p ⊃ □p) ⊃ □p)	(n)	1, PC
3.	~(◇□p ⊃ □p))	(n)	1, PC
4.	◇□p	(n)	3, PC
5.	~□p	(n)	3, PC
6.	◇~p	(n)	5, MN
7.	nAk		6, R◇
8.	~p	(k)	6, R◇
9.	nAl		4, R◇
10.	□p	(l)	4, R◇
11.	p	(l)	10, □ T

We need to be able to get the *p* from □*p* in line 10 into world *k* in order to close the tree. (Don't be diverted by the big antecedent in line 2: it is irrelevant.) It is clear that **T** rules will not do the trick. Nor will **S4**. We need **S5**.

12.	p	(k)	10, □S5
	×		

S5-Valid.

(c)

1.	~(◇□p ⊃ p)	(n)	NTF
2.	◇□p	(n)	1, PC
3.	~p	(n)	1, PC
4.	nAk		2, R◇
5.	□p	(k)	2, R□
6.	p	(k)	5, □T

But the tree will not close with either **T** or **S4** rules. So we try the orthodox **Sym** rule for **S5**:

7.	kAn		4, **Sym**
8.	p	(n)	7, 5, **R** $\square$
	$\times$		8, 3

S5-Valid.

(j)

| 1. | $\sim(\square\Diamond p \equiv \square\Diamond\square\Diamond p)$ | | (n) | NTF |

2.	$\square\Diamond p$ (n)	$\sim\square\Diamond p$ (n)
3.	$\sim\square\Diamond\square\Diamond p$ (n)	$\square\Diamond\square\Diamond p$ (n)
4.	$\Diamond\sim\Diamond\square\Diamond p$ (n)	$\Diamond\sim\Diamond p$ (n)
5.	nAk	nAk
6.	$\sim\Diamond\square\Diamond p$ (k)	$\sim\Diamond p$ (k)
7.	$\square\sim\square\Diamond p$ (k)	$\square\sim p$ (k)
8.	$\Diamond p$ (k)	$\Diamond\square\Diamond p$ (k)
9.	kAl	kAl
10.	p (l)	$\square\Diamond p$ (l)
11.	$\sim\square\Diamond p$ (l)	$\Diamond p$ (l)
12.	$\Diamond\sim\Diamond p$ (l)	lAm
13.	lAm	p (m)
14.	$\sim\Diamond p$ (m)	

The access in the **left path** is nAk, kAl and lAm. Only if access is *transitive* can we get nAm. The left path closes if, and only if, the access were nAm and the $\square\Diamond p$ (n) on line 2 was resolved to $\Diamond p$ (m).

The access in the **right path** is nAk, kAl and lAm. Only if access is *transitive* can we get kAm. The right path closes if, and only if, the access were kAm and the $\square\sim p$ (k) on line 7 was resolved to $\sim p$ (m).

T rules will not do the job. So we apply **S4** rules according to the orthodox strategy.

14.	$\sim\Diamond p$ (m)	kAm	(**Trans**)
15.	nAm	$\sim p$ (m)	
16.	$\Diamond p$ (m)	$\times$	
17.	$\times$		

S4-Valid

3.4 Exercises

1.

(a) p $(n) = q$ $(n) = r$ $(n) = s$ $(n) = 0$

(b) p $(n) = q$ $(n) = 1$; p $(k) = q$ $(k) = 0$; p $(l) = q$ $(l) = 1$

(c) p $(n) = 0$; q $(n) = 1$; p $(k) = 1$; q $(k) = 0$

(d) $p(n) = 0; q(n) = 1; p(k) = 0; q(k) = 1; p(l) = q(l) = 1; p(m) = q(m) = 1;$
$p(i) = 0; p(i) = 1$

(e) $p(n) = 0; q(n) = 1; p(k) = 1; q(k) = 0$

2.   The accessibility relation has to be set out in this and the rest of the questions in 3.

(a) $p(n) = 0; q(n) = 1; p(k) = q(k) = 1; p(l) = q(l) = 0;$
$nAn; kAk; lAl; nAk; kAl; nAl$
n has access to *n*, *k* and *l*
k has access to *k* and *l*
l has access to *l*
$\Diamond p(l) = 0$ [Since the only world to which *l* has access is *l*]
$(\Diamond p \,\&\, {\sim}q)(n) = (\Diamond p \,\&\, {\sim}q)(k) = 0$
$(\Diamond p \,\&\, {\sim}q)(l) = (0 \,\&\, 1)(l) = 0$
$\Diamond(\Diamond p \,\&\, {\sim}q)(n) = 0$
[Since $(\Diamond p \,\&\, {\sim}q)$ is false in all worlds to which (n) has access]
$\Box q(n) = 0; \Box q(k) = 0; \Box q(l) = 0$
$(p \,\&\, \Box q)(n) = 0; (p \,\&\, \Box q)(k) = 0; (p \,\&\, \Box q)(l) = 0$
$\Box(p \,\&\, \Box q)(n) = 0$
So we have an **S4** counter-example.

(b) $p(n) = q(n) = 1; p(k) = 1; q(k) = 0; p(l) = 0; q(l) = 1;$
$nAn; kAk; lAl; nAk; nAl$

(c) $p(n) = 1; p(k) = 0; p(m) = 1$
$nAn; kAk; mAm; nAk; nAm$

3.
(a) $p(n) = q(n) = 1; p(k) = q(k) = 1; p(m) = q(m) = 0;$
$nAk; kAm; nAn; kAk; mAm$
$\Box p(n) = 1$ [Since the worlds to which *n* has access are *n* and *k*]
$\Box q(n) = 1$ [Since the worlds to which *n* has access are *n* and *k*]
So, $(\Box p \lor \Box q)(n) = 1$
$\Box p(k) = 0$ [Since the worlds to which *k* has access are *k* and *m*]
$\Box q(k) = 0$ [Since the worlds to which *k* has access are *k* and *m*]
So, $(\Box p \lor \Box q)(k) = 0$
So, $\Box(\Box p \lor \Box q)(n) = 0$
So, the formula has a true right-hand expression and a false left, so we have a
T counter-example.

(b) $p(n) = q(n) = 1; p(k) = q(k) = 1; p(m) = 1; q(m) = 0;$
$nAk; kAm; nAn; kAk; mAm$

(c) $p(n) = 1; p(k) = 1; p(m) = 0;$
$nAk; kAm; nAn; kAk; mAm$
$\Diamond p(n) = \Diamond p(k) = 1; \Diamond p(m) = 0;$
$\Box\Diamond p(n) = 1; \Box\Diamond p(k) = \Box\Diamond p(m) = 0;$

[Note the true LHE in n]

$\Diamond\Box\Diamond p$ $(n) = 1$; $\Diamond\Box\Diamond p$ $(k) = \Diamond\Box\Diamond p$ $(m) = 0$;

$\Box\Diamond\Box\Diamond p$ $(n) = \Box\Diamond\Box\Diamond p$ $(k) = \Box\Diamond\Box\Diamond p$ $(m) = 0$;

So, the formula has a true left-hand expression and a false right, so we have a T counter-example.

Chapter 4

4.4 Exercises

1.

(a)

1.	$\sim(\Box\Box p \supset \Box\Box(q \supset p))$	(n)	NTF, $n \in \mathbf{N}$
2.	$\Box\Box p$	(n)	
3.	$\sim\Box\Box\,(q \supset p)$	(n)	
4.	$\Diamond\sim\Box(q \supset p)$	(n)	3, MN
5.	nAk		4, $\Diamond$RN
6.	$\sim\Box(q \supset p)$	(k)	4, $\Diamond$RN
7.	$\Diamond\sim(q \supset p)$	(k)	6, MN
8.	$\Box p$	(k)	2, 5, $\Box$RN
9.	kAl		7, 8, $\Diamond$RS2
10.	$\sim(q \supset p)$	(l)	7, 8, $\Diamond$RS2
11.	q	(l)	
12.	$\sim p$	(l)	
13.	nAl		5, 9, Trans
14.	$\Box p$	(l)	2, 13, $\Box$ RS2
15.	p	(l)	14, $\Box$T
	×		

The formula is S3-Valid but not S2-Valid. In S2 lines 13–15 would be missing and the tree not close.

(b) S2-Valid   (c) S0.5-Valid.
(d) S2-Valid.   (e) S0.5-Valid.

4.5 Exercises

1. Since (a) is S3-Valid but not S2-Valid it will not be S1-Valid. Since (c), (d) and (e) are S0.5-Valid, they will be S1-Valid. This leaves (b) which is S2-Valid. Is it S1-Valid?

(b)

1.	$\sim (\Box\Box p \supset \Box\Box(p \supset p))$	(n)	NTF
2.	$\Box\Box p$	(n)	1
3.	$\sim\Box\Box(p \supset p)$	(n)	1
4.	$\Diamond\sim\Box(p \supset p)$	(n)	3, MN
5.	nAk		4, ($\Diamond$RN)
6.	$\sim\Box(p \supset p)$	(k)	4, ($\Diamond$RN)

7.	$\Box p$	(k)	2, 5, ($\Box$RN)
8.	$\Diamond \sim (p \supset p)$	(k)	6, MN

We cannot go further in **S0.5**.
It is not **S0.5**-Valid. So, for **S1**:

9.	$\sim (p \supset p)$ (k)		not $kN \mid \sim\sim (p \supset p) \mid$			8, (S1R$\Diamond$)
10.	p	(k) 9	$kN \mid p \mid$			7, (S1R$\Box$)
11.	$\sim p$	(k) 9				
12.	$\times$		$\sim\sim (p \supset p)$ (l)	p	(l)	9, 10, NN
13.			$\sim p$ (l)	$\sim (p \supset p)$ (l)		9, 10, NN
14.			$\uparrow$			

Since this **S1** tree will not close, the formula is not **S1**-Valid.

4.6 Exercises

1. All are valid in **E2**, so all will have *two* closed trees.

(e) Consider the tree above for 3.3, 1(a). The **E2** trees for both **N** and **Q** worlds will be the same as that tree.

4.7 Exercises

1.

(a)

1.	$\Box (p \supset q)$	(nP)	Pr
2.	$\Box p$	(nP)	Pr
3.	$\sim \Box q$	(n)	NC
4.	$\Diamond \sim q$	(n)	3, MN
5.	$\sim q$	(k)	4, $\Diamond$PN
6.	$\Box (p \supset q)$	(k)	1, $\Box$PN
7.	$\Box p$	(k)	2, $\Box$PN

The tree will not close in **N**. But in **T**, because we have the standard rule for $\Box$, it will close:

5.	nAk		
6.	$\sim q$	(k)	4, $\Diamond$R
7.	$(p \supset q)$	(k)	1, 5, $\Box$R
8.	p	(k)	2, 5, $\Box$R

by standard propositional logic.

(b) The same situation applies as in (a).

(c)

1.	$\Box p$	(nP)	Pr
2.	$\sim \Box\Box p$	(n)	NC
3.	$\Diamond \sim \Box p$	(n)	2, MN
4.	$\sim \Box p$	(k)	3, $\Diamond$PN
5.	$\Box p$	(k)	1, $\Box$PN
	$\times$		

The argument is valid in **N** but not in **T**. It will, of course, be valid in **S4**.

(d)   This is not valid in **N**, but is valid in **T**.
(e)   This is valid in **N**, but is not valid in T.

Chapter 5

5.8 Exercises

1.   Solution for 3.3 Exercises, **2(d)**

To prove: $(\Box(p \equiv q) \supset \Box(\Box p \equiv \Box q))$ is S4-Valid:

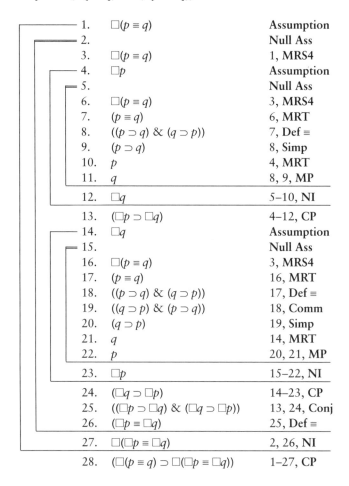

1.	$\Box(p \equiv q)$		**Assumption**
2.			**Null Ass**
3.	$\Box(p \equiv q)$		1, **MRS4**
4.	$\Box p$		**Assumption**
5.			**Null Ass**
6.	$\Box(p \equiv q)$		3, **MRS4**
7.	$(p \equiv q)$		6, **MRT**
8.	$((p \supset q) \mathbin{\&} (q \supset p))$		7, **Def** $\equiv$
9.	$(p \supset q)$		8, **Simp**
10.	p		4, **MRT**
11.	q		8, 9, **MP**
12.	$\Box q$		5–10, **NI**
13.	$(\Box p \supset \Box q)$		4–12, **CP**
14.	$\Box q$		**Assumption**
15.			**Null Ass**
16.	$\Box(p \equiv q)$		3, **MRS4**
17.	$(p \equiv q)$		16, **MRT**
18.	$((p \supset q) \mathbin{\&} (q \supset p))$		17, **Def** $\equiv$
19.	$((q \supset p) \mathbin{\&} (p \supset q))$		18, **Comm**
20.	$(q \supset p)$		19, **Simp**
21.	q		14, **MRT**
22.	p		20, 21, **MP**
23.	$\Box p$		15–22, **NI**
24.	$(\Box q \supset \Box p)$		14–23, **CP**
25.	$((\Box p \supset \Box q) \mathbin{\&} (\Box q \supset \Box p))$		13, 24, **Conj**
26.	$(\Box p \equiv \Box q)$		25, **Def** $\equiv$
27.	$\Box(\Box p \equiv \Box q)$		2, 26, **NI**
28.	$(\Box(p \equiv q) \supset \Box(\Box p \equiv \Box q))$		1–27, **CP**

Theorem Schema 3

To prove $(\sim A \supset (A \supset B))$:

	1.	$\sim A$	Assumption
	2.	A	Assumption
	3.	$(A \lor B)$	2, **Add**
	4.	B	1, 3, **DS**
	5.	$(A \supset B)$	2–4, **CP**
	6.	$(\sim A \supset (A \supset B))$	1–5, **CP**

Chapter 6

6.3 Exercises

1. All are theorems, and I show the proof for **(a)** only. The remainder are left for the reader (you might find it helpful to read G. E. Hughes & M. J. Cresswell, *A New Introduction to Modal Logic* [London & New York: Routledge, 1996]).

(a)
1.	$(\sim\Diamond(\sim p \,\&\, \sim q) \prec \sim\Diamond(\sim p \,\&\, \sim q))$	T1, $(\sim\Diamond(\sim p \,\&\, \sim q)/p)$
2.	$((p \,\&\, q) \prec (p \,\&\, q))$	S1.1
3.	$((q \,\&\, p) \prec (p \,\&\, q))$	2, $(p/q)\ (q/p)$
4.	$(((p \,\&\, q) \prec (q \,\&\, p)) \,\&\, ((q \,\&\, p) \prec (p \,\&\, q)))$	2, 3, *Adjunction*
5.	$((p \,\&\, q) \equiv (q \,\&\, p))$	4, Def $\equiv$
6.	$((\sim p \,\&\, \sim q) \equiv (\sim q \,\&\, \sim p))$	5, S1.R1 $(\sim p/p)\ (\sim q/q)$
7.	$(\sim\Diamond(\sim p \,\&\, \sim q) \prec \sim\Diamond(\sim q \,\&\, \sim p))$	1, 6, S1.R2
8.	$((\sim p \prec p) \prec (\sim q \prec p))$	7, Def $\prec$

6.4.1 Exercises

1. **MP'**$_>$
1.	p	(n)	**Pr**
2.	$(p > q)$	(n)	**Pr**
3.	$\sim q$	(n)	**NC**
	$\uparrow$		

Nothing can be done. So the argument, surprisingly, is invalid in C. **MT'**$_>$, **Contra'**$_>$, and **HS'**$_>$ are invalid in C.

2. **Para1**$_>$
1.	$\sim(p > (q > p))$	(n)	**NC**
2.	$nA_p k$		1, $\sim{>}$R
3.	$\sim(q > p)$	(k)	1, $\sim{>}$R
4.	$kA_p m$		3, $\sim{>}$R
5.	$\sim p$	(m)	3, $\sim{>}$R
	$\uparrow$		

So, **Para1**$_>$ is not a theorem of C, nor are any of the other three.

6.4.2 Exercises

1. **UP′$_>$.**

1.	p	(n)	Pr
2.	$\sim q$	(n)	Pr
3.	$\sim (p > q)$	(n)	NC
4.	$nA_p k$		$3, \sim>R^+$
5.	$p\ (k)$		$3, \sim>R^+$
6.	$\sim q\ (k)$		$3, \sim>R^+$
	$\uparrow$		

So, **UP′$_>$** is invalid in **C$^+$** as is **UPCon′$_>$**.

MP′$_>$

1.	p	(n)	Pr
2.	$(p > q)$	(n)	Pr
3.	$\sim q$	(n)	NC

4.	$\sim p$	(n)	p	(n)		2, Refl
5.	$\times$		$nA_p n$			2, Refl
6.			q	(n)		2, 5, $>$R
			$\times$			

So **MP′$_>$** is valid in **C$^+$**.
Wk′$_>$, **Contra′$_>$**, and **HS′$_>$** are invalid in **C$^+$**.

2. **Para1$_>$**

1.	$\sim (p > (q > p))$	(n)	NC
2.	$nA_p k$		$1, \sim>R^+$
3.	p	(k)	$1, \sim>R^+$
4.	$\sim (q > p)$	(k)	$1, \sim>R^+$
5.	$kA_p m$		$4, \sim>R^+$
6.	q	(m)	$4, \sim>R^+$
7.	$\sim p$	(m)	$4, \sim>R^+$
	$\uparrow$		

So, **Para1$_>$** is not a theorem of **C$^+$**, nor are any of the other three.

6.5.2 Exercises

1. **UP′$_\rightarrow$.**

1.	t p	(n)	Pr
2.	t $\sim q$	(n)	Pr
3.	nt $(p \rightarrow q)$	(n)	NC
4.	f q (n)		2, Neg
5.	nAk		3, nt$\rightarrow$

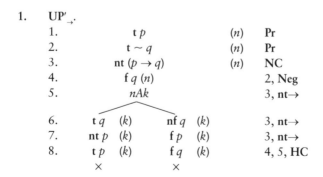

6.	t q	(k)	nf q	(k)	3, nt$\rightarrow$
7.	nt p	(k)	f p	(k)	3, nt$\rightarrow$
8.	t p	(k)	f q	(k)	4, 5, HC
	$\times$		$\times$		

So **UP'**$_\rightarrow$ is valid, as are **MP'**$_\rightarrow$, **MT'**$_\rightarrow$, **Contra'**$_\rightarrow$, and **HS'**$_\rightarrow$. For **Wk'**$_\rightarrow$ we have:

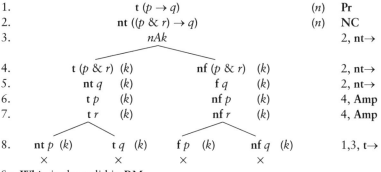

1.		**t** $(p \rightarrow q)$		(n)	**Pr**
2.		**nt** $((p \,\&\, r) \rightarrow q)$		(n)	**NC**
3.		nAk			2, **nt**$\rightarrow$
4.	**t** $(p \,\&\, r)$ (k)		**nf** $(p \,\&\, r)$ (k)		2, **nt**$\rightarrow$
5.	**nt** q (k)		**f** q (k)		2, **nt**$\rightarrow$
6.	**t** p (k)		**nf** p (k)		4, Amp
7.	**t** r (k)		**nf** r (k)		4, Amp
8.	**nt** p (k) **t** q (k)		**f** p (k) **nf** q (k)		1,3, **t**$\rightarrow$
	× ×		× ×		

So, **Wk'**$_\rightarrow$ is also valid in **RM**.

2. **Para2**$_\rightarrow$

1.		**nt** $(\sim p \rightarrow (p \rightarrow q))$		(n)	**NTF**
2.		nAk			1, **nt**$\rightarrow$
3.	**t** $\sim p$ (k)		**nf** $\sim p$ (k)		1, **nt**$\rightarrow$
4.	**nt** $(p \rightarrow q)$ (k)		**f** $(p \rightarrow q)$ (k)		1, **nt**$\rightarrow$
5.	**f** p (k)		**nt** p (k)		3, Neg
6.	kAm	4, **nt**$\rightarrow$	**t** p (k)		4, **f**$\rightarrow$
			f q (k)		4, **f**$\rightarrow$
7.	**t** p (m) **nf** p (m)		×		
8.	**nt** q (m) **f** q (m)				4, **nt**$\rightarrow$
9.	↑	×			

So, **Para2**$_\rightarrow$ is not a theorem. Note how in the last two trees the 'falsehood' paths close. That is because the **RM** tree rules for **f**$(\alpha \rightarrow \beta)$ are essentially classical.

Chapter 7

7.2 Exercises

1. All are valid, so each should have a closed tree. **(a)** is in the text: find it!

7.3 Exercises

1.

(a) S5QT-Invalid. A counter-example is:

$Fa\ (n) = 1$; $Fb\ (n) = 0$; $Fa\ (k) = 0$; $Fb\ (k) = 1$

$(\exists x)Fx\ (n) = (Fa \lor Fb)\ (n) = 1$ [by predicate logic]

$(\exists x)Fx\ (k) = (Fa \lor Fb)\ (k) = 1$ [by predicate logic]

So: $\Box(\exists x)Fx\ (n) = 1$ [since $(\exists x)Fx$ is true in all worlds]

$\Box Fa\ (n) = 0$ [since Fa is not true in all worlds]

$\Box Fb\ (n) = 0$ [since Fb is not true in all worlds]

So: $(\Box Fa \vee \Box Fb)\ (n) = 0\ (n)$

So: $(\exists x)\ \Box Fx\ (n) = (\Box Fa \vee \Box Fb)\ (n) = 0\ (n)$

So: $(\Box(\exists x)Fx \supset (\exists x)\ \Box Fx)\ (n) = (1 \supset 0)\ (n) = 0\ (n)$

(b)   S5QT-Invalid. A counter-example is:

$Fa\ (n) = 0;\ Fb\ (n) = 0;\ Fa\ (k) = 0;\ Fb\ (k) = 1$

(c)   S5QT-Valid

(d)   S5QT-Valid

(e)   S5QT-Invalid. A counter-example is:

$Ga\ (n) = 1;\ Fa\ (n) = 0;\ Ga\ (k) = 0;\ Fa\ (k) = 0$

$(x)(Gx \supset Fx)\ (n) = (Ga \supset Fa)\ (n) = 0$

$(x)(Gx \supset Fx)\ (k) = (Ga \supset Fa)\ (k) = 1$

So: $\Box(x)(Gx \supset Fx)\ (n) = 0$ [since $(x)(Gx \supset Fx)$ is not true in all worlds]

$\Box Ga\ (n) = 0$ [since Ga is not true in all worlds]

$\Diamond Fa\ (n) = 0$ [since Fa is not true in even one world]

So: $(\Box Ga \supset \Diamond Fa)\ (n) = (0 \supset 0)\ (n) = 1\ (n)$

So: $(x)(\Box Ga \supset \Diamond Fa)\ (n) = (\Box Ga \supset \Diamond Fa)\ (n) = (0 \supset 0)\ (n) = 1\ (n)$

So: $(\Box(x)(Gx \supset Fx) \equiv (x)(\Box Ga \supset \Diamond Fa))\ (n) = (0 \equiv 1)\ (n) = 0\ (n)$

7.4 Exercises

1.

(a)

1.	$\sim(a = b \supset \Box(a = b))$	(n)		NTF
2.	$a = b$	(n)		1, **PC**
3.	$\sim\Box(a = b)$	(n)		1, **PC**
4.	$\Diamond\sim(a = b)$	(n)		3, MN
5.	$\sim(a = b)$	(k)		4, $\Diamond$S5

Without necessary identity the tree goes no further. We get the counter-example below. But with necessary identity we go on to closure.

6. $\sim(a = a)$ (k) 2, 5, **NSI**   (substituting a for b)

          ×

S5QT $\Box$ =-Valid

S5QT=-Invalid. A counter-example is:

$a = b\ (n) = 1;\ a = b\ (k) = 0;$

So: $\Box\ (a = b)\ (n) = 0$

So: $(a = b \supset \Box(a = b))\ (n) = (1 \supset 0)\ (n) = 0\ (n)$

(b)   S5QT $\Box$ =-Valid

S5QT=-Invalid. A counter-example is:

$a = b\ (n) = 0;\ a = b\ (k) = 1$

(c)   S5QT □ =-Valid
       S5QT=-Invalid. A counter-example is:
           $Fa\ (n) = Fb\ (n) = 1; Fa\ (k) = 1; Fb\ (k) = 0$
           $a = b\ (n) = 1; a = b\ (k) = 0;$

(d)   Invalid in both S5QT= and S5QT□=. A counter-example is:
           $Fa\ (n) = Fb\ (n) = 1; Fa\ (k) = Fb\ (k) = 0$
           $a = b\ (n) = 1; a = b\ (k) = 1;$

(e)   S5QT=-Valid and S5QT □ =-Valid

Chapter 8

8.6 Exercises

1.
(a)   1. $\sim((x)Fx \supset (\exists y)Fy)$ (n)   NTF
      2. $(x)Fx$ (n)
      3. $\sim(\exists y)Fy$ (n)
      4. $(y)\sim Fy$ (n)   3, QN
      No universal instantiations can be made in free logic. We need to have a formula
      of the form $(\exists\eta)(\kappa = \eta)$ already in the path for **FUI**.
      But we can do ordinary UI.
      5. $\sim Fa$ (n)   4, UI
      6. Fa (n)   2, UI
                    ×
      S5QT=-Valid
      The free logic counter-example simply requires that world n has nothing in
      $Q(n)$. So, $(x)Fx(n) = 1$ and $(\exists y)Fy(n) = 0$.

(b)   1. $\sim (x)(y)(x = y \supset (Fx \supset Fy))$ (n)   NTF
      2. $(\exists x)(\exists y)\sim (x = y \supset (Fx \supset Fy))$ (n)
      3. $(\exists x)(x = a)$ (n)   2, FUI
      4. $(\exists y)\sim (a = y \supset (Fa \supset Fy))$ (n)   2, FUI
      5. $(\exists y)(y = b)$ (n)   4, FUI
      6. $\sim (a = b \supset (Fa \supset Fb))$ (n)   4, FUI
      7. $a = b$ (n)
      8. $\sim (Fa \supset Fb)$ (n)
      9. $\sim (Fa \supset Fa)$ (n)   7, 8, CSI
      10. Fa (n)
      11. $\sim Fa$ (n)
                    ×

      This tree closes for free logic, but would also close for S5QT=, because lines
      3 and 5 would just not appear. Those two lines are not needed for closure.
      S5QT=-Valid and free logic valid.

(c)   S5QT=-Valid and free logic invalid.
        A free logic counter-example is:
        World n has nothing in $Q(n)$ but $a \in D(n)$ and Fa $(n) = 1$
        $(\exists x)(a \neq x)$ $(n) = 1$; Fa $(n) = 1$; $(\exists y)Fy$ $(n) = 0$ $((1$ & $1) \supset 0)$ $(n) = 0$ (n)

(d)   S5QT=-Valid and free logic valid.

(e)   1. $\sim (x)\sim (\exists y)(x = y)$ (n) NTF
        2. $(\exists x)\sim \sim (\exists y)(x = y)$ (n)
        3. $(\exists x)(\exists y)(x = y)$ (n)
        4. $(\exists x)(x = a)$ (n) 3, FUI
        5. $(\exists y)(a = y)$ (n) 3, FUI
        6. $(\exists y)(y = b)$ (n) 5, FUI
        7. $(a = b)$ (n) 5, FUI
                    ↑

        This tree will not close for either logic.
        A counter-example for both is $(a = b)$ $(n) = 1$ and $\{a, b\} \subseteq Q(n)$
        If we eliminate the quantifiers for two items we get:
        $(\sim(a = a \vee a = b)$ & $\sim(b = a \vee b = b))$ $(n) =$
                $(\sim(1 \vee 1)$ & $\sim(1 \vee 1))$ $(n) = (\sim 1$ & $\sim 1)$ $(n) = 0$ (n)

2.

(a)   1. $(x)Fx$ (n) **P**
        2. $(x)Gx$ (n) **P**
        3. $\sim (\exists x)(Fx$ & $Gx)$ (n) **NC**
        4. $(x)\sim (Fx$ & $Gx)$ (n)
        No universal instantiations can be made in free logic. We need to have a formula
        of the form $(\exists \eta)(\kappa = \eta)$ already in the path for FUI.
        But we can do ordinary **UI**.
        5. Fa (n)
        6. Ga (n)
        7. $\sim (Fa$ & $Ga)$ (n)
                    ×   by normal PC
        S5QT=-Valid
        The free logic counter-example simply requires that world n has nothing in
        $Q(n)$.
        So, $(x)Fx$ $(n) = (x)Gx$ $(n) = 1$ and $(\exists x)(Fx$ & $Gx)$ $(n) = 0$

(b)   S5QT=-Invalid. A counter-example is a one item world $\{a\}$ and $Fa = Ha = 0$,
        $Ga = 1$. So with quantifiers eliminated for one item we have:
                $(Fa \supset Ga) = 1$
                $(Ha \supset \sim Ga) = 1$
            $\therefore (Ha$ & $\sim Fa) = 0$
        It is free logic invalid.

Index